HOW DOES
PSYCHOTHERAPY WORK?

CONFER SERIES
SERIES EDITOR: Jane Ryan

Confer has grown from a single event, the Supervision Masterclass held in 1999, to a multi-faceted organization providing extensive continuing education for GPs and psychotherapists, each project being assembled by a team of experts. A core aim of the project is to provide affordable continuing professional development (CPD) that develops the practice of good psychotherapy and the advancement of theory. Confer has also run events about psychoanalysis with the Institute for Contemporary Arts (ICA) in London and is constantly developing new projects to keep abreast of the rapidly developing fields of psychotherapy, integrated approaches to medicine, and the cross-fertilization of ideas between mental health disciplines.

HOW DOES
PSYCHOTHERAPY WORK?

Edited by

Jane Ryan

KARNAC
LONDON   NEW YORK

Published in 2005 by
Karnac (Books) Ltd.
6 Pembroke Buildings, London NW10 6RE

British Library Cataloguing in Publication Data

A C.I.P. for this book is available from the British Library

ISBN 1 85575 306 5

Edited, designed, and produced by The Studio Publishing Services Ltd,
Exeter EX4 8JN

Printed in Great Britain by Hobbs the Printers Ltd, Totton, Hampshire

www.karnacbooks.com

CONTENTS

For Ben, Sonia and Elijah

ACKNOWLEDGEMENTS

My thanks go to Josephine Klein for her careful reading of the manuscript and her advice in the editing process; to all the authors for so generously contributing their time, knowledge, and expertise to the writing of this book. I am indebted to Brett Kahr, Joseph Schwartz, Chris Shingler and Sally Berry for their constant support of the Confer project and to the many others who have contributed as speakers and staff.

ABOUT THE EDITOR AND THE CONTRIBUTORS

The editor

Following a career in community development, Jane Ryan trained as a psychoanalytic psychotherapist in the early 1990s. She is the founder and director of Confer, an independent organization that provides cutting-edge continuing professional development for psychotherapists and medical doctors and that forms a non-partisan space for the exchange of views between approaches.

The contributors

Neil Altman, PhD, is Associate Clinical Professor in the Post-doctoral Programme in Psychotherapy and Psychoanalysis at New York University, co-Editor (with Jody Messler Davies) of *Psychoanalytic Dialogues: A Journal of Relational Perspectives*, author of *The Analyst in the Inner City: Race, Class, and Culture through a Psychoanalytic Lens* and co-author of *Relational Child Psychotherapy*.

Roz Carroll is a body psychotherapist and a Member of the Society for Neuro-Psychoanalysis. She is a trainer and supervisor at the

Minster Centre, London and the Chiron Centre for Body Psychotherapy, London. She has specialized in integrating concepts from
neuroscience, psychoanalysis, and body psychotherapy, and has
lectured and run courses in a wide range of clinical training contexts. Her recent publications include chapters in *Advances in Body
Psychotherapy* (Ed. T. Staunton) and *Revolutionary Connections:
Psychotherapy and Neuroscience* (Ed. Corrigall and Wilkinson).

Sue Cowan-Jenssen is a psychotherapist, trainer and founder
member of the London Association of Primal Psychotherapists,
which runs a UKCP accredited training programme for psychotherapists. She has published interviews, reviews, and articles
in psychotherapy journals, particularly around the theme of the
relationship between social pressures and individual problems. She
also works as a psychotherapist at the Trauma Unit at Watford
General Hospital.

Nicola Diamond, PhD, was formerly a university lecturer in the
social sciences and is currently a Senior Lecturer at the Regent's
College School of Psychotherapy and Counselling in London,
where she is responsible for the PhD programme. Her clinical interests as a practising psychotherapist focus on developmental and
attachment theories, psychosomatics, neuroscience, and the theoretical advancement of embodiment. She holds a PhD in
Psychoanalytic Studies and is a Member of the Steering Committee
of the International Attachment Network. Her most recent writings
can be found in *Attachment and Interaction* (Marrone & Diamond,
1998) and *Attachment and Subjectivity* (Marrone & Diamond).

Carol Holmes, PhD, trained as a communicative psychotherapist
and is a chartered counselling psychologist and supervisor. Prior to
moving to Western Australia, where she now lectures at Notre-
Dame University on the MA in Counselling, she was the head of
post MA training in psychotherapy at the Regent's College School
of Psychotherapy and Counselling in London. She is the recipient
of two awards for outstanding contributions to the field of communicative psychotherapy and designed the first communicative
training in Europe. Her most recent book, *The Paradox of Countertransference*, was published in January 2005 by Palgrave Macmillan.

Carol Holmes is a past chair of the European Society for Communicative Psychotherapy.

Brett Kahr is Senior Clinical Research Fellow in Psychotherapy and Mental Health at the Centre for Child Mental Health in London, and the Winnicott Clinic Senior Research Fellow in Psychotherapy at the Winnicott Clinic of Psychotherapy. He is also Visiting Clinician at the Tavistock Centre for Couple Relationships, and Senior Lecturer in Psychotherapy in the School of Psychotherapy and Counselling at Regent's College, London. He is the author of several books including *D. W. Winnicott: A Biographical Portrait*, which won the Gradiva Prize for Biography, as well as books on infant mental health, exhibitionism, and forensic psychotherapy. He is the Series Editor of the Forensic Psychotherapy Monograph Series for Karnac , and, most recently, he has been appointed as the Resident Psychotherapist on BBC Radio 2, hosting the BBC campaign "Life 2 Live".

Dianne LeFevre (MRCPsych) originally worked as a physician. She is now a Consultant Psychiatrist in Psychotherapy and runs a psychotherapy unit at Basildon Hospital, where they specialize in the treatment of severe mental illness. In collaboration with Anglia Polytechnic University, she also runs an MSc in the Psychodynamics of the Psychoses. She is an advocate of an integrated approach to the treatment of severe mental illness that includes family work, psychotherapy, nutritional therapies, social therapy, and pharmacotherapy.

Susie Orbach, PhD, is a psychotherapist and writer whose theoretical worked is centred on the therapy relationship, the construction of femininity, and rethinking the relationship between the body and mind. She has published extensively on these themes. In addition to her work as a writer she has established two organizations: she was co-founder, with Luise Eichenbaum, of both the Women's Therapy Centre (London) and the Women's Therapy Centre Institute (New York). She holds an academic post as Visiting Professor in Gender Studies Institute at the London School of Economics. Her recent books include *The Impossibility of Sex, Towards Emotional Literacy,* and *On Eating.*

James Pollard is a psychotherapist in private practice in Cambridge and London. He is a training therapist and supervisor for the Centre for Attachment-based Psychoanalytic Psychotherapy in London, and an Associate Member of the Cambridge Society for Psychotherapy. He has taught on a variety of training programmes, and lectures widely on attachment theory and clinical practice. He is currently Chair of the United Kingdom Council for Psychotherapy (UKCP).

Joseph Schwartz, PhD, is a psychoanalytic psychotherapist, supervisor and trainer at the Centre for Attachment-based Psychoanalytic Psychotherapy in London. Trained originally as an experimental physicist at the University of Berkeley, he worked for many years in mental health research before becoming a clinician. His interests include the history of psychoanalysis, intersubjectivity and the psychology of men. Having published widely on the social context of science, his latest book is *Cassandra's Daughter: A History of Psychoanalysis in Europe and America.*

Robert M. Young, PhD, is a psychoanalytic psychotherapist in private practice in London. He is the founder of Free Associations Books, editor of the *Free Associations* journal, co-editor of the human-nature.com web site and moderator of various e-mail forums. Until his retirement he was Professor of Psychotherapy and Psychoanalytic Studies at the University of Sheffield. He is the author of *Mind, Brain and Adaptation; Darwin's Metaphor; Mental Space; Whatever Happened to Human Nature?; The Culture of British Psychoanalysis*, and various other writings on human nature, psychotherapy and psychoanalysis, evolutionary theory, and the history and philosophy of science. His writings are available on-line at http://human-nature.com/rmyoung/

Introduction

What kind of imperatives bring people into psychotherapy? A middle-aged social worker, who has such urgent feelings of need that she eats straight from the freezer. A man whose money, energy, and desire for life are consumed by a compulsion to visit prostitutes. A young woman whose identity collapses when she discovers her boyfriend has been unfaithful. An older woman, whose numerous losses have never been mourned and who no longer wishes to live.

How might these people feel and act in the world when their therapy is complete? The social worker becomes able to take regular meals and to enjoy food. The man becomes able to sustain a relationship with a woman who is a real partner—neither idealized nor denigrated. The young woman has developed a sense of herself that is not threatened by turbulent events but which is resilient and flexible. The older woman has grieved for the people she has lost and can now open herself to those who are available in the present. But how do these transformations occur? What goes on between the two individuals in the psychotherapeutic relationship that can cause such change? What is it exactly that makes this possible?

This book originated in a lecture series hosted by Confer in 2003, when ten well-established psychotherapists were invited to answer these questions. I asked them to identify what goes on in the therapeutic relationship that might account for the client or patient's progress towards improved emotional well-being and ease with life, and what might be difficult about knowing this. Several of the original contributors to that lecture series have adapted their papers to become chapters for this book and other authors have joined the project on the way.

It is widely believed that psychotherapy *does* work, both subjectively from the positive statements of those who have undertaken this form of personal development, and statistically from before-and-after research into its efficacy. Interestingly, the results of some studies suggest that the basic components of successful psychotherapy are common to all therapeutic approaches and that possibly all models share the significant features that make the relationship effective. These are thought to include the existence of a special relationship that exists uniquely for the client's well-being, the use of a consistent method, the therapeutic value of hope through experiencing the possibility of change and, something which is little discussed, the willingness and capacity of the client or patient to commit to this challenging process and to be a partner in making it work.

These findings, while offering reassuring and important signposts, also raise some interesting problems. If the use of a consistent method is known to be important, will not some approaches be more useful than others? If the quality of the relationship is crucial, what are the special interactions that make it so? Is the client's capacity to benefit from the work a prerequisite or an outcome?

These questions and indeed the title of this book presuppose causality: if the therapist takes a specific step then predictable consequence is likely to follow. The very question "How does psychotherapy work?" rests on an assumption that it is possible to reach into the depths of interpersonal complexity and pluck out the truth. But I believe that each explanation of the psychotherapeutic process will be strongly influenced by the implicit values, personal history, and other subjectivities of each author's personal process. We know that the question cannot be answered as though it is an arithmetic problem. None the less, the process of attempting to untangle and articulate core aspects of the psychotherapeutic process is a fascinating project that I believe contributes to the continuing development of good theory, and thus good practice.

You will find that each contributor subscribes to particular notions of what should occur between therapist and client, and uses a specific language to describe that process. But although they come from a wide range of theoretical influences and describe the process in very individual ways, I am struck by how similarly the authors tackle the core of the matter, in particular, in the recurring emphasis on the constancy of the therapist in providing a space in which a profound and complex level of intersubjective encounter can safely occur.

A word about modalities: this book offers a representative sample of psychoanalytical, relational, and object-relational approaches to psychotherapy. These emphasize early developmental experiences as the core of the adult psyche, and the importance of unconscious processes in our relationships with others, in particular with the psychotherapist. Regrettably, it has not been possible to include chapters from the many other important schools of psychotherapy in this volume.

I asked the authors to speak about the issues raised by the question of how psychotherapy works, using accessible language and fully explaining concepts that may be new or unusual for readers beyond the professional community. My hope is that this book will be useful to anyone interested in psychotherapy. In Chapter One, responding warmly to the spirit of user-friendliness, Brett Kahr has contributed a piece that begins with a witty parody of the psychotherapeutic journey as a sophisticated cooking process—highlighting, by paradox, its actual complexity and irreducibility. Whether we can gather together all the necessary ingredients of good practice and produce a good result is the question he both poses and answers. There are certain key ingredients that can be identified. However, he argues, there is also an absurdity in trying to provide an easy answer to the question of how psychotherapy works. This chapter provides an excellent introduction to some of the basic tools a psychotherapist must offer and reasons why: permission to confess, supreme reliability, an interest in the smallest detail of the patient's life, an understanding, and the providing of an empathic and appropriately responsive tone. In all, he lists fifteen "key ingredients". This text is a transcript of his original lecture in the Confer series of talks.

It has seemed essential that this book should contain some historical context for this discussion. In Chapter Two, Neil Altman, a relational psychoanalyst practising in New York, offers a lucid introduction to the history of psychoanalytic theories about how psychotherapy works, from Freud to contemporary relational psychoanalysis. He explores how each theoretical school has developed its own distinct understanding about how psychological transformation occurs, and the precise therapeutic function of the analyst in that process. Tracing a developmental line from the work of Freud to Ferenzi and then via Fairbairn, he leads us to the contemporary approach of "relational psychoanalysis"—a method that gives us a new way of understanding the interaction between psychotherapist and patient. He demonstrates how therapy, if underpinned by a shared understanding of the intersubjective experience by both analyst and analysand, leads to psychic integration, interpersonal competence, insight, and a sense of personal meaningfulness. His contribution also incorporates a very welcome discussion about the values implicit in each metapsychology that underpin its conceptualization of both mental health and pathology.

In Chapter Three, Joseph Schwartz continues the theme of psychotherapy as an intersubjective, relational endeavour. He explores how therapy works by utilizing the unique space of the analytic hour in order to re-experience the relational difficulties that exist in an individual's present and past. Within this space, he argues, an exceptional level of interpersonal exchange is made possible by the therapist's distinctive skills—that are unlike those offered in any other relationship: a special level of listening combined with a profound understanding of human nature, and a vocabulary that can articulate the complexities of relationships and feelings. He makes a compelling case for the significance of psychoanalytic insights into human nature and urges us to value these deeply, especially in a cultural climate that is so questioning of psychotherapy's worth.

Susie Orbach's most welcome contribution to this book (Chapter Four) further develops the new theoretical framework and practices of relational psychoanalysis through a lucid exploration of the skills necessary to transform the individual's sense of self so that they become flexible, adaptive agents in the "theatre of life". Like Brett Kahr and Joseph Schwartz, she emphasizes the special capacity of the therapist to listen and be affected by the patient's words. Through communication to another person the unknowable can become conscious as the therapist gains insight into the internal world of the patient through the potency of the narrative upon her own psyche. The two subjectivities in the room become a vibrant intersubjective realm in which the patient's internal objects can become understood, articulated and revised. This chapter further elucidates the role of repetition and other psychological defences, exploring how we can articulate—with the patient—the unseen helplessness, shame, and conflicts that underlie apparently self-destructive patterns.

Relational psychoanalysis is a relatively new concept, which subscribes to a form of psychotherapeutic practice that pays particular regard to the impact of the client's psyche upon that of the therapist. In this respect there is an equal valuing and weighting of both participants in the process. Practitioners of this approach, which can be seen as a synthesis of American self-psychology, British object relations and developmental theory, regard "relational configurations between self and others (whether real or perceived) as the primary units of human interaction". They give special attention to the creative management of countertransference as a therapeutic tool.

In Chapter Five, Roz Carroll demonstrates how countertransference (the therapist's complex and multi-layered emotional responses to the client's transferences) can be a crucial guide to finding a spontaneous point of intervention—a relational experience with the therapist that will precipitate the deep reorganization of the client's psychic structures. Embracing the concepts of recent neuroscience, she argues with great clarity and through clinical illustration that these points occur at pivotal moments in psychotherapeutic work that are unplanned and cannot be prescribed. Rather, she proposes, they take place through a dialectic of spontaneity and discipline; they are simultaneously relational, bodily, perceptual, and reflective. What occurs in therapy, she proposes, is an expansion of the client's relational capacity (and that of the therapist). This shift embraces both verbal and non-verbal processes; it takes place in an integrated mind–body space.

This theme is central to Nicola Diamond's contribution (Chapter Six), which also anticipates a theoretical future in which psychotherapists will more generally perceive the work of psychotherapy to be taking place with an integrated mind–body system. She argues that therapy works when the practitioner witnesses, understands, shares, and processes the patient's emotional world at the points where the somatic (bodily) and affective (emotional) worlds are joined. Process in this context means the procedure by which both practitioner and patient can come to make affective–somatic links within the relational experience that the patient holds of self and other. When that attachment history is shared and processed at that core level then the body, relational experiences, and resulting emotional structures can become integrated. She illuminates the "procedural" method with a most moving case history in which her analysand recovers from disabling somatic symptoms via an integration of the unconscious feelings she has towards herself, parents, and siblings. Nicola Diamond suggests that the key emotional shifts that took place in the therapy were not reducible to verbal exchanges or interpretations, but were more fundamentally rooted in her open reception to the patient's symptoms as a mode of communication.

In Chapter Seven, Sue Cowan-Jenssen, whose work is strongly influenced by both primal and relational psychotherapies, examines the importance of feelings in psychotherapy and the uses and dangers of regression as a means of reaching early developmental crises. She argues that the need for emotional expression is not in conflict with the discipline and boundaries of more conventional psychotherapies and that in fact both elements are needed if therapy is to be effective. She considers the role of memory and the need to understand how memory works in the light of current neuroscience research. Clinical vignettes are given to illustrate how painful recollections can be evoked and then worked through safely in a therapy setting, and how touch might be used appropriately and creatively to facilitate this process. Like many cutting-edge psychotherapists, including Roz Carroll, Susie Orbach, and Nicola Diamond, Sue Cowan-Jenssen understands the psychotherapeutic process to be embodied, that is, to be simultaneously physical, cognitive, and emotional.

The theme of maintaining disciplined boundaries is at the core of Robert Young's paper (Chapter Eight), in which he offers a powerful argument for the importance of structure in the psychotherapeutic process. By exploring the multiple elements of the relational frame inside which the therapy relationship occurs, he illustrates how a disciplined management of safe and predictable limits is necessary for a shift to occur in the patient's internal world. Opportunities for therapeutic change arise in particular scenarios: when the patient puts pressure on that frame, thus alerting the therapist to a bubbling up of unconscious material; when transferred objects are imported into the therapy relationship—that is, when significant people occupying the patient's internal world become experienced by the patient to be (like) the therapist himself; or when the patient's projections—the split-off elements of the psyche that cannot be borne—are experienced by both participants to be part of the therapist. When such pressures occur in the relationship, "resonance at the level of the deepest subjectivity is required". Then toxic matter can be digested, processed, and represented to the patient in benign form, and the opportunity may also arise for the therapist to make an interpretation. Through this multi-faceted interplay, past hurt is gradually verbalized and symptoms are resolved.

When John Bowlby formulated attachment theory from his observations of children who experienced separation and loss, he created a theoretical framework that would become one of the most important developments in psychoanalysis. From the nature of the child's attachment ties we are able to learn a great deal about the internal relationship structures of the adult in psychotherapy, both in the relationships that the client needs to speak about, and also as way of understanding how the relationship develops with the therapist. In James Pollard's paper (Chapter Nine) we have a most welcome elaboration of how he experienced the therapeutic task in his psychoanalytic work with an "avoidantly attached" male patient. At the core of this work was a process of loosening the patient's established attachment structure, that of his insecure relationship to his mother, so that a greater differentiation of his own sense of self could be established. From this base an increased capacity for free association develops, a strengthening of reflective function, and ultimately the establishment of new structures that permit greater emotional flexibility and inclusiveness. In this sophisticated exploration James Pollard offers an elegant account of the fundamental link between relationships, feelings, and cognitive processes.

Carol Holmes' theoretical and clinical approach (Chapter Ten) is focused on the interface between communicative principles developed by Robert Langs, existential philosophy, and dynamic systems theory. Her chapter begins with a brief summary of the difference between classical psychoanalysis and Langs' radical theory of psychoanalytic communicative reconstructions. In order to highlight the significance of the interpersonal components of communicative psychotherapy, she draws on the fundamental relational propositions that are emphasized in existential philosophy. Communicative psychotherapy, she explains, "is organized around the therapist's recognition and confirmation of the patient's unconscious perceptions of the therapist's management of the relationship" and it is centred on a belief in the patient's innate ability to comprehend interpersonal reality. Successful therapy, she proposes, rests upon deep interpersonal contact between therapist and patient and, like many of the authors here, she emphasizes the complexities of countertransference. In light of her interest in current scientific ideas, she uses the basic axioms of the hologram to metaphorically support and explain the essential holistic and interconnected nature of the therapeutic dyad. Finally, she examines a clinical example of time-limited therapy as a means of illustrating the holographic process in the therapeutic encounter.

In the moving and inspiring final chapter, Dianne Lefevre talks about her belief that the authenticity of the psychotherapist is a fundamental prerequisite for therapeutic change in the patient. The concept of authenticity is theoretically unravelled and then illustrated in vignettes from a case study based on her work with a psychotic patient. Dianne Lefevre's clinical practice is pioneering. She runs a hospital unit that offers an integrated approach to the treatment of severe mental illness. Her work rests on an understanding of the psychoses being complex psycho-social, neurological conditions that are none the less amenable to psychotherapeutic intervention because the mind is plastic in its structures and can respond to new relational configurations at a neurological level. This chapter contains an elucidating account of the traumatic roots of psychosis, and how we each have potentially psychotic tendencies that are managed by other, stronger psychic structures and cognitive capacities. She demonstrates that psychosis can be contained by a strengthening of the non-psychotic parts of the patient's internal world if the therapist has the capacity to create a relationship and an alliance with the healthy personality within the patient. Then, in the place of murderous madness, we see a grief and terror that the therapist feels fully with her patient. This authentic experience, Dianne Lefevre demonstrates, occurring at a meditative, pre-verbal, alpha level, is the basis of the relational connection that facilitates recovery.

I have found the reading of these chapters in the editing process to be an enriching and illuminating experience and I have learnt something significant about psychotherapeutic practice: there is a remarkable degree of overlapping theory and practice from chapter to chapter, despite the range of theoretical approaches represented in the book. It seems as though each author has taken their own unique route to arrive at a very similar account of how psychotherapy works: that transformation of internal objects occurs through a real experience of profound, resonating, and felt relatedness between therapist and patient that expands and strengthens that person's internal world so that they can safely embrace secure attachments in the present. I find this good reason to be optimistic that areas of agreement will grow—and that psychotherapy may become more widely culturally understood to be underpinned by a coherent and effective system, and to be offering a quality of relatedness that exists in no other professional domain.

Jane Ryan
Editor

CHAPTER ONE

The fifteen key ingredients of good psychotherapy*

Brett Kahr

T urn on your television set any night of the week, and you will be able to gorge yourself upon any number of new-fangled cookery experts, or so-called celebrity chefs, who attempt to communicate the secrets of their trade to us in a stylish, entertaining fashion. Each evening at eight o'clock, we too, the ordinary viewer at home, can perch on our sitting room sofas, notepads nestling on our knees, as we learn an eminently trans-missible sequence of culinary steps. First, we must choose our ingredients; then we rinse, slice and dice, baste and bake, heat or chill, lightly season, garnish with fresh parsley, and . . . hey presto . . . we have concocted a veritable replica of a British Broadcasting Corporation feast.

If only those of us who work as professional psychotherapists could communicate the nitty-gritty details of our craft with such grace and dexterity, and still manage to do so in an entertaining twenty-four minute broadcast. If only we could transform our ponderous, arcane, and stodgy textbooks into a foolproof do-it-at-

---

* Lecture transcript

1

home recipe, then psychotherapy would be available at the flick of a switch, and the mental health problems of Great Britain would be solved. And just imagine if some very visionary commissioning editor from the Channel Four Television Corporation did indeed commission a six-part half-hour slot on how psychotherapy works, how on earth would we translate our hard-won clinical expertise into a snappy format that would engage the attention of millions of viewers?

> "First, we need a suitable patient. A full-fee patient would be preferable, but if you are still in training, then a reduced-fee patient will work equally well. Next, assess thoroughly for signs of psychotic functioning and suicidal ideation. When you have done this, leave the patient to stew for a week or more so that he or she will really have time to think about whether psychotherapy can be managed. Next, set your timer to fifty minutes. It is very important that you do not exceed this time, otherwise the patient will be over-cooked, and you might experience unconscious resentment. Place the patient on a leather-clad couch. If you haven't got a leather one, then a cloth covered one will do, or, if you are more relationally orientated, you might put the patient in a comfortable chair located approximately six feet away from your own. Carefully scrutinize your countertransference for unprocessed affects, stir up the internal world with pointed interpretations—not too many, but not too few, just enough to target the point of maximal anxiety. Analyse the resistances and the character defences, discuss in supervision, and prepare for termination, but only after the bill has been paid in full. In next week's episode, I'll be in Bolton, teaching you how to deal with addictions. Until then, good night from Shrink Shop."

I have indulged in this parodic and satirical interlude as a means of illustrating both the utter absurdity of articulating an easy answer to the question of how psychotherapy works, but also as a means of demonstrating, however inadequately, the increasing necessity of being able to write about our work, and to talk about our work, in an infinitely more approachable manner than many of our more stolid colleagues have managed to do in the preceding decades.

As professionals who have spent much time and money on our trainings, we do not wish to give away the secret family recipes, in part because we wish to preserve an air of mystery about what we actually do in clinical sessions, and in part, I suspect, because of a widely held sense of shame that what we do is, in fact, sit in a chair, and listen quietly, with ordinary compassion, occasionally proffering an illuminating comment. Although I remain very committed to the idea that a lengthy course of psychotherapy should be facilitated only by a very well analysed, well trained, clinically experienced, and mentally healthy person, I wish to assert that the key ingredients of the recipe for a good psychotherapy are all very ordinary, wholesome, organic items, all available not only to the practising mental health worker, but to the ordinary citizen as well. Though deeply impressed and influenced by our predecessors' grand theories on the metapsychology of technique, from Sigmund Freud's insistence on the role of "working-through" to James Strachey's (1934, p. 138) emphasis on the mutative function of the transference interpretation, and of the analyst's intrapsychic agency as an "auxiliary super-ego", I have become increasingly convinced that the factors that promote cure cannot be readily learned in the academy or in the training institution, but that these factors are, in fact, the ordinary and admirable components of valiant human relatedness.

In the pages that follow, I wish to highlight fifteen ingredients of what I have come to regard as good psychotherapy, based on my quarter of a century of clinical work, and on my personal acquaintance with a great many psychotherapists, psychotherapy students, and psychotherapy patients. I make no pretence that my manifesto represents anything other than a personal perspective, based on direct experience, particularly of moments of therapeutic engagement when a patient seems to have felt recognized in some very moving manner. I present these ingredients—some universally appreciated, some more idiosyncratically so—in a Winnicottian spirit as a list to be used, either engaged with, or discarded (Winnicott, 1969).

Herewith, the fifteen key ingredients of good psychotherapy:

Permission to confess

In our psychotherapeutic work, we strive to create a quiet and confessional atmosphere in which an individual can verbalize what the early medical psychologists called "the pathogenic secret", a private secret so painful and so shameful that one dare not articulate this to anyone. In my past week of clinical work alone, a sexually confident, compulsive womanizing male patient confessed in shame the scarring taunts that he had to endure at boarding school for having the smallest penis in the class; a female patient revealed her self-loathing and self-disgust for the first time by bravely speaking about the occasion when her father told her that she smelled; another female patient spoke of a fellatio trauma that had occurred at the age of five years; and a male patient admitted to an illicit homosexual encounter in a public toilet, sweating in terror in case his wife or children should discover.

The sheer beauty of Freud's psychoanalytical invention has never paled. Psychoanalysis began, first and foremost, as a means of cathartic purging—a form of secular confession, devoid of the potentially punitive and judgemental overtones of organized religion. Although we recognize the value of verbalizing secrets, we also appreciate that some secrets cannot be shared outside of the consulting room, and some secrets must not ever be shared. A male patient who enjoyed a very warm and affectionate and companionable relationship with his wife revealed the agonizing secret that during coitus he has never, ever thought of his wife, nor has he done so while masturbating. As the gentleman admitted to me, "I have sex with my wife, and I enjoy it, but only because I am thinking about other women, including her sister. I could never tell her this. It would kill her. But I feel better knowing that at least I can tell you." Needless to say, the patient and I talked endlessly about his fears of deeper mental intimacy with his wife, his private anger towards her for various perceived injustices, his hatred of his mother transferred on to his wife, and all the other predictable lines of analytical enquiry, much of which proved quite fruitful and facilitative in his marriage. This work helped the patient in many respects, but the greatest relief, I suspect, came from the sheer direct and private confession of an aching, festering secret that gnawed away at the mind of the patient, and that he knew, perhaps rightly so, that he could never report to his spouse. In a moment of deep pleasure at having revealed this marital secret, the patient exclaimed, "Gosh, talking to you is like . . . well, it's like mouthwash for the mind."

The clinical value of talking, and of confession, has received extensive empirical support (e.g., Dreher, 1995; Pennebaker, 1995; Wallerstein, 2002), and it remains, in my opinion, a veritable cornerstone of psychological healing; and yet, the revelation of the secret must be handled with great tact and diplomacy. What do we do when a patient taunts us with a secret that can never be spoken about? How do we manage the disclosure of a secret that might incriminate the patient in an illegal activity, or that might represent a source of danger to a third party? And can we ever respect and appreciate the wish or the need of the patient to preserve some secrets forever, even from the clinician? In 1963, Dr Donald Winnicott (1963, p. 187) spoke about the "incommunicado" part of the patient's mind, and he dared to wonder whether it might be in the best interests of the analysand to have at least some part of the mind that remains so private and precious that it must be never be shared. The technical aspects of secrecy and confession cannot readily be summarized in a series of clinical sound-bites; but whatever the correct management of the vicissitudes of a secret, we should never underestimate how many secrets our patients will be harbouring, how toxicogenic these secrets may be, how much courage will be required to disclose the secrets, and how healthfully freeing the hard-won verbalization of the secret may prove to be.

Supreme reliability

A great humourist once quipped that death and taxes might be the only certainties upon which we may rely in the course of our lives. Sadly, this pessimistic epithet may well be true, especially for those untold individuals who have had to endure innumerable separations and bereavements, disappointments and rejections, as well as daily hurts and betrayals along the way. If psychotherapy accomplishes nothing else as an enterprise, it certainly provides a bedrock of reliability, predictability, and some reasonable expectation of certainty in an otherwise turbulent and haphazard world. As clinical practitioners, we can be relied upon to start our sessions on time, and to end them on time. We can be counted on to remember the patient's history. And we can be depended upon to act in a predictable manner, confining ourselves to the benign expression of concern and interest and curiosity, without any expectation of reward other than a token economic payment in the form of what can only be regarded as a reasonable fee.

Ancient psychoanalytical practitioners have sometimes created a veritable fetish of reliability by ending the session with obsessional precision before permitting the patient to complete his or her last phrase. I suppose that nowadays we would all regard such an action as a very perversion of psychoanalytical technique. I would not regard such a scenario as an expression of reliability.

Rather, I regard reliability, as Donald Winnicott did, as that which provides an antidote to the pains of dependency. One of my patients, a young female who spoke in a whingeing and whining voice, often had to suffer the indignity of friends cancelling social engagements. This young lady began to become very paranoid and very persecuted on the one hand, but also able to work with growing insight on the other hand, as she began to acknowledge how she would often drive people away. On one occasion, I announced that I would have to be absent from my consulting room on a certain date in the middle of the term, and I told her about this anticipated cancellation some ten days in advance. Upon my return, the patient began to make insulting remarks about an older male colleague at work who had failed to appear for her annual staff appraisal meeting. As one might imagine, I made a comment about her feelings of anger and disappointment towards me for having cancelled her "staff appraisal" meeting with me. To my astonishment, the patient replied: "I knew you were going to say that, and yes, maybe I am a bit upset that you cancelled my session, but you know something, your track record with me is so good, it really doesn't matter. I know I can rely on you, and you are the only one who won't cancel on me without a very good reason."

As the years have progressed, I have found that the concept of reliable time-keeping has served as a template with which patients can identify. As a result, patients themselves attend sessions more promptly and regularly, but they also become better friends to their own friends and family by becoming more respectful. A charming male patient used to arrive more than two hours late to every dinner party, boasting to me: "I'm the funniest one there, so they don't mind waiting." I reflected that this may well be true, and that perhaps he did deliver good value when he finally arrrived, but

I also wondered whether he could entertain the notion that although his friends found him amusing, they might also harbour feelings of contempt and hatred for him as well? This thought—a new thought—greatly shocked the patient, but he did listen, and some weeks later, he reported with great pride that he had arrived on time to his last dinner, and that he enjoyed himself greatly, as well as the conversation, and that he finally realized that one need not make a grand and unreliably late entrance in order to be liked and appreciated. I suspect that my reliability of attitude and style became a remedy against the flighty unpredictability that this man had internalized from his two alcoholic parents.

As a young student working in the forensic field, I had the great privilege of undergoing supervision with the late Dr Murray Cox, a brilliant forensic psychiatrist who pioneered psychotherapeutic work in British prisons and who established the psychotherapy service at Broadmoor Hospital. A gifted impressionist, Dr Cox used to tell me about his many violent and colourful patients, offering impeccable renditions of their rich, regional accents. I shall never forget his imitation of a violent murderer who had ghoulishly dismembered his victim. Dr Cox had asked the patient to describe his most pressing memory from childhood. The patient did not miss a beat and responded: "I remember one day, when I was eight, and my mother went out to buy a loaf of bread . . . but she never came back. She never came back." Such instances of almost unthinkable abandonment can be found with great regularity in the childhood histories of most forensic patients, instances of extreme unreliability and undependability, all of which exact a punishing toll on psychic development. By providing a context in which patients can experience our reliability as a privileged feature, I find that we will have done good psychotherapeutic work.

Interest in the smallest detail

We will all have had the experience of talking with a mentally healthy child in a state of excitement, perhaps returning home from a day at primary school with a newly painted picture, perhaps describing the thrill of a class outing. Any emotionally intelligent person will appreciate the vital developmental need of the child to belabour every detail of the expedition, and it will be our job to listen, and woe betide us if in relating the story to our partner we should dare to make a mistake, as we find ourselves in great trouble. In my work with psychotherapy patients, I have found that some of the most extraordinarily touching encounters have occurred when I have expressed an overt interest in the minutiae of the patient's life, and also when I have then demonstrated a correct memory for these small details some weeks, months, even years, later.

A middle-aged lady arrived one day for her very first consultation, wracked with diffuse pelvic pains, migraines, and a host of other crippling psychosomatic manifestations. Curiously, she wore a striking orange suit, complete with an orange blouse, an orange skirt, and orange pumps. Although very well groomed and very pleasantly dressed, the profusion of orange seemed somewhat unusual, at least to my sartorially undersensitized eyes. This lady struggled through the consultation, and she seemed extremely uncomfortable about engaging with any of my preliminary trial hypotheses or interpretations. As the hour neared its end, this prospective patient looked anxious and she exclaimed, "Well, thanks for seeing me, but I don't really think this sort of thing is for me." I asked whether she might want to have a week to think about treatment, and perhaps return for a second consultation before making her decision, but she seemed steadfast, and she asked me to post her a bill. As the woman reached for her handbag, I found myself still very preoccupied by her orange costume, and I took a risk. In a soft voice, I dared to comment: "I know that you are getting ready to leave, and that you perhaps found this meeting somewhat unusual, as you have never met a psychotherapist before; but I must say that I am very struck by the fact that you have come dressed completely in orange, which is the international colour for rescue, and perhaps you will feel quite unsatisfied if you think that I have not noticed your need to be rescued." The lady looked at me with bewilderment and incomprehension, but she shed a tear and she offered to return for a second meeting. She stayed in psychotherapy three times per week for a period of seven years, often referring to the so-called "orange episode" as a catalytic moment. Until that point, the patient could not at all imagine that anyone else would treat her clothes as an expression of her psychological life, or that such details could even matter.

Another patient, a forty-year-old man who suffered from quite marked agoraphobia, spoke with great pleasure about having finally managed to go to a West End theatre show for the very first time in his life. The patient finally allowed himself to join a party of work colleagues for an outing to see Andrew Lloyd Webber's musical *Sunset Boulevard* at the Adelphi Theatre; and to his great delight and surprise, my patient enjoyed himself much more than he had expected. Three years later, the patient reported a very elaborate and very cryptic dream that took place in a mysterious location called Adelphi House. This detail confused the agoraphic man as he could not appreciate the significance of this dream image. I asked the patient for associations to Adelphi House, but he claimed that he had none.

At this juncture, I offered a suggestion. I remembered that some three years ago, the patient had experienced rather a breakthrough when he went out to the theatre for the very first time, and that if I recalled correctly, he went to see the musical *Sunset Boulevard* at the Adelphi Theatre, on the Strand; and I then wondered whether this incident might be linked in some way to the presence of Adelphi House in his dream. The patient sat bolt upright on the couch, and he began to shed some tears, utterly amazed that I could remember such a trivial detail from three years previously, as no one else in his life had ever bothered to remember anything about him. I replied that I did not regard his visit to the Adelphi Theatre as trivial, but rather, as transformational, and that he might have felt very dropped had I not recollected something so critical.

Lest one imagine that the psychotherapist will be forced to remember every tiny detail of an analysand's material, I should confess that I had no great difficulty recalling that *Sunset Boulevard* had premiered at the Adelphi Theatre for the simple reason that a very old friend of mine—a musician—worked as the keyboardist in the orchestral pit at *Sunset Boulevard*, and I had seen the show many times; and so, the Adelphi Theatre represented common, readily available knowledge to me, rather than arcane knowledge. Regardless of whether one recalls a small detail of the patient's narrative with great ease or with great difficulty, in my experience the healing potentiality might be enormous for the patient. How many of us, I wonder, will know, for example, the actual first names of our patients' mothers and fathers? Such knowledge may be fundamental to the later decryption of psychic material, and we would do will to make a mental or physical note of such data.

The provision of tonal factors

Although I shall fail miserably in my attempt to highlight the importance of what I shall call "tonal factors", I believe very strongly that the musicianship of the psychotherapist may well prove to be one of the most transformational ingredients in the clinical encounter. In other words, I suspect that the patient will be deeply affected by our tone of voice, our accent, the volume of our voice, the pitch of our voice, its cadence, its flow, its pressure, as well as by our sentence structure, our knowledge of grammar, and by the richness or paucity of our actual vocabulary. These components of the voice, arguably the most important physical items that we bring into the session—especially if we work with analysands on the couch who cannot see our faces—remain among the most shamefully undertheorized and underinvestigated components of psychological work.

When librettist Alan Jay Lerner adapted George Bernard Shaw's classic play *Pygmalion* into the timeless musical comedy *My Fair Lady*, he wrote a memorable lyric for Professor Henry Higgins about the perils of dangerous relationships. You will no doubt recall Higgins's euphonious warning label about certain women:

> "She'll have a booming, boisterous family
> Who will descend on you en masse.
> She'll have a large Wagnerian mother
> With a voice that shatters glass."

Evidently, the human voice can pierce the eardrums of the vulnerable with a cruel intensity, and I do know of many psychotherapy patients who have dropped out of treatment, or who have felt injured by clinicians who speak in a particularly strident voice. I do not wish to suggest that mental health workers ought to talk to their patients in a gooey, cosseted, saccharine tone of voice; that might be rather artificial and revolting. But, many clinicians with whom I have conversed over the years speak in a markedly biting tone, devoid of warmth and musicality. As a musician, I regularly find myself plotting the vocal tonality of colleagues' voices on an imaginary stave, and I have become increasingly convinced that the psychological workers whom I most admire speak with a rich verbal texture, utilizing a free range of notes from the middle of the scale. It will not therefore surprise you that one of the psychoanalysts whom I have found most cruel always speaks in intervals of augmented fourths, in other words, alternating between notes such as Middle C and F#, a sort of vocal relatedness that I regard as impoverished, and potentially betokening an impoverishment of the creative imagination as well.

In my personal discussions with the noted developmental psychologist and psychobiologist Professor Colwyn Trevarthen (2003), he and I have begun to theorize certain correspondences between the tones of healthy mothers cooing to their babies, and healthy clinicians engaged in discussion with their patients, clients, or analysands. Though tricky to quantify, Professor Trevarthen certainly agrees that the more flexible, mellifluous voice might well promote greater psychic growth. Of course, a beautiful voice with limited content will not be of much help at all, but a smart interpretation rendered with vocal warmth, diplomacy, and concern might prove very potent indeed.

The voice can be so useful as a diagnostic indicator that I have often found myself advising prospective psychotherapy patients to ring their psychotherapist-to-be on the telephone before making an appointment for a first consultation so that the patient can hear the outgoing message on the answering machine. I have found the outgoing answering machine message to be very indicative of the tonal quality of the practitioner in everyday conversational life.

One of my patients, a man in his thirties, arrived at his session in a flood of tears. Shortly before he had left his flat, only a stone's throw away from my office, his mother had left a message on his answering machine to say that she missed him, and that she had not heard from him in ages. Though the content of the mother's message could not be faulted, the patient described the volume and the timbre of the mother's voice as "deafeningly acidic", so much so that he felt as though her message had sliced into his eardrum. As the patient lay on the couch, he soaked up the relative silence of my consulting room, and he said, "You have a firm voice, but it never explodes. Thank you."

Needless to say, vocal tone may not be the only tonal feature to which we must be sensitive; for instance, we must consider posture, gait, facial texture, bodily expressions, mannerisms, dress, and so on. Each of these variables has its own language, awaiting an intuitive researcher to decipher their various vicissitudes.

In order to preserve sufficient time for discussion, I shall enumerate the remaining ingredients in a much more economical manner, in the hope that these may be engaged with by us all as a group. In addition to the permission to confess, the psychotherapist's supreme reliability, the psychotherapist's interest in the smallest detail, and the tonal qualities of the psychotherapist, I would add the following components:

- the psychotherapist's emotional intelligence and cognitive intelligence, which permit the clinician to disentangle the secret unconscious meanings of the patient's material;
- the psychotherapist's guarantee of absolute confidentiality, where this can be provided, which facilitates the willingness of the patient to engage and to confess;
- the psychotherapist's extreme neutrality of purpose, neither pushing the patient in any direction, except that of mental health, nor divesting oneself of concern for the patient's ultimate outcome;
- the psychotherapist's anonymity, refraining from taking up the patient's time and mental space with irrelevant details of the psychotherapist's private life;
- psychotherapy and the psychotherapeutic exchange as a template for loyalty, relatedness, and that which Donald Winnicott called "going-on-being" in the patient's life;
- the psychotherapist's posture of benignity and concern, as well as advocacy, transmitting first and foremost a sense that the clinician is "on the patient's side";
- identification with the joyfulness, zestfulness, playfulness, and vitality of the clinician;
- the staying power of the psyychotherapist, who displays the capacity to "sweat it out", as Dr Hanna Segal (1988) has noted;
- the rich private life of the psychotherapist, which allows the psychotherapist to practise in an unembittered fashion;

- the dedication of the psychotherapist to principles of account-ability and to further development, allowing his or her work to be liberally and appropriately scrutinized by trusted colleagues;
- the cooperation of the patient to a reasonable extent.

In other words, if we dared to summarize how and why psychotherapy works in one crisply constructed sentence, it might read thus:

> Psychotherapy may be defined as that very special, very private, very confidential professional interaction between an emotionally and cognitively intelligent, well-analysed, well-educated, well-resourced, and mentally zestful clinician, and a reasonably cooper-ative patient, in which the patient engages in the cathartic process of talking or communicating, assisted by the interest, benevolence, curiosity, and memory of the psychotherapist, who helps the patient to verbalize, to confess, to tolerate, to mourn, and to grow, through compassion, understanding, and deciphering of uncon-sciously coded material.

This possibly cumbersome and arguably idiosyncratic distillation does, I believe, represent the essence of the last quarter of a century of my work with the irked, disquieted, or indeed miserable people who have entrusted me with their narratives. I have witnessed tremendous growth in many of my patients during this period of time; and I trust that through such public arenas we can all continue to share and discuss our work, and that by doing so we can influ-ence one another in a positive, healthful manner, and thus improve the patient's experience of us as workers in the psychological field.

References

Dreher, H. (1995). *The Immune Power Personality: Seven Traits You Can Develop to Stay Healthy*. New York: Dutton.

Pennebaker, J. W. (1995). Emotion, disclosure, and health: an overview. In: J. W. Pennebaker (Ed.), *Emotion, Disclosure and Health* pp. 3–10. Washington, DC: American Psychological Association.

Segal, H. (1988). Sweating it out. *Psychoanalytic Study of the Child*, 43: 167–175.

Strachey, J. (1934). The nature of the therapeutic action of psycho-analysis. *International Journal of Psycho-Analysis*, 15: 127–159.

Trevarthen, C. (2003). Personal communication, 8 March.

Wallerstein, R. S. (2002). The generations of psychotherapy research: an overview. In: M. Leuzinger-Bohleber & M. Target (Eds.), *Outcomes of Psychoanalytic Treatment: Perspectives for Therapists and Researchers* pp. 30–52. London: Whurr Publishers.

Winnicott, D. W. (1963). Communicating and not communicating leading to a study of certain opposites. In: D. W. Winnicott, *The Maturational Processes and the Facilitating Environment: Studies in the Theory of Emotional Development* (pp. 179–192). London: Hogarth Press and the Institute of Psycho-Analysis, 1965.

Winnicott, D. W. (1969). The use of an object. *International Journal of Psycho-Analysis*, 50: 711–716.

CHAPTER TWO

Relational perspectives on the therapeutic action of psychoanalysis

Neil Altman

An historical perspective

L ewis Aron (1995) once commented that in order to make a creative contribution to the psychoanalytic literature, one has to be prepared to revise, even overturn, all of psychoanalytic theory. Psychoanalytic theory is an integrated set of conceptions that forms a system in which each part depends on all the other parts. Not everyone has agreed with this systemic conception of psychoanalysis; for example, it has been argued (Gill, 1976) that the metapsychology of psychoanalysis (e.g., the structural theory of id, ego, and superego) is independent of the clinical theory (of transference and resistance). Thus, one could get rid of the metapsychology without affecting the clinical theory. On the other hand, much of the literature in relational psychoanalysis over the past twenty years has been concerned with developing the far-reaching implications for psychoanalytic theory and practice of the "relational turn", i.e., the shift from regarding drives as fundamental to mental life, to regarding relational configurations as fundamental in the external world and in the internal world. In 1983, Jay Greenberg and Stephen Mitchell shook up the psychoanalytic world by systematizing and making explicit this shift that they claimed was taking place across a range of psychoanalytic schools of thought, from drive theory to relational theory. Since then, the implications that have emerged include, but are not limited to: redefinitions of the notion of neutrality (Aron, 1996, 2003; Greenberg, 1986), the emergence of the concept of "enactment" (Aron, 1996; Bass, 2003; Black, 2003; Jacobs, 1986), the re-emergence of dissociation as a fundamental organizing principle of the mind (Bromberg, 1999; Davies, 1999), a reconsideration of self-disclosure in psychoanalysis (Aron, 1992), new psychoanalytic epistemologies (Hoffman, 1998; Mitchell, 1993), new concepts of "mutuality" and "asymmetry" (Aron, 1992), reconsiderations of gender (Benjamin, 1995; Dimen, 2003; Goldner, 1991; Harris, 1991), race (Altman, 2000; Leary, 1997, 2000), and sexual orientation (Domenici & Lesser, 1995). In this paper, I spell out some of the implications of the relational turn for the theory of the therapeutic action of psychoanalysis. In the background of this discussion are considerations of what constitutes health and pathology; thus moral judgments, considerations as to what constitutes a good life, will be inevitably implicated and I attempt to make them explicit when I notice them in the background of the theories being discussed. We will see that ideas as to what constitutes a good life will also be found in ideas about what constitutes a good analysis. Let us begin with the first generation of analysts: Freud and his contemporaries.

Freud

At the outset, one must acknowledge that one cannot make monolithic statements about Freud's point of view. He said too many, sometimes contradictory, things at various points in the development of his thought, sometimes in the course of a single article (see Dimen, 2003, for comments about the role of footnotes as the medium through which Freud complicated his own thinking in his writing). It can, however, safely be said that Freud had reservations about the therapeutic potential of psychoanalysis. For example, he once commented that he had "never been a therapeutic enthusiast" (Freud, 1933a, p. 151). Freud often seemed to be more interested in psychoanalysis as a research method than as a therapy, although it is also clear that he believed that psychoanalytic therapy was superior among psychotherapies: "Compared with the other psychotherapeutic procedures, psycho-analysis is beyond any doubt the most powerful" (1933a, p. 153). The therapeutic potential of psychoanalysis, for Freud (Breuer & Freud, 1895d), consisted in its ability to liberate people from neurotic suffering, after which ordinary human suffering would remain. For all his caveats, it is none the less possible to draw out Freud's vision of what constituted a good life and what it was about psychoanalysis that facilitated the living of such a life.

Let us begin with one of Freud's epigrammatic statements, "where id was there ego shall be" (1933a).What is implied about a good life in this statement? The ego, in Freud's structural theory is the mediator among the contradictory demands of id impulses, superego prohibitions, and the need to adapt to the external world. Freud here seems to be saying that the good life consists in making room for all these demands given inherent conflicts among them. Some of Freud's therapeutic pessimism may derive from a tragic vision of endemic conflict, similar to that of Isaiah Berlin (1969) who posited inevitable conflicts among our various values (e.g., justice *vs.* freedom) such that we are always sacrificing something near and dear to us in the course of pursuing something else equally near and dear. The idea of the ego is that to some extent the mind is capable of calculating, as it were, the best possible resolution of conflicts among the various agencies of the mind and the external world.

Freud also implicitly privileges consciousness in this statement. While all ego functions are not conscious, the ego's domain is expanded when id–superego conflicts that had been resolved in childhood in untenable ways and then repressed are re-opened in adulthood and brought to the conscious attention of the more mature ego of adulthood. New resolutions can then be considered by an ego with more resources at its disposal than were available to the weak ego of childhood. Here is the point where Freud has a degree of therapeutic optimism. There is also a value placed on rationality over irrationality here, in so far as the ego is thought to have rationality at its disposal in the management of conflict. At this point, Freud reveals his enlightenment-bred faith in reason, or, rather, his belief that if the irrational workings of the unconscious mind, holdovers from childhood, could be placed into the illuminating rays of conscious rationality, irrationality could be superceded by rationality. In his effort to make the unconscious conscious, Freud was both pursuing a research agenda and acting in a way he considered therapeutic, based on an implicit equation of consciousness with rationality.

The means to this end of making the unconscious conscious is via language, i.e., through verbal interpretation or decoding of the derivatives of the unconscious that appear in free association. The conditions under which this therapeutic action could occur are well known, so I will only briefly summarize them: under conditions of abstinence, transference wishes (drive derivatives) will emerge. Under conditions of anonymity, the analyst will appear as a blank screen on to which the transference can be projected and validly interpreted as having nothing to do with the analyst as a person in the external world.[1] Interpretation renders the unconscious conscious, but the unconscious will only be subdued gradually through repeated interpretations in the longer-term process of working through.

Ego psychology

Freud's daughter, Anna, amended this picture of therapeutic action in connection with her concentration on the psychology of the ego and her work with children. Anna Freud (1966) noted the problems involved in working with people, all children and some adults, whose egos are not strong enough to tolerate the frustration and anxiety entailed in psychoanalytic work under conditions of abstinence and anonymity. In such cases, she believed a period of ego-supportive activity, educational in large part, might be necessary as preparation for analysis proper. By restricting this type of activity to a preparatory period with only certain patients, Anna Freud did not challenge her father's ideas about the therapeutic action of psychoanalysis *per se*. Others following in this tradition, like Elizabeth Zetzel (1958) and Ralph Greenson (1967), went further to maintain that all patients need a more supportive relationship with their analysts, but they segregated (one might say split off) this aspect of the relationship as non-transferential and characterized it as the working alliance. Nunberg (1932) challenged this dichotomy between the transference relationship and the working alliance by claiming that the working alliance, too, is based in transference, an "unobjectionable" positive transference, in Freud's words. Meanwhile, however, if one considers ego-strengthening to be a proper therapeutic goal, the ego psychologists had fundamentally revised the notions of psychoanalytic therapeutic action to include educational and supportive activities as therapeutic in their own right.

Fred Pine (1983) elaborated on this point of view by claiming that interpretation could take place either in the context of support (for those who need it by virtue of ego weakness) or in the context of abstinence (for those who have strong or normal egos). Pine here differs from the Freudian idea that the transference emerges properly only in the context of abstinence. He seems to imply that the need to support the ego takes precedence over fostering the emergence of transference when the ego is weak. Pine gives many detailed examples of the therapeutic effect of educational and supportive activities, such as naming feelings, being available consistently, and so on. Such activities go on in the background, silently, in all analyses, but need to be in the foreground in the analyses of ego-deficient people. At times, Pine goes further to note that such supportive activities are often cited by analysts themselves (who presumably have strong egos) when looking back at what seemed most important in their own training analyses. Pine and many others working in the ego psychological tradition, thus, both expanded the applicability of psychoanalytic treatment to more disturbed and developmentally less advanced people and brought in the idea that ego strengthening could be a valid therapeutic goal in a psychoanalytic treatment. In other language, one might say that the ego psychologists conceived of the analyst as a new and good object (in her supportive activities) to supplement the analyst as old and bad object (in her role as transference figure).

James Strachey (1934) took up the question of therapeutic action, emphasizing modification of the superego rather than the ego. He saw the operative factor as entailing the analysand's internalization of the analyst as a less harsh superego figure than the patient's pre-existing superego. Hans Loewald (1960) emphasized the analyst's higher level of ego function, compared to that of the patient. In the interaction between patient and analyst, Loewald emphasized how bridges could be formed between the patient's lower level of functioning and the analyst's higher level of functioning.

Ego psychology became the psychoanalytic mainstream in the USA, where life was more comfortable for analysts and others, and where analysts sought a privileged place among elite medical practitioners. In general, ego psychology seems to privilege functionality and adaptation. Their notion of the good life seems to revolve around fitting in, living up to conventional social expectations. With this emphasis on adaptation, the ego psychologists earned the scorn of analysts with a more critical attitude towards society, such as those with a more Marxist leaning, like Fromm (1947, 1955). Loewald's theory of therapeutic action sounds, at first blush, as if it fits in with rather an extreme version of this adaptational ethic, whereby health is equated with functionality and the analyst is the embodiment of this higher level of functioning. However, a fuller reading of Loewald's work (see, especially, Loewald, 1988) reveals that he was actually quite a maverick within the ego psychological community of the USA. He saw pathology in terms of a disconnect between higher and lower levels of functioning, so that the therapeutic task became that of reconnecting primary process and secondary process levels of thinking, rather than to replace primary process with secondary process. Loewald believed that secondary process without primary process would be as sterile as primary process without secondary process would be incomprehensible. Loewald's version of health, then, has to do with access to a wide range of developmental levels, as it were. Loewald thus laid the groundwork for revisions of developmental theory by Mitchell (2000), Harris (2005), and others who would move away from a more linear model with simplistic notions of health equated with maturity. Melanie Klein (1975), from a different angle, made a similar move in speaking of "positions" rather than "stages" in her developmental theory, the latter term implying more than the former a linear movement from immaturity to maturity; in the developmentally "delayed" or "fixated" individual, a move from sickness to health. Like Loewald, Klein saw health more in terms of access to a range of positions, rather than achievement of the later position *per se*.

Klein and the Kleinians

Melanie Klein differed sharply with Anna Freud on the role of ego-supportive interventions in psychoanalysis. Klein and her followers did not compromise on the centrality of interpretation in psychoanalytic technique, although the object of interpretation in Kleinian psychoanalysis differs from that in Freudian psychoanalysis. Whereas Freud saw the unconscious as consisting of drives, Klein saw the unconscious as structured by internal objects. Where Freudian interpretation focused on drives and defences against awareness of drive derivatives, Kleinian interpretation focused on anxieties with bad, i.e. destructive, internal object relationships and defences that entail the disavowal and projection of destructiveness. Where Freudian interpretation aims to bring repressed material to consciousness, Kleinian interpretation aims to help the patient reintegrate split off psychic content. Contemporary Kleinians (e.g. Joseph, 1978), since Bion (1959), emphasize not simply the return to the patient of split off psychic content via interpretation, but also the processing of that material while it is contained in the analyst so as to make it more digestible for the patient. There has also been increasing recognition that the analyst's interpretation must take account of the patient's degree of readiness to reintegrate anxiety-laden material. Klein (1975) delineated two basic psychic positions, the paranoid–schizoid and the depressive. In the former, badness is split off and projected. The interpersonal and intrapsychic worlds are sharply divided into good and bad objects. In the latter, people and internal objects are recognized as at once good and bad, including the self. Badness can be owned, along with goodness. The Kleinian value system centres on depressive position integration and tolerance for anxiety and complexity, though not to the exclusion of the passionate love and hate associated with the paranoid–schizoid position.

Freud's dissidents: the role of resistance in the psychoanalytic process

Meanwhile, Alfred Adler (1929) and Carl Jung (1953) were taking psychoanalysis in radically different directions. Each differed from

Freud with respect to the fundamental organizing power in the human psyche. Whereas Freud postulated sexuality, later adding aggression, as fundamental driving forces, Adler postulated a will to power and Jung postulated an integrative force. Adler's ideas led to fundamentally different ideas about the therapeutic action of psychoanalysis, specifically around the idea of resistance. For Freud, who was fond of military metaphors, resistance was the enemy, to be overcome through interpretation and confrontation. For example, he writes "the patient brings out of the armory of the past the weapons with which he defends himself against the progress of the treatment—weapons which we must wrest from him one by one" (1914g, p. 151). On the other hand, for Adler and his follower Otto Rank (1945), resistance was an expression of the patient's will and thus a manifestation of his healthy will to power. Adler, however, saw this will to power as compensatory to a feeling of inferiority, while Rank saw will as primary and healthy. Rank (1945, p. 457) wrote: "Where Freud met the will of the other he called it 'resistance' (to his will) and where Adler came upon this counterwill he called it masculine protest—. At the basis of both presentations lies a moral evaluation: it is 'bad'". But: "It is important that the neurotic above all learn to will".

In the other branch of classical psychoanalysis, Melanie Klein, like Freud, did view resistance as a force to be overcome, going further than Freud in regarding many instances of resistance as an expression of a destructive, envious drive directed toward the analyst's generative power. This destructive force was to be confronted by interpretation and by a determination on the analyst's part to stand firm, not to be seduced or bullied into departing from the analytic stance as traditionally defined. More contemporary Kleinians, particularly Anne Alvarez (1992), advocate looking for the healthy strivings in what might look like defensive activity, but she did not go so far as to regard instances of resistance to the analyst's interpretations as possibly healthy. Among later generations of psychoanalysts in the Freudian tradition, some, following Adler and Rank, redefined "resistance" in ways that led to a less confrontational attitude than Freud often took. The ego psychologists, believing that one needed to proceed "from surface to depth", from ego to id, in one's interpretations, saw resistance interpretation as ego-building and thus therapeutic in itself, not merely preparatory to interpretation proper, or id-interpretation. For the ego psychologists, resistance was also a sign of a relative weakness in the ego, an incapacity to tolerate the anxiety associated with a psychic content, and so was a therapeutic problem to be addressed, not simply an obstacle to be overcome. Relatively recently, Roy Schafer (1983) pointed out that the language associated with Freud's theory tended to portray the individual as passive, buffeted about by id impulses, paralysed by conflict. In proposing a shift to "action language", Schafer, like Adler and Rank, was suggesting that agency be regarded as a fundamental and healthy part of being human. Not surprisingly, Schafer (1983) proposed that we no longer speak of "resistance" but of the patient as agent "resisting", sometimes as an expression of a healthy assertive striving. The therapeutic power of psychoanalysis thus could derive not from the overcoming of resistance, but sometimes, to the contrary, from the mobilization of "resistance", now redefined as an expression of agency. The shift from id psychology to ego psychology thus had as a corollary that resistance came to be regarded more as part of the regulatory function of the ego; additionally, there evolved a focus on the self, as well as the ego as a set of functions, that led to a view of resistance as potentially an expression of an agentic self.

These theorists, from Adler to Schafer, privilege agency and activity in their view of the good and healthy life. There is a divergence between this point of view and that which sees the ego as a mere mediator among forces larger than the individual, as well as the more adaptational versions of ego psychology. The theories of Adler, Rank, and Schafer differed from those (Freudian and Kleinian) that emphasized transpersonal drives in being more individualistic.

Theorists of the self

In putting the self at the centre of their theories, Kohut (1977) and Winnicott (1950–1955, 1960), and their followers went even further in reframing "resistance". For Kohut, resistance could often be seen as an iatrogenic phenomenon, a reaction to the analyst's failure to recognize the patient's valid need for the analyst to meet self–object needs for mirroring and idealization. This focus on the patient's needs set up a conflict with the Freudian and Kleinian focus on the prominence of the destructive forces in the patient. Around the concept of idealization, for example, there could not be a sharper contrast between Kernberg (1975), who, operating in a Kleinian framework, saw the patient's idealization of the analyst as a defence against destructive envy, and Kohut, who saw idealization as a basic human need. In the self-psychological tradition, resistance is thought of as a fear of being retraumatized (Ornstein, 1991; Stern, 1994) and/or as an expression of a self–object need for an adversarial relationship (Lachman, 1986). It is important to recognize, however, that for Kohut the therapeutic action of psychoanalysis did not derive from the meeting of self–object needs *per se*. Rather, change occurred as a function of the analyst's failures that were followed by empathy with the patient's response to the failure. In this way patients were helped to internalize, to take over, the self-esteem regulating functions of the object, thus progressing to a more mature form of narcissism. It is thus all-important, in a self-psychological framework, not to interpret the patient's negative reactions to the analyst as a manifestation of a destructive or envious reaction to the analyst's constructive power. This response on the part of the analyst would make "transmuting internalization", in Kohut's terms, impossible. It is in the empathic response to the patient's sense of failure that the therapeutic potential lies. It should be noted here, parenthetically, that despite Kohut's emphasis on the importance of the human environment in psychological development and in psychoanalysis, maturity is defined in terms of the patient's increasing independence from that environment. Kohut's vision of the good life seems to centre on self-esteem and the ability to regulate self-esteem autonomously.

Winnicott, like Kohut, developed a theory of the self. Winnicott emphasized the self as a source of spontaneous gestures or actions that could be deformed by being required to adapt prematurely to the outside world. For those patients who had developed a "false self on a compliance basis" (Winnicott, 1960) the analyst's job was, first, to recognize the falseness of the patient's seeming compliance with the analyst and the analytic procedure, and second, to maintain a non-intrusive stance that would make room for the patient's spontaneous gestures. "Resistance", from this point of view, could be seen, to the extent that it is reactive to the analyst's intervention, as a manifestation of false self (the essence of false self is its reactivity). On the other hand, there is some striving towards true self in the resistance to compliance. For the analyst to expect compliance with the analyst's interpretations is perhaps the most anti-therapeutic thing an analyst could do from a Winnicottian point of view. Here, obviously, is a point of radical departure from Kleinian and classical Freudian technique and theory of therapeutic action.

Winnicott's ideal of health had to do with the ability to inhabit "transitional space", defined as a space in which subjectivity and the recognition of externality could co-exist. This is a creative space in which there is room for personal reality without negation of consensual reality. There is room for both true-self living and accommodation to external reality. The paradigmatic activity in transitional space is play. The child or adult at play is creating a world within a world, a fantasy space that co-exists with the world of consensual reality. The ability to play, to live life playfully is, for Winnicott, the goal of psychoanalytic therapy and the ideal mode of being for patient and analyst within the analysis. In particular, interpretations should be offered by the analyst in a spirit of play that leaves room for the co-creation of meaning between patient and analyst, as opposed to dogmatic interpretations that leave no room for any response except compliance and resistance. For those patients unable to play, the process of analysis is towards the ability to play, and the mode of therapeutic action has to do with the fostering of a play space in which that ability can be unlocked or developed. Creativity and the ability to inhabit subjectivity playfully and without the loss of objectivity, along with the sense of meaningfulness that derives from authenticity and spontaneity, are at the core of the Winnicottian notion of a good life.

Jung and the Jungians[2]

While one can find many precedents for relational concepts in Jung, there has been very little direct connection between Jungian analysis and relational psychoanalysis due, no doubt, to the fall-out, on all levels including that of institutional politics, following the Freud–Jung split. Contemporary post-Jungian analysts (e.g., Samuels et al, 2000) have little difficulty in resonating with many of the ideas and practices evolving within the tradition of relational psychoanalysis.

Jung asserted that analysis was a "dialectical process", intending to highlight the fact that two people are involved in a relationship, that emotionally charged interactions between them are two-way, and that, in the deepest way, they are to be conceived of as equals (1935, p. 8). Analysis, Jung goes on to say, is "an encounter, a discussion between two psychic wholes in which knowledge is used only as a tool". The analyst is a "fellow participant in the analysis". Jung's focus was often on "the real relationship" (Greenson, 1967), making his point in very challenging terms: "In reality everything depends on the man [sic] and little on the method" (Jung, 1931, p. 7) In a manner strikingly reminiscent of Ferenczi, to whom we will soon turn, Jung's perspectives encouraged post-Jungian analysts to explore the extent to which they themselves were "wounded healers", bringing their strengths and weaknesses to the therapy situation (see Samuels, 1985, pp. 173–206). The focus on the analyst is balanced by Jung's understanding of countertransference, which, in many ways, anticipates contemporary psychoanalytic attitudes. In 1929, he stated that

> You can exert no influence if you are not susceptible to influence . . . The patient influences the analyst unconsciously . . . One of the best known symptoms of this kind is the countertransference evoked by the transference . . . countertransference is a very important organ of information. [Jung, 1929, pp. 71–2]

In spite of his relational perspectives, Jung's intricate model of the psyche tended to concentrate on inner structures that were considered by him to be innate ("archetypal"). Hence, he is also a proponent of a "one-person psychology". For example, between the ego and the outside world, he discerned the "persona", the necessary social mask that a person puts on. Between the ego and the inner world, lies the "contrasexual component", "animus" for a woman and "anima" for a man. These figures, whose anatomical sex is the opposite of the subject's, guide her or him in a journey to reach what Jung sometimes called "the undiscovered self". They may symbolize what is, at present, out of the psychological reach of the individual. This journey would take place under the aegis of the

"Self", a sort of internal, guiding intelligence to whose voice patient and analyst had better attend. The "shadow" was Jung's term for "the thing a person has no wish to be", the irreducibly destructive, envious, and immature part of the personality. These archetypal structures can be encountered inwardly via reflection and what Jung termed "active imagination". Or they could be encountered in the relational world—but this would be via projection on to others, including the analyst.

There is, therefore, a tension between Jung's interactive, relational, dialogical side and his orientation towards the internal world. His attempt to resolve the tension is found in his seemingly surprising preoccupation with alchemy exemplified in "The psychology of the transference" (1946). The processes and imagery of alchemy were understood by Jung as facilitating a consideration of intrapsychic processes occurring in both patient and analyst and their interpersonal relationship at the same time.

Jung (1953) differed from Freud in de-emphasizing sexuality as the primary driving force in human life. Jung believed there was a healthy tendency towards individuation, which he defined in terms of the integration of polarized parts of the psyche. For example, the male principle (animus) tends to get split off from the female principle (anima) in both men and women. Whatever is emphasized consciously, the opposite is emphasized unconsciously. Psychoanalysis is a process of reconnecting with the "shadow" self through dreams and free associations. The analyst's job is to recognize the emergence of the "shadow" and to promote the patient's recognition of disowned aspects of himself. In this way, Jung's ideas anticipated the Kleinian idea of health in terms of the reowning of previously split-off aspects of self. Jungians, like Kleinians, privilege psychic integration in their notion of the good life, though Jung, unlike Kleinians, saw a spiritual dimension to the sought-after wholeness.

Lacan and Lacanians

Lacan (1972) considered the psychoanalytic project from a radically different perspective from those we have so far considered. Lacan understood the Freudian unconscious as a transpersonal factor structured by language, or the symbolic network of human culture (there is a resonance here with the Jungian collective unconscious). For Lacan, the individual personality or ego belongs to the "imaginary" register, the realm of appearances and illusions. A patient's speech, then, can and should be heard on two levels, much as one can listen to a dream and hear the manifest and latent content. One can hear the imaginary level of an interpersonal transaction, a transaction between two egos, and one can listen for the discourse of the unconscious. An individual's personality, or an interpersonal exchange, cannot be considered outside the context of the unconscious discourse that speaks through persons, just as the manifest content of a dream cannot be considered apart from the latent content that speaks through it. A therapy that seeks to strengthen the ego or the personality outside the context of the unconscious that constitutes that personality trades in mirages from this point of view. A modern Lacanian, such as Bernstein (1999), takes care to point out that she does not ignore the realm of the ego and the personality, nor does she dismiss the significance of the patient–analyst interaction. Rather, she insists that one not confuse the individual personality with the subject of the unconscious. The influence of this point of view is not limited to Lacanians: Thomas Ogden (1994), for example, pays close attention to his reveries in a session as a point of entrée into what he calls the "analytic third", a subjectivity that subsumes and speaks through the individual subjectivities of patient and analyst. For Lacanians and others influenced by their point of view, then, the good life is not about adaptation to the social world or about having a strong ego or personality. On the contrary, attachment to the ego, the individualized self, is the disease to be cured by psychoanalysis.

From Ferenczi and Fairbairn to interpersonal psychoanalysis

Finally, among those in Freud's circle who differed with him there is Sandor Ferenczi. Ferenczi (1933) believed that Freud underemphasized the impact of the analyst as a person on the patient and on the analytic process. In particular, Ferenczi came to believe that the analyst's denial of his own feelings towards the patient retraumatized the patient in ways similar to the pathogenic situations of childhood. Where the analyst had negative feelings towards the patient, the analyst's neutral, anonymous stance amounted to "professional hypocrisy". Where the analyst had blockages in his ability to love the patient, his capacity to receive the patient's love would be inhibited. Ferenczi was so concerned not to mystify or deprive the patient that he was willing to submit himself to mutual analysis (Ferenczi, 1933) in order to transcend any blockages in his ability to heal the patient. Ferenczi thus mounted a very radical critique of Freudian technique, a technique that emphasized an unvarying reserve regardless of the analyst's true underlying feelings. Ferenczi's view of the analytic situation as interactive, of the therapeutic action of psychoanalysis as very much implicating the analyst's personal influence on the patient, anticipated much of American interpersonal psychoanalysis and the relational tradition that emerged from its integration with British object relations theory. Meanwhile, Fairbairn (1958), in Scotland, was similarly coming to the conclusion that the analyst's personal influence was core to the therapeutic action of psychoanalysis. Fairbairn saw pathology as consisting of the patient's incapacity to see other people objectively, as they truly are in external reality, because of the distorting influence of a fixed, internal, reality. Whereas for Klein the world of internal objects was a given, for Fairbairn it was a pathological response to frustration. In the Kleinian epistemology, the external world is always known through the prism of internal reality. For Fairbairn, this is a pathological development. Fairbairn believed in the possibility of objective perception of other people, and this constituted his ideal of health. The therapeutic action of psychoanalysis thus derived from the analyst's making himself available as a person to the patient to help make a breach in the patient's closed system of internal reality. To take an anonymous stance only reinforces the patient's closed inner world. Fairbairn and Ferenczi thus concurred in believing that Freudian reserve was not only not helpful, but actually pathogenic. They both saw the analytic process as helping the patient take in the analyst's influence as a new and good object.

Sandor Ferenczi influenced American interpersonal psychoanalysis, as Clara Thompson travelled to Budapest for a brief analysis with Ferenczi, reporting back on her experience to Harry Stack Sullivan. Interpersonalists picked up on Ferenczi's idea that there is

a certain hypocrisy in the classical analyst's denial of personal feelings towards the analysand. Analytic hypocrisy repeated an earlier
parental hypocrisy that mystified the child by denying the presence
of negative feelings towards the child on the part of the parent that
the child could sense were present. Note here that Ferenczi is
propounding a relational theory of pathogenesis, i.e., that psychopathology results from environmental failure of one kind or
another. He is considering the analytic situation to be relational as
well, in which the fate of the analysis depends on how the analyst
actually behaves in comparison to how the child was treated by his
primary objects. Ferenczi (1933) came to believe that the analyst's
ability to love the patient was key to the therapeutic action of
psychoanalysis and even submitted himself to analysis by one of
his patients in order to better analyse her.

Clearly, by the end of his life Ferenczi had departed sharply
from Freud's ideas about the therapeutic action of psychoanalysis
and the technical principles that flowed from these ideas. Ferenczi
was ahead of his time in many ways; as a pioneer in considering the
psychoanalytic situation as an interactive one, prepared to take
radical action if that's where his ideas led him, he went off in some
misguided directions, e.g., mutual analysis, in the absence of a
community of like-minded people with whom to develop the implications of his ideas. His ideas in the longer term, however, were
developed by others to form the foundation of contemporary
psychoanalysis. We have already noted his view of the analytic situation as interactive. In pointing out the powerful impact of the
analyst's efforts to be anonymous and abstinent, Ferenczi did more
than demonstrate the inadvisability of this technical stance. He
demonstrated that anonymity is impossible in principle, in that the
analyst as a person is revealed in the choice to try to be anonymous.
Sullivan (1953) captured the essence of this point of view in his
description of the analyst as a participant–observer. Freud had
conceived of the analyst as an observer and a commentator. As a
participant–observer, the analyst still observes, but since the analyst
participates inevitably and continuously, the object of observation
must be the interpersonal field, rather than the patient in isolation.

What are the implications for the therapeutic action of psychoanalysis from this interpersonal point of view? Sullivan, following
Ferenczi, stressed the role of mystification in promoting psycho-

pathology. Psychopathology consists of disordered interpersonal relationships, and these result from failure to see and understand clearly what is going on in the interpersonal field. Sullivan believed that this failure resulted from a need to avoid awareness of anxiety-provoking interpersonal stimuli. In thorough-going interpersonal fashion, Sullivan believed that anxiety was transmitted by contagion from parent to child. The child's anxiety arose from the parent's anxiety. The child could not afford to make the parent anxious, and so would collude with the parent's anxiety-driven selective inattention. The goal of psychoanalytic therapy, then, came to be conceived of as undoing this process by helping the patient perceive the interpersonal world clearly. The analyst's job was to notice the patient's blind spots, then seek to promote heightened awareness in those anxiety-laden areas. Sullivan considered that his expertise consisted in his ability to probe these blind spots without counterproductively stimulating an overflow of anxiety that would simply reinforce the patient's selective inattention. There is a contradiction here, however. As an expert in interpersonal relations, as the one who knows what's going on in the patient's interpersonal world, the analyst is being seen again as the very same objective observer that the interpersonal point of view denied was possible.

Edgar Levenson (1982) developed this conundrum further by filling in the details of just how it is that the analyst is a participant in the analytic situation. Drawing on speech act theory (Austin, 1962) Levenson pointed out that when we say something to a person we are simultaneously acting in relation to that person. There is always the message and the meta-message, and the meta-message is an action. A psychoanalytic interpretation, then, inevitably involves some sort of action on the patient. Levenson believed that the action level of an interpretation would be isomorphic with its content, i.e., it would enact the content being discussed. He illustrated this point with a simple example: if one comments on a patient's sensitivity, one is likely to hurt his feelings. The analyst always participates as a function of the nature of speech. The nature of the analyst's participation is likely to be obscure to the analyst himself, especially if he is directing his attention to the content of what he is saying. The analytic procedure, then, consists of progressively and endlessly explicating what is going on between the patient and analyst. The therapeutic action depends on the ability of patient and analyst to examine carefully the nature of their inter-action. The greatest analytic obstacle is the analyst's anxiety, her own blind spots that transmit to the patient that she, in turn, doesn't dare explore certain aspects of their interaction. It is inter-esting to compare this interpersonal perspective with the ideas being developed by Merton Gill (1982) contemporaneously with Levenson. Gill believed that the exploration of transference was the heart of psychoanalysis, and that resistance to the awareness of transference took the form of the patient's making indirect allu-sions to feelings about the analyst, e.g. by talking about someone other than the analyst. Gill believed further that transference reac-tions were always a plausible reaction to some action on the analyst's part. Unlike Levenson, Gill believed that transference also had roots in pre-existing, preformed templates in the patient's mind. Transference arose when one of these preconceptions found a plausible basis in something the analyst actually did. The tech-nical principle that one should explore the here-and-now analytic interaction as thoroughly as possible was similar, but Gill more than Levenson wanted the patient to develop a heightened aware-ness of what the patient brought to the interaction in the form of preconceptions, biases, positive and negative expectations, and so on.

Relational perspectives on the therapeutic action of psychoanalysis: contemporary issues

Relational psychoanalysis arose out of the desire to take account of the interpersonal and intrapsychic domains without collapsing one into the other. In other words, relational psychoanalysis seeks to integrate interpersonal psychoanalysis, with its focus on the exter-nal world, with British object relations theory with its focus on the internal world. With respect to the analytic space itself, a move towards this integration becomes necessary once it is acknowl-edged that the analyst as a person is inevitably a participant in the analytic situation, even by virtue of trying not to be a participant. There is then no way to study the patient's mind except in the context of the analyst's presence and activity. Likewise, there is no way to study the interaction between patient and analyst without taking account of the meaning-making system through which each person processes what happens between them. Studying the patient's internal world, and studying the interpersonal field: you can't have one without the other. One implication of this principle is epistemological; since both patient and analyst know the other through a particular meaning-making system (including the analyst's theory), there is no such thing as infallible or purely objective knowledge about either the patient's mind or the nature of the analytic interaction. There are no certainties, whether they be Freudian or Kleinian or derived from any of the other schools of thought. This is the basic tenet of constructivism. It is important to note that it does not follow that "anything goes", that any construction is as good as any other. What I am describing is epistemological constructivism, not ontological constructivism. In other words, what is constructed is our understandings of reality, not reality itself. Reality, including the nature of a person's mind or an interpersonal interaction, is what it is. But we cannot know that reality except through our constructions because we are human and our constructions are always tentative and revisable. This is a basic principle of the scientific method: any conclusion based on experimental evidence is potentially revisable in the light of the results of the next experiment, or even in light of the next interpretation of an old experiment. Irwin Hoffman (1991, 1992) has described psychoanalytic constructivism as "social constructivism", in that the understandings arrived at are constructed between patient and analyst, as the patient conveys his understanding and experience of the analytic interaction and the analyst conveys her understanding and, sometimes, the experience on which that understanding is partially based, to the patient.

From this relational–constructivist perspective, then, part of the therapeutic action of psychoanalysis arises from a process of ongoing exploration and negotiation of the analytic interaction. In the process the patient's interpersonal competence is enhanced as a function of the joint inquiry. At the same time, the patient's perspective on his internal world, from which his meaning-making system is derived, is enhanced as his experience of the analytic interaction is examined in an intersubjective context. The word "intersubjective", widely used in relational psychoanalysis (Benjamin, 1988,

1995, 1998, Stolorow & Atwood, 1992) conveys the intrapsychic–intersubjective integration I have been discussing. The "subjective" part of the word conveys the focus on personal experience that derives in part from pre-existing, or internal, meaning-making systems. The "inter" part of the word conveys the focus on the interpersonal field, the space between patient and analyst. Finally, we should note that recently theorists such as Benjamin (2004) and Ogden (1994) have spoken of an intersubjectively derived "third" to convey the idea that there is experience generated in an intersubjective field that both subsumes each individual's experience and transforms their interaction. Ogden uses his experience of this intersubjectively generated third to derive hypotheses about the patient's experience, i.e., in the service of understanding the patient's mind; Benjamin, with more of a focus on interpersonal interaction, looks to the "third", using the analogy of the relationship of the dance to the dancers, as a way to break out of impasses that she calls "split complementarity".

The notion of split complementarity brings us to another mode of therapeutic action often discussed in the relational literature. Mitchell (1997) refers to "impasses and outbursts" (p. 53), a sequence of events initiated by a situation in which patient's and analyst's experience of their interaction is discrepant in such a way that their respective notions of how to carry the analysis forward imply opposite actions. In one example taken from Mitchell (1997, pp. 53–58) the patient wants the analyst to help her with her graduate school application; the analyst feels that to do so would be demeaning or infantilizing of the patient, and demurs. The patient feels abandoned by the analyst; the analyst feels the patient is holding on to an archaic self-image as incompetent and dependent. This kind of situation often devolves into a power struggle; this is what Benjamin (1998) refers to as a "split complementarity". Benjamin's idea is that there is a splitting process involved in such situations, in which the analyst is taking one side of the split while the patient takes the other. In the case of Mitchell's just cited, the analyst is seeking to promote the patient's autonomy, the patient seeks what she feels is a needed or desired support. With reference to the Kleinian notion of the depressive position, Benjamin believes that the analytic process is advanced by an intersubjective negotiation in which patient and analyst struggle to see the other's point of view without abandoning his or her own. Thus, each party to the interaction achieves an intrapsychic integration while fostering a "meeting of the minds" (Aron, 1996) between them. In Mitchell's case, having found a way to contain both the patient's point of view and his own, he shares his dilemma with the patient (an act he calls an "outburst") that allows them to transcend their power struggle. Benjamin (2004) looks for a way for patient and analyst to surrender themselves to the larger process in which they are both swept along (the "third") as a way to achieve such an integration.

Note the comparison and contrast with a more classical position, whether Freudian or Kleinian or Sullivanian. Patient and analyst do seek understanding of the way the patient's mind works, and they do seek understanding of the interaction that evolves between them. But Mitchell and Benjamin, along with others in the relational tradition, also seek to revise internalized self–other paradigms through falling into an impasse that is presumed to contain important aspects of what makes the patient unhappy and unsatisfied in daily life outside the analysis, and then working their way out of it. Hoffman (1998) believes that the special "mystique" of the analyst and the analytic situation provides a special power to new experience that takes place therein. He believes that the specialness of parents to children accounts for the rigidity of the patterns developed in early family interactions, and that it takes new experience in an equally enchanted situation to counter their power. This process of working one's way out of situations that at one point might seem inevitable and insoluble demonstrates that there are many more options than one had thought.

In relational psychoanalysis, then, the therapeutic action occurs through understanding and through action itself. The analyst seeks a position in which "old object" paradigms come alive (summoning ghosts, in Loewald's, 1960, terms) in the context of a relationship that has "new object" properties as well. Greenberg (1986) commented that in the absence of a new object transference the analysis would never begin (the patient would simply play out old self–object patterns as she does in the rest of her life) while in the absence of an old object transference the analysis would never end (this being the fate of simple "corrective emotional experiences"). Hoffman points out that the analyst is never just an old object, in that he plays that part in a new way, conditioned by the particularity of his idiom (Bollas, 1987), his personality, or way of being. At the same time the analyst is never simply a new object; the patient will be selectively attentive to those aspects of the analyst's behaviour that signal danger on the basis of the patient's past history and current meaning-making system. Given an adequate new object–old object balance, the patient's internalized paradigms of self–other interaction become open to change. In Winnicott's terms, one might say that this balance is characterized by the optimally playful enactment of old object paradigms and danger situations. In more traditional terms, one might say that the role of insight and understanding is to gain perspective on old object interactions so as to reduce the sense of inevitability about them, thus to make possible an element of flexibility and playfulness.

Relational analysts see interpretations as actions, as discussed above, and actions as potentially interpretive, in terms of the commentary about the patient embedded in an action such as answering or not answering a question, accepting or not accepting a gift, and so on. Ogden (1994) notes that it is now widely accepted that patients communicate important unconscious meanings to the analyst through their actions, as part of a process of projective identification, for example, but that it is less widely noted that analysts convey important transference interpretations to their patients via their actions. In one of his examples, he comes to an understanding that the function of a patient's speech is primarily to get the analyst to speak, as if everything of value in the analysis had to come from the analyst. Ogden, as analyst, realizes that any verbal interpretation to this effect will only serve to further enact what he considers a perversion of verbal communication of meaning. So he resorts to what he considers an action, i.e., silence, as a mode that more effectively communicates, in his view, his understanding of what his speech means to the patient. Ogden notes that "interpretation is a form of object relationship, and—object relationship is a form of . . . interpretation (in the sense that every object relationship conveys an aspect of the subject's understanding of the latent content of the interaction with the object)" (1994, pp. 109–110), thus perhaps undercutting any distinction between interpretive action and verbal interpretation. It should be noted that Ogden's example can be understood as a form of "outburst" from an impasse

(Mitchell, 1997), i.e., a variation on the theme of the renegotiation of self–other relationships, in Frankel's (1998) words, without necessarily involving an interpretation *per se*, except in so far as an interpretation of the intersubjective situation is part of the backdrop of meaning-making that informs any action.

In another example of what might be called interpretive action, Lewis Aron (1996) describes a clinical case in which a patient who is contemplating breaking up with his girlfriend because of some perceived faults asks Aron, "Are there important things about your wife that you don't like?" Aron,

> after a moment of hesitation, responds "Yes, there are important things about my wife that I don't like—More significant, perhaps, there are important things about me, that my wife doesn't like— you know there are important things about myself that I don't like—why should she have to like them?" [p. 225]

Aron suggests that this vignette demonstrates that self-disclosure can work "in the service of interpretation". Self-disclosure thus can constitute a form of interpretive action. In this case, Aron seems to be making an interpretation of defence, something like "I think you are focusing on your girlfriend's faults to avoid thinking about your own faults". Aron (1992) elsewhere makes the complementary point, following Levenson as noted above, that interpretations also constitute a form of action. If actions (such as self-disclosures) can be interpretations, and interpretations are actions, then any principle of technique relying on the distinction between the two needs to be revised. If we then note the social constructivist point that the meaning of any interaction can never be fully known to either patient or analyst, any interpretation can be seen, not as the end point of meaning-making, but as the beginning of a process of meaning-making focusing on the analyst's interpretation itself. For example, Aron's comments about he and his wife not liking things about each other, and about Aron not liking certain things about himself, clearly have much more potential meaning than is contained in the idea that Aron is making an interpretation of his patient's defence. Aron might be thought to be claiming that he is superior to the patient because he is free of that particular defence, or that he has worked through that particular defence. Simultaneously, he might be thought to be making a statement of commonality with the patient because they both have things they don't like about themselves. He might be thought to be piquing the patient's curiosity about what he doesn't like about himself, maybe in the interaction with this patient in particular. And so on and so on.

It is interesting to compare Ogden's ideas with Mitchell's ideas about "impasse and outburst". In the case Mitchell uses to illustrate this concept (Mitchell, 1997, p. 53ff), a patient who had been seen once a week at a reduced fee comes into some money and finds herself in conflict about whether to spend it by increasing the frequency of sessions or whether to save it. She also had questions about whether this treatment justified spending the money. She asks her analyst's advice about whether she ought to arrange more frequent sessions. There was a background with her father and previous analyst of going along with their advice in a way that felt somewhat unreflectively compliant. Mitchell finds himself feeling suffocated, torn between feeling that it would be seductive to urge her to spend the money on more frequent sessions, but withholding and abandoning if he should refrain from offering that opinion. In the end, he has what he calls an "outburst", which consisted of telling the patient how stymied he felt, and how he might be struggling with the choice if he were her. Mitchell views the impasse as reflecting a necessary engagement with the "old object" transference; i.e., he finds himself on the cusp of acting in a way that would seem seductively reminiscent of the patient's father and other father-like figures in her life. But it is not so simple to refrain from this sort of engagement; the alternative is to seem unengaged, a prospect that does not seem to offer much therapeutic value. In meta-communicating about the dilemma, Mitchell believes that he has found a way to construct something new out of something old. Old relational structures need to be activated, followed by an unexpected and creative engagement with the analyst's own participation from a position partly embedded in and partly outside of the old object role, in order to maximize the potential to foster fundamental change in relational structures. This is what Frankel (1998) calls the renegotiation of self–other relationships in action. Interpretation is not a central aspect of this process, except in so far as the construction of meaning is in the background as the analyst constructs his intervention.

In both Ogden's cases, and in Mitchell's case, the analyst is on the verge of playing out the complementary role to the patient's in an old object interaction. The difference between the two theorists is that Ogden believes he can refuse the gambit, decline the old object participation, e.g., by silence, by deferring taking the poems, by asking a question rather than answering one. The old object transference is interpreted, in a sense, in the course of declining to participate in it. For Mitchell, by contrast, there is no simple way to decline participation. To decline to participate in one scenario is to fall into another old object scenario (abandonment in the case cited). His choice is to metacommunicate and to seek creative ways to break out of "damned if you do and damned if you don't" scenarios. For Ogden, the activation of an old object pattern is the occasion for an interpretation, through words or actions, from a position of non-participation. For Mitchell, the analyst's ability to reflect, to metacommunicate, on the nature of the interaction from a position on the verge of falling into, or having partially fallen into, an old object participation, is crucial. Ogden's interpretation focuses on the patient's intrapsychic struggles, while Mitchell's focuses on the relational situation. Although Mitchell does not say so in this particular case, it would be consistent with his point of view to believe that any metacommunicative comments offered in the hope of transcending an enactment might well constitute an unreflective participation in another enactment. For example, Mitchell's sharing his thoughts about what he would be thinking if he were his patient might be seen as self-involved, a failure to address the patient's unique dilemma. If the patient were to perceive Mitchell's comment that way, indeed if Mitchell perceived his comment that way in the course of speaking it, this would simply create another impasse that one would need to seek to reflect on with the patient. For Mitchell and other relational analysts, enactments are continuous and potentially useful, a royal road to the relational, co-constructed, unconscious. The interpretive element is addressed to the interaction, as well as to the patient's intrapsychic situation, and takes the form of metacommunication about the interaction, as well as reflective comments about the patient's, and his own, participation in it. Mitchell sees a great deal of the therapeutic action as deriving from the analyst's authentic and good-faith struggle with being an old and a new object. For

Ogden, therapeutic action is much more associated with the maintenance of an interpretive position.

In short, from an evolving relational point of view, the therapeutic action of psychoanalysis arises from the nature of the process between patient and analyst. It is not tied to any particular mode of action on the part of patient or analyst but rather depends on the negotiation of meaning between the two parties What Stern (1997), following Gadamer (1975), calls a "fusion of horizons". This development of meaning is an endless process; the end point of an analysis cannot be defined in terms of an end point of the process of developing meaning. Rather, one might think of analytic termination in terms of the patient's ability to continue the process on her own and in the rest of her life with other people without needing the analyst's assistance (although it is not as though the analyst's assistance could not always be helpful).

Clinical illustration

I will conclude with a clinical example[3] that illustrates some of these points. Rosa was a seventeen-year-old high school student who came to a public clinic in which I worked with panic attacks and severe intermittent depression, triggered at the time by a breakup with a boyfriend. She was a bright young woman who went to an elite high school out of her neighbourhood in a poor section of the Bronx. Her mother and father were immigrants from the Dominican Republic who had lived here for over twenty-five years. Rosa's mother was an intelligent woman, but moody and sometimes depressed, who had never learned English. She stayed at home raising her three children, of whom Rosa was the youngest. The father, an intelligent and energetic man, had worked his way up from being a stock clerk in a store to being store manager. Rosa began therapy talking about her anger that her boyfriend had left her for another young woman they both knew. Rosa was enraged, depressed, with suicidal thoughts. I began seeing her twice a week.

After the first few sessions, Rosa began missing appointments. A pattern developed between us: Rosa would come to one or two sessions and then miss one. At first she would call to cancel. Something had come up at school, or she needed to be home to help her mother. After some time, she began missing sessions without calling. I was in conflict about how to respond. I felt caught between intruding by pursuing her and abandoning her by seeming to ignore her absence. I also felt caught between revealing to her, by an overly eager phone call, how much I wanted her to show up and revealing to her, by withholding contact, how angry I was. My compromise solution was to wait a day or two to see if she would call; if she did not, I would write her a letter noting that she had missed an appointment and saying that unless I heard otherwise, I would expect to see her at our next appointment. Rosa would show up at the next appointment with some concrete reason she had been unable to come to the appointment and apologize for having forgotten to call me.

After a couple of months, Rosa did not respond to one of my letters, so I wrote again asking her to contact me about her plans for our next appointment. After a week's delay, Rosa called, saying she had not got my first letter and asking for a new appointment.

When we met, I asked Rosa what she had been thinking about our work while we had not met. She said she had been feeling better and thought perhaps she did not need to come so regularly. I asked if she had considered contacting me to tell me so. She said that she felt uncomfortable about that; she anticipated that I would think she needed to continue her sessions, and that since I was the doctor, it was not her place to disagree. I asked her how she thought I had experienced her absence, and she said she had actually thought about me at one point, and wondered how I would fill the time when she did not show up. When I pressed her to speculate about my state of mind, she said she thought I was probably angry to be "stood up". I said perhaps this was not unlike what she had felt, although more intensely, when her boyfriend had "stood her up", and she agreed.

In the next session, Rosa expressed anger at her mother for insisting that she be home at midnight the previous weekend when she had gone to a party. She felt that her mother could not accept that she was pretty much grown up. What if she wanted to go away to college the next year? Would her mother even let her go? Rosa felt that her mother had no life of her own, that she would go into a depression if Rosa did not stay home with her. I suggested that Rosa might feel similarly about me, that she had to hide her thought that she was feeling better and might not need me any more. Rosa agreed, and said that she had been angry at me for pursuing her when she thought she was making it clear by her absence that she did not want to come to her sessions, at least on a regular basis. Her mother and I were both standing in the way of her developing autonomy. Over the next few sessions, none of which was missed, we had the opportunity to explore her guilt about wanting to be more independent. She felt that she was leaving behind her mother, as well as her childhood friends, by going "downtown" to school.

I want to highlight in this vignette the analytic impasse that developed precisely around Rosa's point of maximum intrapsychic conflict. It seemed that to encourage Rosa to attend her sessions simultaneously expressed a wish to foster her independent functioning, and maintained her in a dependent position in relation to me. In the former respect I was a new object, in the latter an old object. My new object position, seeking to promote growth and change towards independence, needs to be qualified with recognition of my attachment to and dependence on her in the light of my feeling abandoned by her when she missed appointments. My old object position, as manifest in this dependence on her, needs to be qualified by my over-riding commitment to use our relationship to foster her independent development. As Mitchell (1997) pointed out, this is just the position in which the analyst needs to be for therapeutic change to occur. Since Rosa herself had both independent and dependent strivings, I needed to be in a position to resonate with both sides of her conflict. The problem, ultimately, was the lack of integration of these various strivings, the polarization between her and her mother, and between her and me, whereby it seemed that we were holding her back, rather than that she had an internal conflict at that point in her life. Our enactment of this polarization around my pushing her to attend sessions was necessary for these issues to come into focus, but not sufficient for her to reown her internal conflict. For this to occur we had to find a way to work our way out of the enactment. In this case, talking, metacommunicating, about the bind we were in served an integrative function as Rosa could acknowledge that she had guilt about leaving her mother and her childhood friends behind as she moved ahead in the larger world. A precondition for this integration to occur was that I could recognize that in pursuing Rosa to come to her sessions, I was enacting more than I knew. I had to be open to recognizing my own dependence on Rosa, my personal need for her to attend her sessions with me. Not recognizing my own personal investment in this regard would have conduced to "acting out" these feelings, in the sense of enacting them unreflectively. For change to occur, both of us needed to grow, in the sense of being able to recognize a multiplicity of feelings in relation to each other, being able to "stand in the spaces" (Bromberg, 1999) among them and reflect on them together in the midst of emotionally charged enactments.

Conclusion

The relational psychoanalytic ideas I have been developing in this chapter integrate some aspects of American interpersonal psychoanalysis with various aspects of British object-relations psychoanalysis. I have drawn on neo-Kleinian notions of the importance of integration of the paranoid–schizoid and depressive positions in the course of psychoanalysis and in life in general. That is, I have argued for the necessity of both engaging in enactments (paranoid–schizoid mode), and in reflecting on them (depressive mode). The notion that psychic health consists in integration of various self-states, in psychic unity amidst diversity and psychic diversity in the context of unity, is consistent with the Kleinian notion of psychic integration. There is a divergence from the neo-Kleinian position, however, in the notion that the analyst needs to have access to the paranoid–schizoid mode as well, in terms of engaging in enactments. This emphasis on the inevitability and usefulness of analyst enactments derives from the American interpersonal focus on the analyst's inevitable and useful participation in, as well as observation of, the analytic process. A further divergence from the neo-Kleinian position is evident in the exploratory, as opposed to definitive, nature of the analyst's interventions. Herein one can see a Winnicottian stress on non-intrusiveness and a playful approach both to enactments themselves and to the exploration of their meaning. One might say, in summary, that, in terms of process, both the means and the end of psychoanalytic therapy derive from the exploration and development of meaning in a playful interpersonal context. In terms of substance, the end of a psychoanalytic treatment has to do with psychic integration without losing the capacity for passion, and with a loosening up of psychic structure (in terms of internalized self–other patterns) that makes for a more flexible approach to the interpersonal world and a capacity for more openness to experience.

What is the notion of the good life in this relational perspective? Clearly, there is value placed on interpersonal competence, insight and understanding, psychic integration, and a sense of personal meaningfulness (Mitchell, 1993), many of the values we have found associated with the various schools of psychoanalytic thought. I see two distinctive and inter-related relational values: intersubjectivity, and tolerance for contradiction and paradox, i.e., apprehension of the underlying commonality in, and the ability to sustain a tension between, seeming opposites. The basic project of relational psychoanalysis itself involves an effort to transcend a seeming contradiction between the intrapsychic and the interpersonal, the social and the personal. Intersubjectivity, too, entails a potential contradiction, that between being able to inhabit one's own subjectivity and recognizing and respecting the experience of others. To the extent that self and other are conceived of as opposites, there is a polarization of the kind that leads to impasses, split complementarities, relationships organized around dominance and submission. Resolutions, Mitchell's "outbursts", entail the achievement of intersubjectivity, the recognition of the other without giving up one's own point of view. Intersubjectivity involves the (paradoxical) recognition that another person is similar to and different from oneself. There are critiques of relational psychoanalysis that claim that it overemphasizes either the interpersonal or the intrapsychic elements of intersubjectivity. Bollas (2001) sees the relational focus on the interpersonal field as a distraction from the focus on the interplay of two unconsciouses, an overdevelopment of American empiricism, while some American interpersonalists are suspicious of the relational focus on the inner world. Bernstein (1999), a Lacanian analyst, also sees relational psychoanalysis as potentially overly focused on the interpersonal field, over-emphasizing the imaginary world of personality and ego, and under-emphasizing the way that the individual is constituted by the social surround and the discursive field. All these critiques are valuable in the never-ending project of developing theory adequate to contain the complexity and contradictoriness of human life.

There are political implications to intersubjectivity; implications for how one can conceive of the process of negotiation on all levels from the dyadic to the international have been developed by Pizer (1998). On the other hand, Botticelli (2004) argues that relational psychoanalysis, as a kind of dyadic utopianism reflecting despair about the possibility of making the world a better place, constitutes a retreat from the political world. Further political implications follow from the recognition, intrinsic to intersubjectivity, that one's self has unity and multiplicity; this unity and multiplicity may be organized around gender (Harris, 1991; Dimen, 2003; Goldner, 1992; Benjamin, 1988, 1995), sexual orientation (Domenici & Lesser, 1995), race and culture (Altman, 1995, 2000; Leary, 1997, 2000). The inability to tolerate internal multiplicity around these categories leads to the splitting off and projection of discordant elements, leading to racism, sexism, and homophobia as the people are denigrated who contain one's own disavowed psychic elements. Psychoanalysis thus contributes an understanding of the psychic dynamics of discrimination and hatred that may be useful to those who intervene on the political level.

I conclude here on a note that links psychoanalysis with current thinking in the humanities and social sciences. Relational psychoanalysis, like all forms of psychoanalysis, is a product of, and contributor to, its time and place. It is not surprising, then, to find contemporary psychoanalysis struggling with the issues around simultaneity, unity and multiplicity, complexity, and identity that come up in many fields at the intersection of modernism and postmodernism. Finally, in making links with politics at the end of a paper on the therapeutic action of psychoanalysis, I am suggesting that we might consider how psychoanalysis might have a healing potential in the larger world beyond the consulting room.

Notes

1. It is of interest to note that Freud made a distinction between the technical and non-technical relationship, such that in the non-technical relationship, outside the bounds of the session, the analyst was out of role and so free to be revealed as a person and to act in a non-abstinent way. It was only in North America, under the influence of ego psychology,

that the technical relationship came to subsume all aspects of the relationship, in and out of the session (see Lipton, 1977).

2. I am indebted to Andrew Samuels for his guidance in understanding Jung and the contemporary Jungians, the influence of whom was woefully underemphasized in my training and subsequent study.

3. This clinical material is adapted from Altman (1995, pp. 13–14).

References

Adler, A. (1929). *Individual Psychology*. London: Routledge & Kegan Paul.

Altman, N. (1995). *The Analyst in the Inner City: Race, Class, and Culture through a Psychoanalytic Lens*. Hillsdale, NJ: The Analytic Press.

Altman, N. (2000). Black and white thinking: A psychoanalyst reconsiders race. *Psychoanalytic Dialogues, 10*(4): 589–605.

Alvarez, A. (1992). *Live Company*. New York: Routledge.

Aron, L. (1992). Interpretation as expression of the analyst's subjectivity. *Psychoanalytic Dialogues, 2*(4): 475–507.

Aron, L. (1995). The internalized primal scene. *Psychoanalytic Dialogues, 5*(2): 195–238.

Aron, L. (1996). *A Meeting of Minds: Mutuality in Psychoanalysis*. Hillsdale, NJ: The Analytic Press.

Aron, L. (2003). The paradoxical place of enactment in psychoanalysis: introduction. *Psychoanalytic Dialogues, 13*(5): 623–632.

Austin, J. L. (1962). *How to Do Things with Words*. Cambridge, MA: Harvard University Press.

Bass, A. (2003). "E" enactments in psychoanalysis: another medium, another message. *Psychoanalytic Dialogues, 13*(5): 657–676.

Benjamin, J. (1988). *The Bonds of Love*. New York: Pantheon.

Benjamin, J. (1995). *Like Subjects, Love Objects*. New Haven: Yale University Press.

Benjamin, J. (1998). *Shadow of the Other*. New York: Routledge.

Benjamin, J. (2004). Beyond doer and done to. *Psychoanalytic Quarterly, 73*(1): 5–46.

Berlin, I. (1969). *Four Essays on Liberty*. Oxford: Oxford University Press.

Bernstein, J. W. (1999). Countertransference: Our new royal road to the unconscious? *Psychoanalytic Dialogues, 9*(3): 275–299.

Bion, W. (1959). Attacks on linking. *International Journal of Psychoanalysis*, *40*: 308–315.

Black, M. (2003). Enactment: Analytic musings on energy, language, and personal growth. *Psychoanalytic Dialogues*, *13*(5): 633–656.

Bollas, C. (1987). *The Shadow of the Object*. New York: Columbia University Press.

Bollas, C. (2001). Freudian intersubjectivity: commentary on paper by Julie Gerhardt and Annie Sweetnam. *Psychoanalytic Dialogues*, *11*(1): 93–106.

Botticelli, S. (2004) The politics of relational psychoanalysis. *Psychoanalytic Dialogues*, *14*(5): 635–652.

Bromberg, P. (1999). *Standing in the Spaces: Essays on Clinical Process, Trauma and Dissociation*. Hillsdale, NJ: The Analytic Press.

Davies, J. M. (1999). Getting cold feet, defining "safe enough" borders: dissociation, multiplicity, and integration in the analyst's experience. *Psychoanalytic Quarterly*, *68*(2): 184–208.

Dimen, M. (2003). *Sexuality, Intimacy, Power*. Hillsdale, NJ: The Analytic Press.

Domenici, T., & Lesser, R. (Eds.) (1995). *Disorienting Sexualities*. New York: Routledge.

Fairbairn, W. R. D. (1952). *Psychoanalytic Studies of the Personality*. London: Routledge & Kegan Paul.

Fairbairn, W. R. D. (1958). On the nature and aims of psychoanalysis. *International Journal of Psychoanalysis*, *19*: 374–385.

Ferenczi, S. (1933). Confusion of tongues between adults and the child. In: M. Balint (Ed.), E. Mosbacher (Trans.), *Final Contributions to the Problems and Methods of Psychoanalysis* London: Karnac, 1980, pp. 156–167

Frankel, J. (1998). The play's the thing: how the essential processes of therapy are seen most clearly in child therapy. *Psychoanalytic Dialogues*, *8*(1): 149–182.

Freud, A. (1966). *The Ego and the Mechanisms of Defense*. Madison, CT: International Universities Press.

Freud, S. (1914g) Remembering, repeating, and working through (further recommendations on the technique of psycho-analysis). *S.E., 12*. London: Hogarth.

Freud, S. (1933a). New introductory lectures in psychoanalysis. *S.E., 22*. London: Hogarth.

Freud, S., & Breuer, J. (1895d). Studies in hysteria. *S.E., 2*. London: Hogarth.

Fromm, E. (1947). *Man For Himself*. Greenwich, CT: Fawcett.

Fromm, E. (1955). *The Sane Society*. Greenwich, CT: Fawcett.

Gadamer, H.-G. (1975). *Truth and Method*. G. Barden & J. Cumming (Eds. and Trans.). New York: Seabury Press.

Gill, M. (1976). Metapsychology is not psychology. In: M.Gill & P. Holzman (Eds.), *Psychology versus Metapsychology: Psychoanalytic Essays in Honor of George S. Klein* (pp. 71–105). New York: International Universities Press,.

Gill, M. (1982). *Analysis of Transference*. New York: International Universities Press.

Goldner, V. (1991). Toward a critical relational theory of gender. *Psychoanalytic Dialogues*, 1(3): 249–272.

Greenberg, J. (1986). Theoretical models and the analyst's neutrality. *Contemporary Psychoanalysis*, 22: 87–106.

Greenberg, J., & Mitchell, S. (1983). *Object Relations in Psychoanalytic Theory*. Cambridge, MA: Harvard University Press.

Greenson, R. (1967). *The Technique and Practice of Psychoanalysis*. New York: International Universities Press.

Harris, A. (1991). *Gender as Contradiction*. Psychoanalytic Dialogues, 1(2): 197–224.

Harris, A. (2005). *Gender as Soft Assembly*. Hillsdale, NJ: The Analytic Press.

Hoffman, I. Z. (1991). Discussion: Toward a social-constructivist view of the psychoanalytic view of the psychoanalytic situation. *Psychoanalytic Dialogues*, 1(1): 74–105.

Hoffman, I. Z. (19920). Some practical implications of a social constructivist view of the analytic situation. *Psychoanalytic Dialogues*, 2: 287–304.

Hoffman, I. Z. (1998). *Ritual and Spontaneity in the Psychoanalytic Process*. Hillsdale, NJ: The Analytic Press.

Jacobs, T. (1986). On countertransference enactments. *Journal of the American Psychoanalytic Association*, 34: 289–307.

Joseph, B. (1978). Different types of anxiety and their handling in the clinical situation. In: M. Feldman & E. Spillius (Eds.), *Psychic Equilibrium and Psychic Change* (pp. 106–115). London: Tavistock/Routledge, 1989.

Jung, C. G. (1929). Problems of modern psychotherapy. *CW*, 16: 53–75, R. F. C. Hull (Trans.). Princeton, NJ: Princeton University Press.

Jung, C. G. (1931). Commentary on "The Secret of the Golden Flower". *C.W.*, 13: 1–56, R. F. C. Hull (Trans.). Princeton, NJ: Princeton University Press.

Jung, C. G. (1935). Principles of practical psychotherapy. *C.W.*, *16*: 3–20, R. F. C. Hull (Trans.). Princeton, NJ: Princeton University Press.

Jung, C. G. (1946). The psychology of the transference. *C.W.*, *16*: 163–236, R. F. C. Hull (Trans.). Princeton, NJ: Princeton University Press.

Jung, C. G. (1953). Two essays on analytical psychology. *C.W.*, *7*, R. F. C. Hull (Trans.). Princeton, NJ: Princeton University Press, 1966.

Kernberg, O. (1975). *Borderline Conditions and Pathological Narcissism*. Northvale, NJ: London: Jason Aronson.

Klein, M. (1975). On the theory of anxiety and guilt. In: *Envy and Gratitude and Other Works* (pp. 25–42). New York: Delacorte.

Kohut, H. (1977). *The Restoration of the Self*. New York: International Universities Press.

Lacan, J. (1972). *Ecrits* (Alan Sheridan, Trans.). New York: Norton.

Lachman, F. (1986). Interpretation of psychic conflict and adversarial relationships: a self-psychological perspective. *Psychoanalytic Psychology*, *3*(4): 341–355.

Leary, K. (1997). Race, self-disclosure, and "forbidden talk": race and ethnicity in contemporary clinical practice. *Psychoanalytic Quarterly*, *66*: 163–189.

Leary, K. (2000). Racial enactments in dynamic treatment. *Psychoanalytic Dialogues*, *10*(4): 639–653.

Levenson, E. (1982). Language and healing. In: S. Slipp (Ed.), *Curative Factors in Dynamic Psychotherapy* (pp. 91–103). New York: McGraw.

Lipton, S. (1977). The advantages of Freud's technique as shown in his analysis of the Rat Man. *International Journal of Psychoanalysis*, *58*: 255–273.

Loewald, H. (1960). On the therapeutic action of psychoanalysis. In: *Papers on Psychoanalysis* (pp. 221–256). New Haven, CT: Yale University Press, 1980.

Loewald, H. (1988). *Sublimation*. New Haven, CT: Yale University Press.

Mitchell, S. A. (1993). *Hope and Dread in Psychoanalysis*. New York: Basic Books.

Mitchell, S. A. (1997). *Influence and Autonomy in Psychoanalysis*. Hillsdale, NJ: The Analytic Press.

Mitchell, S. A. (2000). *Relationality: From Attachment to Intersubjectivity*. Hillsdale, NJ: The Analytic Press.

Nunberg, H. (1932). *Principles of Psychoanalysis*. New York: International Universities Press, 1955.

Ogden, T. (1994). *Subjects of Analysis*. Northvale, NJ: Jason Aronson.

Ornstein, A. (1991). The dread to repeat: comments on the working through process in psychoanalysis. *Journal of the American Psychoanalytic Association, 39*: 377–398.

Pine, F. (1983). *Developmental Theory and Clinical Process*. New Haven, CT: Yale University Press.

Pizer, S. (1998). *Building Bridges: the Negotiation of Paradox in Psychoanalysis*. Hillsdale, NJ: The Analytic Press.

Rank, O. (1945). *Will Therapy and Truth and Reality* (Jessie Taft, trans.). New York: Knopf.

Samuels, A. (1985). *Jung and the Post-Jungians*. London: Routledge & Kegan Paul.

Samuels, A. (2000). Post-Jungian dialogues. *Psychoanalytic Dialogues, 10*(3): 403–426.

Samuels, A. et al. (2000). Analytical psychology after Jung with clinical case material from Stephen Mitchell's *Influence and Autonomy in Psychoanalysis. Psychoanalytic Dialogues, 10*(3): 377–512.

Schafer, R. (1983). *The Analytic Attitude*. New York: Basic Books.

Stern, D. B. (1997). *Unformulated Experience*. Hillsdale, NJ: The Analytic Press.

Stern, S. (1994). Needed relationships and repeated relationships: an integrated relational perspective. *Psychoanalytic Dialogues, 4*: 317–346.

Stolorow, R., & Atwood, G. (1992). *Contexts of Being*. Hillsdale, NJ: The Analytic Press.

Strachey, J. (1934). The nature of the therapeutic action of psychoanalysis. *International Journal of Psychoanalysis, 15*: 127–159.

Sullivan, H. S. (1953). *The Interpersonal Theory of Psychiatry*. New York: Norton, 1965.

Winnicott, D. W. (1950–1955). Aggression in relation to emotional development. In: *Through Pediatrics to Psychoanalysis*. New York: Basic Books, 1975, pp. 204–215.

Winnicott, D. W. (1960). Ego distortion in terms of true and false self. In: *The Maturational Processes and the Facilitating Environment*. New York: International Universities Press, pp. 140–153.

Zetzel, E. (1958). Therapeutic alliance in the analysis of hysteria. In: E. Zetzel (Ed.), *The Capacity for Emotional Growth* (pp. 182–196). New York: International Universities Press, 1970.

CHAPTER THREE

The questions we have to ask (ourselves) before we answer the question: "How does psychotherapy work?"*

Joseph Schwartz

I was an experimental physicist before I became a psychotherapist. The experimental part of my previous career has been very helpful in dealing with theoretical issues in psychoanalysis. Traditionally, experimentalists have always been very, very critical of theory. The important thing for an experimentalist is that the theory be right, not that it be intriguing, or interesting, or even beautiful. The experimental question is not "Well, could it be that?" The experimental question is "*Is* it that?"

Although there always needs to be space for exploration of theoretical issues, my appraisal of the field of psychoanalysis over the past twenty years is that psychoanalysis is at a particular point in its historical development where too many people are playing around with psychoanalytic ideas and not enough colleagues are asking, "Is it that?"

There are very many different ideas being put forward to answer the question "How does therapy work", or indeed, "Does therapy work?" But what the field has lacked is a disciplined

---

*Lecture transcript

engagement between practitioners with a view to sorting things out. It is not good enough for us to sit in our separate corners, slag each other off, and turn up our noses at how our colleagues have understood the experience of the consulting room. There is a certain discipline in natural science, not very well understood within psychoanalysis, that our field sorely needs. My psychoanalytic colleagues seem to carry around a lot of the ambient mythology about the so-called precision, and the so-called objectivity of natural science that appears not to apply to the subjectivities involved in psychoanalysis. The result has been that our community has lost track of the salient point of any exploration of human experience: it takes discipline to get results.

While I will be offering some very definite statements about how therapy works, I hope they can be taken in the spirit of engagement with an important issue together rather than dismissed as "Oh well, that's one point of view". Jane Ryan has done a fine job in putting together this series of lectures. It has permitted a certain kind of engagement, and we very much need that at this point in our development.

I'd like to bring to your attention what I consider to be two or three major categories—questions to ourselves—to hold in mind in addressing the question of the effectiveness of psychotherapeutic action: the external context in which this question is being asked, the internal context, and third, the epistemological question of what constitutes an answer.

First I would like to situate the external context in which the question, "How does therapy work?" is being asked. By external context I mean insurance companies, psychiatrists, intellectuals of one kind or another, usually hostile literary critics, people like Frederic Crews (1998). We live with attacks on therapy all the time. One BBC religious programme found it necessary to mount an attack on psychotherapy for all the usual reasons—too painful, makes matters worse, what are friends for, and so on. This negative social context affects how we approach the question of how psychotherapy works because it tends to make us defensive. If you have society against you, it is pretty hard to keep a fairly open stance and explore a question in the face of continued questions about one's legitimacy.

The internal context within psychotherapy in which the question "How does psychotherapy work?" is posed is one in which we have difficulty engaging each other. Our theoretical differences can be held very, very strongly, usually quite destructively in my opinion. Our internal defensiveness against difference keeps us from assimilating together what psychotherapy has learned over the past 100 years. We have a century of clinical practice under our belts now and there is an awful lot to be learned from it. Over the past fifteen or twenty years we have had a period of neutrality where different views have been tolerated. But we now need to be moving on, into a spirit of engagement with each other in the interest of advancing our field as a whole rather than continuing to defend fixed positions.

I wrote a history of psychoanalysis (*Cassandra's Daughter*, 1999), because I felt we'd lost our intellectual history. What we'd had in the way of history was a series of biographies of the great people in the field, usually great men, with the exception of Klein. We tended to engage each other by quoting what the greats had said as if we were dummies to the ventriloquist. We were making the great speak to us from the past by mouthing in the present what they had to say then without bothering to make the effort to think the issue through for ourselves now.

I tried to write a book that was much more about the development of the ideas of the field as a whole, a real history of psychoanalysis in its social context, not a biography of Freud, which usually is a chronology of Freud's thinking, or any of the other greats. From a perspective of taking in the historical development of psychoanalysis as a whole one can get a sense of where we are now in our internal development.

We are not at a point to have a definitive answer to the question of how psychotherapy works. But perhaps, if we work at it, we can begin to create a constructive, safe enough space to advance our thinking, to have a lot more confidence and openness in our response to sceptics if not actually to hostile critics.

First, then, the external context. One of the big features in the history of the development of Western civilization, beginning with the English revolution 350 years ago as a marker, is the development of hostility to the inner world of human feeling in favour of the presumed superiority of so-called rational thinking, thinking without emotion, which we now know is impossible. We inhabit a culture where feelings tend to be marginalized, ignored, and ridiculed. A frequent statement in arguments is "I believe I'm being completely objective when I say . . .". In this kind of discourse, feelings are seen to be dangerous things. They subvert our judgment and make us incapable of acting—how shall we put it—rationally. This sensibility is pervasive in our culture.

But one needs affect to be able to think. The things that one thinks about have to be loaded with affect. They have to carry an emotional meaning in order for us to be able to think about them. The whole business of rationality is a bit of Western ideology tied by many commentators to the rise of the money economy in general and the existence of the slave trade in particular. If one makes so-called rational calculations, you can deal with the human misery that one inflicts by being rational about it. What does that mean? Well, you'll make money. That is where we can locate, at least in principle, the origin of rationality as a value in the West as coming from the deep depersonalization of human culture in the service of personal profit.

That is one way to think about where the supremacy of the idea of rationality comes from, and why feelings need to be driven out. There was money in it. While men were out dealing with the money economy, women were left to deal with feelings. Women have been meant to pick up the pieces from our inhuman economic relationships. A profession like psychotherapy that has attempted to deal with human emotional life has been denigrated because at some level, in a patriarchal society, psychotherapy has been seen as women's work, not quite worthy of respect in the same way as our culture respects the so-called objective process of cutting somebody open.

At the Royal Geographical Society in March 2003, there was a debate titled "Anyone who visits a psychotherapist needs to have their head examined" (IQ, 2003). The organizers thought this was a very cute, humourous way to debate people's fears about psychotherapy. I wasn't amused. I don't see any other profession subject to that kind of public ridicule. In spite of all the horrors that we know that can happen in operating theatres, surgery as a whole is not critiqued in the same way.

There are, of course, counter trends such as the growth of victim support groups organized by, of all groupings, the police, whom one might not expect to be sensitive to emotional issues. There has been a rise in disaster counselling. I was quite impressed by the way resources were made available to the survivors of the *Herald of Free Enterprise*, the ferry involved in a major disaster. In an interview, Ken Doherty, the British snooker star, made public that he sees a sports psychologist, and then as a matter of fact also mentioned that he's married to a psychiatrist.

Things are changing. They need to change. And they will change because human emotional life is fundamental to our existence. Nevertheless, we operate in a situation in which as psychotherapists we are called to justify ourselves and our practices like no other profession. We basically operate in still quite a hostile environment, and because we can become defensive and uncertain about the legitimacy of what we do, we ourselves can make it difficult for our friends to be vocal on our behalf.

It is symptomatic of the environment in which we practise psychotherapy that psychiatry, which addresses similar mental problems, frequently those that are the most severe, has never been called to justify its procedures, certainly not in the twentieth century, not even to itself. Take the pulling of teeth. It was a standard practice for someone suffering mental pain to have their teeth pulled. Freud speaks about this practice in *Studies on Hysteria* in the case of Cäcilie M. who suffered from neuralgia, a psychosomatic face ache:

> Earlier in her life, her teeth were accused of being responsible for her neuralgia, that's the face ache. They were condemned to extraction, and one fine day, the sentence was carried out on seven of the criminals. This was not such an easy matter. Her teeth were so firmly attached that the roots of most of them had to be left behind. This cruel operation had no result, either temporary or permanent. At that time, the neuralgia raged for months on end. Even at the time of my treatment, at each attack of neuralgia, the dentist was called in. On each occasion, he diagnosed the presence of diseased roots and began to get to work on them. But as a rule he was soon interrupted for the neuralgia would suddenly cease and at the same time the demand for the dentist's services. [Freud & Breuer, 1893, p. 249]

This is Freud at his sardonic best.

Frau Cäcilie M. was not an isolated case. Andrew Scull, an historian of psychiatry, dug out the case of Henry Cotton, the head of the

Trenton State Hospital in New Jersey in America (Scull, 1984). Cotton, a former student of Adolf Meyer, one of the leading psychiatrists and psychotherapists in America, was not a marginalized man at all. Cotton ran this hospital as his personal fiefdom. Over a period of two years, from 1919 to 1921, he had 10,000 teeth extracted from inmates. This was in the service of what he called the focal infection theory of mental pain. He also extracted pieces of people's colons, colonectomies, as a way to deal with his patients and did tonsillectomies as well.

Some of the other things that have been tried in the history of psychiatry include camphor-induced convulsions, histamine shock therapy, transorbital and prefrontal lobotomies, insulin shock therapy. There still is electro-convulsive shock therapy used for treating clinical depression. There is forced feeding in the case of anorexia, where women are incarcerated, tied down, and force-fed. There was the widespread practice of restraint, the use of the straitjacket with assorted other paraphernalia, bolted chairs, leather wristlets, hand muffs, wire helmets, room lock-ups (Schwartz, 1999).

At the turn of the twentieth century, William Alanson White created a sensation in psychiatric circles when he took charge at St Elizabeth's Hospital in Washington and banned the use of restraint. In more modern times, we have the use of drugs, what can be called chemical coshes, beginning with the use of chlorpromazine in the 1950s. In mental hospitals in the 1960s when I trained, you had the frightful sight on the wards of people being vegetables managed by drugs.

There has been no professional evaluation of these techniques. These are things that that psychiatrists can try out, and when they do not seem effective, they stop. Nobody questions publicly, "What are you doing here?" in the same way that psychotherapy is questioned all the time. That is interesting. We have had some shock-horror films about psychiatric practices. Ken Loach's early film *Family Life* from the 1960s is an excruciating critique of the use of ECT on a young woman. *One Flew Over the Cuckoo's Nest*, with Jack Nicholson, based on Ken Kesey's novel, was an exposé of practices in mental hospitals. We get a bit of muck-raking. But we do not get any systematic evaluation or any visible signs of professional questioning of the efficacy of any of these psychiatric procedures.

What psychiatry gets up to has been called "the desperate manic defence of frustrated therapeutic omnipotence" (Weigert, 1939). One can see what this means. You're faced with someone in very severe, extreme, mental distress and you're meant to do something. And everything you try is hopeless. So you've got to do something, anything. So you can lock them up. You can give people drugs. You can shock them. When a person is sectioned, they lose the right to resist treatments. They don't have any rights. Tom Mayne, who worked at Northfields here in the UK when the insulin shock therapy was brought in, said he didn't think it helped the patients at all in a direct sense, but it gave the staff a feeling that they were doing something for the patients. And because the staff felt better, then the patients were able to feel a bit better because they had a happier staff to deal with, instead of a frightened, frustrated, embattled staff (Schwartz, 1999).

With modern drugs, it would not be good practice in the case of extreme distress not to entertain some form of medication that could alleviate the distress enough for psychotherapy to begin to work. If a person is inaccessible to relationship, we don't have much chance to be effective with the talking cure. But the mechanism of action of psychoactive drugs is almost completely unknown. Lithium carbonate, a drug that has helped a lot of people who have suffered very extreme borderline, even psychotic conditions, was discovered by accident. Nobody knows what lithium carbonate does to the body. Nobody even knows why SSRIs, the prozacs, do what they do. We know they inhibit the uptake of the neurotransmitter involved. But nobody knows why that should have any positive effect on depression. The question "How does drug therapy work?" never gets asked. The question "How does psychotherapy work?" is right up front in the headlines all the time. Why is this?

It helps to recall that medicine did not always have this kind of untouchable legitimacy. For example, the use of cadavers in medical education was prohibited for a long time except in a very few cases. There never were enough cadavers to dissect to learn about the human body. There was a profession of grave robbers who would exhume bodies and sell them to the medical schools. And it was highly illegal. It was an emotionally charged issue with a strong class component. The bodies that were exhumed were invariably those of working people and poor people who were justifiably outraged that their graves were being disturbed and other people's were not.

There was a famous case, that of Burke and Hare, two men who murdered people to sell their bodies to medical schools, to a very famous medical school, to a man by the name of Knox (Walker, 2003). They were caught and convicted and Burke was hanged in 1828 in a public hanging that was attended by 25,000 people. There was a saying on the street: "Burke's the butcher, Hare's the thief and Knox the boy who bought the beef". This was an issue that was not confined to select circles. People did not want their bodies messed with after they were dead.

The analogy today for psychotherapy is that people don't want their minds messed with. That is the fear, that what psychotherapy does is mess with your mind. And that's where some of the more superficial, hostile critiques come in. To some extent we can be sympathetic with those fears. But the attacks against psychotherapy can be so hostile and virulent that we have to defend our field. We have to defend the fundamental humanity and effectiveness of psychotherapy—which is not to say that bad psychotherapy doesn't take place.

To conclude my first point: we operate in a context that makes the asking of the question, "How does psychotherapy work?", very loaded. I'm always very careful, if I'm asked that question, to try to understand where it is coming from, because frequently there is a lot of fear behind the question and we need to learn how to speak to this fear when we are asked "How does therapy work?"

In our internal social context, as I have mentioned above, the difficulties we face are that we tend not to listen to each other. We have a history of splits and schisms. Disagreements between us are interpreted away as resistance. We lack a tradition of a disciplined engagement with each other. The effect of this has been to keep us from knowing with confidence what we know.

Consider what we can know for sure from the history of psychoanalysis. The basic innovation, the basic discovery (Breuer's, elaborated by Freud), was that of the analytic hour. The analytic hour is a unique space in our culture. There's no other domain in our culture, including the confessional box, that offers the kind of concentrated listening that a therapist can give a client. It is fifty minutes. It is incredibly long. And it doesn't exist anywhere else. That has been our instrument, invented by Breuer and developed by Freud.

Freud was very affected by Charcot in France, who was observing hysterical fits. Charcot is sitting there observing and making topologies of various kinds of fit. Freud realizes the way really to learn what is going on here is follow what Breuer did with Anna O. and to listen to what women say about their experience, not to watch them from a distance. That's the beginning of the talking cure. And things then start to happen in the analytic hour that actually happen everywhere else but nowhere else are they really examined. We have learned about the countertransference. We have learned about different forms of countertransference. We have learned about the kind of feelings that a therapist can have that are concordant, in Heinrich Racker's terms, with what our client is feeling (Racker, 1968). We feel with them what they are feeling. Or we can be listening to a narrative and we can end up having complementary countertransference, feelings that significant figures in the past have felt towards our client. There is also projective identification, feelings we have that our client is unable to have, that are projected into us if we want to use that metaphor.

So we have quite a rich literature on what we, as therapists, experience in a consulting room, and we have names for a variety of feelings that we experience. This is far in advance of anything else that is in the culture. Nobody else has names for these things. Nobody else has looked at them as closely as we have, has worked with them as systematically as we have. Nobody. You can get transferential issues coming up, say, in management circles nowadays. People will talk about transferences in the workplace. But it is not worked with. It is managed, not worked with. And we deal with very extreme cases of mental distress way beyond anything that one can find in a workplace.

The analytic hour has let us learn, observe, and experience aspects of the human inner world that nobody knows very much about. We have learned an awful lot in 100 years and there has been some pretty good theory. But we have not learned how to take ourselves seriously enough to be confident that we are on to something valuable.

Consider the following examples of great discoveries in psychoanalysis. Klein discovered the powerful destructive feelings that can come from separation and annihilation anxiety—extremely powerful affects, very, very disruptive, extremely painful. Fairbairn's practice led him to conclude that the individual is not a biological organism seeking reduction of tension from biological urges—pleasure seeking—but was fundamentally relationship seeking. Human beings are object seeking. They're not pleasure seeking. Winnicott echoes this development. There is no such thing as a baby. There is only a mothering pair. René Spitz studied the effect of traumatic, prolonged separation and the destructive effects of separations in hospital, terribly, terribly disruptive (Spitz, 1960). James Robinson made a film *The Child Goes to Hospital* to help change a nation's consciousness about the importance of attachment. One of Bowlby's achievements was to change hospital practice so that the whole British sensibility of how upsetting it would be for the child to have visits from the parents was reversed. The practice on the fever wards, where parents were not allowed to visit their children and children were kept in isolation was changed. And one can see in the new neural localization studies what the neurophysiological correlates of secure attachments are in the development of the human child (Schore, 1994). Psychoanalytic perspectives are now beginning to inform research in neuroscience rather than the other way round.

We can now offer a partial answer to how psychotherapy works. If we take the last 100 years of psychoanalytic psychotherapy, one very strong theoretical theme emerges, and that's basically Fairbairn's observation that human beings are object-seeking, not pleasure-seeking, that is to say, we need human relationships. Bowlby's extensive work on attachment and loss virtually completes the overriding theoretical framework that psychotherapy operates within. The basic principle of psychotherapy is that human beings have a fundamental need for attachment, which if not met in a good enough way, is the source of the psychopathology we see in the consulting-room. That is the basic framework. That is the basic fact of the human organism. We cannot survive without relationships. What we do in the consulting-room then is look for what has gone wrong in relationships.

I think it is useful to make a slight digression here about laws of nature. Take the laws of mechanics, the origin of the concept of lawfulness in natural science. What Newton's second law of motion

(F=ma) says is that if you want to understand motion, if you want to understand dynamics, how things change in the natural world, you look for the forces. Locate the forces and you'll be able then to work out how things are going to move, whether bridges will shake themselves to pieces in high winds, whether aeroplanes will come out of the sky, and so forth. Now, Freud, writing at the end of the nineteenth century, is very, very affected by this quite important achievement of Western culture, and he talks in terms of forces and dynamics, and he looks for the forces within the body. He looks at displacements of energies in the body. He's got a very mechanical, hydraulic kind of model of how we work.

Well, that was a long time ago. We don't think this way any more. We talk about forces in a kind of loose, metaphorical way, but we don't think human dynamics comes from forces, masses, and acceleration. We don't do that. What we do when we're dealing with mental pain and emotional difficulty is look at relationships. That is where we are going to locate the source of mental pain. This is our F=ma. If you want to understand the origins of mental pain look for what has happened in a person's relationships.

The source of mental pain and emotional difficulties is to be located in the individual's relational and attachment history. And, even more strongly perhaps, no matter what our orientation is in therapy, basically we all do that. We may theorize it differently, but everybody is doing that, otherwise they are not going to get results. We are always working with the human relationship. We are always working with the relationship in the room, and that's how therapy works. We work with the relationship in the room and it is in that relationship that the healing happens.

Therapy works by addressing the relational difficulties that exist in an individual's present and past. And the way it works, the way we address it, is by being in the relationship. That is how it works. That is what happens for all our clients.

So what's the big deal? I don't think "we work with the relationship in the room" is much of an answer to the profound uncertainties we can experience in a therapeutic relationship. But it is fundamentally an extremely important basic principle of how psychotherapy works. Our field has been considerably weakened by our inability to address, assimilate, and build on this fundamental insight.

We have got a fundamental principle here, derived from clinical practice, that we could offer for example to the neurobiologists. Think about it. Think about the kind of organism we would be if we grew up as a wild child. Think about what happens in cases of hospitalization. Think about Harlow's monkeys. Think about the agony and suffering caused by broken attachments.

We address these difficulties in relationship histories in the consulting-room. We enter into the relationship. We have a range of responses. We learn to speak about the responses. We learn how to use them. We learn how to relate to our client's difficulties. We don't drop them when they get upset. We don't leave them isolated with the difficulty. We try to create a safe enough place for past cumulative trauma to be worked through. We have concepts that describe it, like working through.

But how do we know when or if it has worked? That is the second, usually unvoiced, part of the question "How does psychotherapy work?" How do we know it works?

We know that in classical terms the dissolving of the transferences is a sign that the therapy or the analysis has been completed. But what does this mean, the dissolving of the transferences? When we are not having to respond defensively to hostile attacks, or to hostile colleagues, this is where we can begin to answer what actually happens. How does it *actually* work?

I'd like to remind you of Diana Spencer's *Panorama* interview. Now, for me, in my generation of psychotherapists, that interview was an example of someone who's had good therapy. What does that mean, good therapy? What am I responding to? I would say someone who comes out of therapy and is able to talk about issues that have caused them, or may continue to cause them, emotional pain in an undefensive way, has had good therapy. We have a lot of metaphors for it. Diana was centred. She owned her experience. She had words to describe her experience—infidelity, bulimia, feelings of being emotionally abused in her social setting—and to talk about it without embarrassment, inner conflict, or rancour. Short report: she had worked it through.

I invite you to think about whether you would agree with that appraisal, whether this woman we saw on our television screens had had a good therapy, whether she talked about her bulimia in a way that showed she was able to talk about the distress she had without embarrassment or shame, and had accepted that yes, that was a phase she had been through, that was the way she dealt with her mental pain then and she had worked it through.

I give the example of Diana's *Panorama* interview as one example we have in common. One can usually tell when somebody's been in therapy and has had a good therapy. Zen study could accomplish the same kind of thing; the same kind of self-under-standing, a certain quality of self-possession, a sense of someone who has made peace with themselves in a way that can be quite apparent.

The quality of narrative that I am alluding to has led to attempts to make a linguistic analysis of self-descriptions. The psycholin-guist Paul Grice (1989) has four maxims indicators of mental health. A person gives a narrative of their life history to an interviewer. The elements Grice looks for are truth, how truthful does it appear, what is the supporting evidence, and how economical it is. Is there too much evidence? Is it over the top? Is it too self-involved? How relevant is what's offered, and what kind of emotional tone exists in the manner of speaking. So truth, manner, economy, and relat-edness. Some of the attachment interviewers use this framework to assess the qualities of the Adult Attachment Interview (Steele, 2002).

Can we as clinicians do better than describing the process as "worked through"? What kind of language do we need to show other people what we mean when we say somebody's got better, when we say somebody's had a good therapy, when we say that therapy worked? We know what's going to make it work. It is the relationship with the therapist that is going to make it work. But can we find better ways of describing it, accurate ways of describ-ing it, ways that will let people say, "Oh, I see what you mean, yeah." That's our challenge—to find a way to put into words what we know is happening in the consulting-room. We know it works, although not always why.

Audience discussion (edited)

AUDIENCE: You ask whether Diana had a good psychotherapy. I saw the interview and I thought I could see the psychoanalytic psychotherapy in it. From that perspective, I couldn't argue with your point at all. I also think I know who the therapist was and their work is fabulous. But as a humanistic psychotherapist, I have questions about what was left out. If I had been her therapist, coming from my own perspective, I would have had to ask myself some very serious questions about the way she died, in terms of the kind of things that *I* might look for in a successful therapy. The things that you mentioned in your successful therapy are not necessarily the same things that I've looked for in mine.

JOSEPH SCHWARTZ: Could you say what they are?

AUDIENCE: Well, her behaviour was quite self-destructive. She may have been having good therapy but actually the fact is that she died. She's a poor example of a good result. One could argue that she shouldn't have died and that actually she was being quite self-destructive. I enjoyed the interview but who knows how good or bad the therapy was since the end result was that she died. She may well have been getting better but it doesn't strike me as a great result—unless she was murdered, we don't know. But, either way, she put herself at serious risk.

JOSEPH SCHWARTZ: There may be an issue of principle but I don't hear it here. This critique is a little after the fact. I wonder what you might say just about the interview?

AUDIENCE (Speaker A): Personally the interview was fantastic. I know a lot of people said that she was being manipulated, and had been coached. I personally felt it was genuine. She came up fantastically well. I just think end result is . . . well, you know, nothing's perfect and one can't blame therapy for that because she may well have been . . . (overlap)

JOSEPH SCHWARTZ: She could have been up against forces that were too strong for any individual.

AUDIENCE (Speaker B): Well, I found that very interesting. I'm a psychoanalytic psychotherapist so I find myself very much in agreement with Joe's evaluation of that interview. And I would add something to that: when Diana spoke about cutting, which I found useful at the time because I was working with a woman who was in danger of being sectioned because she was cutting herself, I could use that interview in the psychiatric team work. What I absolutely agree with you about was that she came to some form of resolution with her terrible pain, and I thought that was what was so moving and so true. But the point I actually want to make about the idea of outcomes is it is hugely complex. A person might have an inner resolution or, in Freudian terms, have managed to commute human misery to common unhappiness and this is a huge gain. Some of my work has been very meaningful on that level. So one might have some form of inner peace about oneself but still not actually be able to negotiate relationships. And one might do very well in work and not be able to negotiate relationships, or the other way round. And what I'm trying to say is, if, if we look just for one factor, we might be missing a whole complexity about being in the world.

AUDIENCE (Speaker C): Well, I enjoyed that. I was very excited about the opening of your seminar on the need for further integration the whole of psychotherapy. I'm absolutely sick and tired to hear constantly about the hostility between the approaches. Hearing you saying that it is 100 years over and we should move on to something that we could find [together], that regardless which approach we're working from we have a sense of the healing process being completed or somehow brought into integration.

AUDIENCE (Speaker D): Are you asserting that if you have a fifty-minute session ongoing with someone who can talk to you about the failings of relationship past and present, in a related way, the therapy will work regardless of the therapist's technical capacity or their technical training?

JOSEPH SCHWARTZ: Actually it is usually the case that people can't talk about what's happened to them that's the significance of the therapy. We stick around for things to be expressed when they can't be talked about. They get acted out is one way. And you sit there with horrible feelings of hating your patient. And now what? Well, outside the consulting room, people do not usually stick around for that. Well, we stick around. We ask ourselves or our supervisors: where's that hate coming from? Why have they made me angry? Why do I feel rejecting? And we work with that. We're in the relationship no matter what, and that's where the healing happens.

AUDIENCE (Speaker E): I remember one of my teachers from long ago said, "The more aggravated society is by psychotherapy and counselling, the more successful psychotherapy and counselling is," because it is actually disturbing something that probably needs to be disturbed. Another thought that I have is, people are not dragged off the streets into the consulting-room. They're not dragged into hospitals, mostly, so there's this odd tension between those people who say, "What a load of rubbish it is", and who probably would have sat here, listened to your talk and still not be convinced that it was worth doing, because I imagine that everyone in this room says, "Well, yes, we know it works, we perhaps have not always found a language to describe how it works." But that the argument is not going to penetrate a set of people who do not wish to investigate an inner world.

AUDIENCE (Speaker F): I always wonder about actually the personality of the therapist. A successful and good therapist needs something else, some kind of wit, some richness, and how many people are like that? I just always feel that there is another element and I don't know how that element is bought or can it be bought. Some kind of, I don't know what it is.

JOSEPH SCHWARTZ: I don't agree with you about the extra element. We train our people and we ourselves are trained in a process, and it is the process that does the work. We can talk about differences in practice. But we engage in a process, we are part of the process. And I don't think there's anything particularly special about us. I mean, for any job I suppose you could say there has to be an affinity for the work, but it is the process that goes with the work, it is not we as individuals. There's nothing particularly special about us. We have learned to listen and it is not so easy. It is not so easy to listen. You know, I would like to make one last point. I do think of something that Winston Churchill once said, "Democracy is a terrible system except for all the others". There's a way in which when we talk about the faults and difficulties of psychotherapy, we lose sight of what's gone on in psychiatry for the past 100 years, thank you very much, right, and it just vanishes, right? All of a sudden, all the problems are the problems of the psychotherapist and all the power and balance, it is a real problem, the power and balance, and how that's manageable. What's the real fear, what are people so afraid of? I don't think I know. It is something about, it is the last area where they, I, can't be got, is my mind, so leave me alone. It is a very defensive posture.

AUDIENCE (Speaker A): It is control.

JOSEPH SCHWARTZ: It is control, right, and control is usually an expression, a feeling of helplessness, and we need a lot of control when we feel really, really vulnerable, so inhabit a social environment that makes people feel afraid that they're going to be invaded, and you know, we're just one small professional grouping, dealing with this large social force, right, and that's why I spent so much time going after the psychiatrists, and there may be some psychiatric colleagues here, I hope they don't take it personally, but the history of psychiatry is something we should keep in mind when we're being self-critical.

References

Crews, F. (Ed.) (1998). *Unauthorised Freud: Doubters Confront a Legend.* New York: Viking.

Freud, S., & Breuer, J. (1893). *Studies on Hysteria.* The Pelican Freud Library, vol. 3, 1974. Harmondsworth: Penguin Books.

Grice, P. (1989). *Studies in the Way of Words.* Harvard University Press. See also Google search: Paul Grice.

IQ (2003), www. intelligencesquared.com

Racker, H. (1968). *Transference and Countertransference.* Madison, CT: International Universities Press.

Schore, A. N. (1994). *Affect Regulation and the Origin of the Self: The Neurobiology Of Emotional Development.* Hillsdale, NJ: Lawrence Erlbaum.

Schwartz, J. (1999). *Cassandra's Daughter.* London: Karnac.

Scull, A. (1984). Desperate remedies: a Gothic tale of madness and modern medicine, *Psychological Medicine, 17*: 561–577.

Spitz, R. (1960). *The First Year of Life.* Madison, CT: International Universities Press.

Steele, H. (2002). Clinical Forum at the Centre for Attachment-based Psychoanalytic Psychotherapy, London.

Walker, V. (2003). From body snatching to bequeathing. Google search: Victoria Walker body snatching, pp. 1–4.
Weigert, E. (1939). Discussion on Psychoanalysis. Reprinted in *Psychiatry*, 46, May 1983.

CHAPTER FOUR

The psychotherapy relationship

Susie Orbach

T here are so many ways of describing how psychotherapy works and the purpose of this book is, of course, to try to address particular facets of it. I shall restrict myself to a discussion of how entrenched ways of being that cause distress can change through the therapy relationship.

The aims, conventions, and experience of therapy makes for an encounter that creates the conditions for reflection, feeling, analysis, and experimentation to occur. Reflection, feeling, analysis, and experimentation lead to a reinscribing of experience in which the individual's present feels *made by, but not bound by history* and in which her or his past is animated by new thoughts and understandings. Transformation of the individual's subjective sense of self is the outcome of a successful therapy: the individual experiences her or himself as an actor in their own life who has the flexibility to respond in novel ways to the emotional demands upon her or himself.

Psychotherapy is a very personal human endeavour. What I mean by this is that unlike psychological treatments, which are essentially procedural such as CBT or phobia desensitization, psychotherapy involves the therapist and patient in a relationship with one another. The therapy relationship itself is akin to a human laboratory for the exploration of change and risk. Although there for the benefit of the patient, the therapy relationship also affects the therapist in often profound ways. It can make the most enormous demand on the therapist as well as delivering considerable emotional and intellectual satisfaction (Orbach, 1999).

The psychotherapist and listening

A critical aspect of psychotherapeutic practice is the extraordinary capacity the therapist develops to listen and hear. Through Freud's invention of the analytic hour (Schwartz, 1999), the therapist develops a quite unique and specialized form of listening and hearing. Circumstances that in ordinary life one might find difficult, unpleasant, painful, shocking, revolting even, and want to avoid or ameliorate by spontaneously providing responses of straightforward sympathy or of telling tales of similar emotional valance, are instead simply welcomed. The therapist listens. She or he doesn't immediately respond. Neither does she or he ignore what they have heard. In the first instance, the difficult, unpleasant, painful, shocking, or revolting utterances stand alone, without elaboration. As the starkness of their emotional timbre reverberates between the two people, these utterances are engaged with in ways that extend our ordinary notion of listening to include a deepening of understanding *of the experience of the individual and what the incident(s) and utterances mean to and for them.*

People come to therapy in great difficulty. It may be that they have a secret, something confidential they need to explore, as Brett Kahr has suggested, and often the secret or the confessional is a gateway to issues more complex than the secret *per se*. For it is frequently the feelings around the secret, it is what the secret represents as a view of themselves, and it is the shame around the secret that needs addressing. I think it is too limiting to see therapy as a confessional for it is often the case that even where the "confessional" aspect seems important in itself, we cannot know which bit of the confessional aspect is critical. What we endeavour to discover with the individual may be the "whys" of the particular secret or confessional. We don't assume to understand why it is compellingly problematic but what in it is for *them* so difficult.

There is, of course, the related issue that until an individual speaks, she or he does not yet know what may be crucial to them or what turns out to require secreting. It is extremely commonplace for an individual to be devoid of language and even images about issues that are troubling them. Thus, while a secret or a confession may form part of a therapy, it may be as Bollas (1987) has written, an unthought known that needs speaking of. Therapy provides the context and the relationship in which the unthought unknown can be spoken of, heard, received, and embraced.

The therapy relationship and transformation

Therapy is a transformational experience that occurs through the therapy relationship. Both individuals are transformed, challenged, influenced, and learn from the therapy. It is an asymmetrical but mutual experience (Aron, 1991; Mitchell & Aron, 1999) in which our efforts are expended to enable our patients to become transformed. In the process we often become transformed ourselves. We extend our emotional vocabulary as we try to extend that of our analysands. In order to understand their distress and to be of use to them we are forced into deep confrontations with ourselves and with our own habitual responses. Being well analysed does not mean clearing up confusions about our emotional lives in such a way that we will not feel challenged. Nor does it mean that we can avoid being personally affected by our patients. What our own training experiences can afford us is the capacity to notice *how* and *that* we are being affected. As Casement (1985) writes, we develop the capacity to be our own internal supervisor and reflect on how our patients are "working" on us.

In order to address the question of how therapy works we need a theory of the therapy relationship. What might constitute such a theory? We have many theories of what has gone wrong in developmental terms, but in trying to understand how therapy works we need theoretical understandings of what gets things going again when things have gone wrong for the individual, the family, the group. What are the elements within the therapy relationship that permit an individual in particular to develop psychologically? What are the ingredients to getting things going right?

A theory to right things

When an individual's life has gone wrong in consistent ways for them we are pretty safe in assuming that there are neural and psychological pathways that have been honed that incline an individual to manage experiences in habitual ways. Usually sets of feelings have been constrained, while others have been arced in particular and limiting ways, and an important aim of therapy is to deconstruct those repetitious pathways in order to enable the individual to have a wider set of responses.

In creating an emotional ambience in the consulting room (and the conditions for the individual to develop the confidence to do so without the actual presence of the therapist) so that what has not been able to be experienced can be felt, thought about, and digested, habitual neural and psychological ways of being are disrupted and new experiences can occur. There is nothing particularly pathological about an individual's tendency to repeat. This is part of the human condition and it is in our repetitive modes of response that we recognize ourselves and our uniqueness. This holds true for all kinds of experiences: those that are enabling as much as for those that are disabling. Interrupting the repetitions by facilitating, provoking, or encouraging the individual in therapy to risk experiencing something fresh involves the therapist demonstrating her understanding of the inevitability and function of these repetitions.

Understanding repetition

Therapy is a partnership and a working alliance. The latter depends upon the therapist conveying to the patient the understanding that people find themselves compelled to do things in the way that they do. It is not that they are stupid, wilful, or contrary, but that their ways of acting, behaving, and feeling make "sense".

They do things that may appear to be stupid, wilful, or contrary, but their involvement in these practices is logical. They are ways of being that encode the individual's sense of her or himself and their internal relationships. Moreover, they can be said to express a positive aspect in the sense that they are perceived as protective or as the assertion of a fragmented aspect of self. To take a commonplace example, the adolescent who doesn't study for his exam and does poorly may be protecting himself with the idea that if he did study he would do well. This idea may soothe him in the face of a deep concern that he doesn't know how to study or learn. This adolescent's habitual non-studying, although apparently self-destructive, protects his sense of potential capacity.

An example

A man, Paul, who had a complex relationship to his twin brothers was in the final stages of disentangling himself from a fraught shared business when he found himself starting a new venture with them. His view of this new involvement was that it was sick and perverse, a sign of his death wish and negativity. His self-criticism was unproductive and kept him entangled in a way that added to his sense of stupidity. The therapy needed to help him discover what psychic issues he was addressing and what problems he is trying to solve for himself by this new entanglement.

Exploring defences

In exploring the various motivations—conscious as well as unrecognized ones—we may discover many contradictory issues expressed by Paul's jumping in again with his siblings. Some of the kinds of ideas we discussed that allowed him to reposition his understanding of himself were as follows. He began to consider the idea that, in re-engaging with them in business, he was trying to enable his brothers, who had disappointed him, and who from Paul's perspective had exploited him, to find a new response and to act decently and equably.

At the same time, Paul considered that this new venture had materialized because he was fearful of separating from the twins. Despite the emotional grief and umbrage he felt towards his brothers, he feared that they could form an even stronger and excluding alliance against him from which he risked being cut off completely.

A third area of enquiry centred on the many ways in which Paul had protected himself from recognizing that it is he who has been looking after his brothers for twenty years, in the guise of them looking after him. Although they were younger than him, he had been a sickly child. A family story emerged about his need of his brothers but tucked into this fable was a more complex tale of Paul's competence and success and his brothers' need of him to grow the family business. He needed their bravado but it was to a large extent his efforts that underpinned his brothers and made them appear substantial and capable.

Appreciating complexity

These, in brief, were the kinds of motivations that formed part of his defence structure. The human psyche is complex, so that there will always be multiple meanings that have significance for the individual at different moments and at times may have to be juggled simultaneously. In articulating the possible motivations, he (and we) can see his human agency, his psychological intention- ality in what otherwise appear to him as foolish and somewhat degrading actions. Recognizing his unseen motivations reveals that Paul is being active rather than a collapsed passive and inevitable repeater, which is what he fears. He is also able to see how much psychic energy goes into keeping things static and how complex and surprising his mind is: how things aren't black and white but that ambiguity and conflict are part of what is going on for him.

For many people, and certainly for Paul, the idea that their minds are messy or complex is initially daunting. Soon this unwel- come notion is part of what becomes exciting and alive for them in therapy. In discovering complexity, one is able to join up the many fragmented experiences one has that can feel alternately stuck, unpredictable, or at times like separate self-states that just emerge impulsively and over which one experiences little control (Blomberg, 1993).

Entering into the experience of others

Understanding the thinking that motivates the repetition compulsion begins the process of entering into the mind of the other. This very special property of therapy involves psychotherapists in a process that goes beyond the normal assumptions and guessings of everyday life to a judicious use of questions to illustrate to the other that we have understood a piece of their experience. We do this because we need not only to enter into the thoughts of the other but to enter into their feelings and to discover which feeling states are so shameful to them. We try to feel *our* way into *their* experience. In becoming their therapist we are not just a technician sorting through the strange thoughts or feelings they have. We are, in a sense, more enveloped by their experience: we feel *with them*, we see things *from their perspective*, while also holding on to a third position, the therapist part that is concurrently focused on the process. Our primary focus is on the patient, of course, but it is the intensity of our focus that yields important information to us about their experience.

If we now return to Paul, we can observe the *feelings states and mind states* that are aroused when he envisions "separating". In his case they are myriad and range from guilt that he doesn't need his brothers quite so much any more, a fear of his own competence, his sense that his brothers would be delighted to exclude him, a fear that he is absolutely dependent on his brothers and, however much he wants to be free of them, he is attached in ways that can only be destructive.

As a therapist we are making pictures, theoretical constructs about why Paul's particular feelings should be so absolutely paralysing or shameful. In Paul's case we might find out that the shame relates to the nature of his attachment to his brothers. We would then ask ourselves and him if he understands what it is about his desire to be attached and dependent that causes him shame. In posing that question I am suggesting that attachment or dependency need not be only shameful. This disruption of Paul's expectation that I will concur with his view instigates a set of unfolding questions that will be going on in our minds and will form part of the discourse of the therapy.

Defences and shame

There will inevitably be historical patterns that would have encouraged Paul to absorb the idea that dependency and wanting were shameful. Like many upper middle class children of his generation he was sent away to boarding school at seven, to the same school as his brothers. His father worked in the Far East and while some holidays were spent with his parents, contact with them was truncated and, for a set of easily imaginable reasons, emotional displays or articulations of loss and missing were discouraged. Indeed, even the attachments to his brothers were undermined in a school setting that frowned on familial ties during school term. His brothers were placed in different houses and the parents were asked to send separate packages and letters to each child. Contact between the brothers, particularly Paul, was kept to a minimum.

It was not surprising to discover that the family psychic *zeitgeist* was one which mirrored aspects of the school culture in, if not condemning, then certainly denying need and attachment. Paul believed his wish to be close to his brothers was a failing and that the missing feelings that he had for his parents were best stuffed away. As we talked it became clear that the psychological adjustments that his parents made for the separation from their children was non-trivial. His father could not bear to hug them goodbye and acted as though the continual severings that occurred were part of the natural order. His mother's upset at the children's departures was ascribed to her frailties, implying that if she were more robust she would have weathered these *without feeling distress*. Between his father, mother, and his brothers (who, *au fond*, had one another) Paul picked up a certain terror around attachment and need that was compounded by denial and shame and by the general cultural sense that despises dependency and substitutes the heroic man on his own as an antidote to dislocation and sorrow. In being able to see the roots of his shame as emerging out of a sense of disallowed dependency, Paul was able not only to question this as a stance towards life and relationships rather than a fact of life, but to recognize that his sense of shame came from his legitimate dependency needs having been thwarted. He understood that it was a consequence of the severing and the psychological preparation for the severings that intensified his conflicts around dependency and attachment. It was historically over-determined: not having his needs addressed instigated the confusion around attachment and dependency.

Defences enacted in the therapy relationship

Discourse about Paul's understanding of relationship, attachment, need, and dependency and the ways in which it was enacted in his present conflicts with his brothers formed a very large element of what occurred in therapy. Alongside this emotional narrative were the ways in which these themes played out between us in the transference–countertransference. Our relationship was a crucial site of the work we did together and Paul's acknowledging, receiving, and accepting his involvement with me and my caring for him was a challenge, a disruption to his normal responses. Paul was uneasy with desires for attachment and acceptance that he experienced in our relationship. He was reluctant to recognize my constancy as of use to him, and we had much working through to do in order for him to open himself up to the relationship that was on offer. It was not so much that he tested me, us, but he didn't initially have the psychological receptors to receive a relationship that accepted his need for attachment without disparaging, denying it, or not knowing how to be inside of it.

The relationship between us involved many enmeshments and entanglement that reflected what he had experienced in his other close relationships. By analysing these emotional excursions when they occurred and welcoming them as data about himself we could see that Paul anticipated certain responses to him and in ingenious ways encouraged others to meet his expectations by inhabiting particular roles for him (Mitchell, 1988; Sandler, 1976). The therapy looked at such dynamics between us and through our enquiry allowed us to intercept these well-established patterns. Together we cleared an emotional space in which he could begin to have a new experience of what it meant to accept a relationship that provided for his attachment needs in the present (Eichenbaum & Orbach, 1982).

Removing fright from feelings

An important dimension to successful psychotherapy is enabling an individual to experience difficult feelings at manageable levels. Many of the people we will see in therapy are frightened by their feelings. This could be because certain kinds of feelings were prohibited, disavowed, or frowned upon in their family of origin, or sets of feelings were so unbearable that they became detached and split off in a dissociated form. Part of our skill as therapists is to pace the introduction of split-off affect. We are not feeling fascists who insist upon the individual engaging with feelings that might appear overwhelming. Rather, our skills lie in making it gradually possible for our patients to approach difficult feelings with diminished or zero anxiety.

We do this by not being frightened by those feelings ourselves. As we know well, part of why fright attaches to feeling sets is that they have no history of being received, experienced, and digested. Patients who are frightened of particular feelings imagine being engulfed or stuck in those feelings. We offer our patients a relationship that can accept, witness, and receive those feelings in such a way that fear is lessened. We demonstrate, through not shying away from those feelings in the therapy room, that all sorts of feelings can be tolerated. And in the bearing of difficult feelings certain potentialities open up *vis à vis* those feelings.

In cases where, as I mentioned above, particular sets of feelings have been off limits, we find that the individual will either have a very flat affect or that certain emotions and feelings are over developed and in effect doing the work of other feelings. The (misplaced) feelings get repeated and repeated and become the emotional chord for the individual. However, because they are a kind of all-purpose emotion they are not accurate enough to provide relief or digestion of the painful experience that is generating the misplaced feeling. They are a template for managing difficulty rather than for working it through.

Feelings as a cover for other feelings

Let's see how psychotherapy expands this reliance on a few notes in a chord to multiple chords. My patient, Paul, has a propensity to become involved in very aggressive business deals. He likes to go to the edge and part of the reason his twin brothers rely on him is that he appears to have nerves of steel in negotiation. He is able to adopt a rather contradictory stance of intense pressure combined with an attitude that he can let a deal go. This combination seems to win him contracts on extremely favourable terms. He is also a heavy user of illegal recreational drugs, which involves him in some risk because he is simultaneously a well-regarded elder in his church and community.

His behaviours show him to be a man who seems to require risk and through the therapy we have deduced that his sense of vitality and aliveness comes from being on the brink. He frequently blows up at key employees, finds fault in restaurants, and is hypercritical of his wife. On the surface he appears to have an insatiable appetite for aggression or risk-taking. If we put this together with what we have understood so far about his difficulty with accepting his dependency and conflicts around attachment, then we discover something rather different about his risk-taking and aggressive feelings.

By pinpointing the states of being that precede his entering into aggression and risk-taking, we can help him to recognize and then change how he manages feelings he finds difficult. Aggression and risk are easy for him. They are the well-trodden mechanism for the immediate "release" or discharge of feelings. What *is* difficult is vulnerability, longing, wanting, fear of not existing, collapse, bleakness, emptiness, depression. It is in our naming of such difficult feeling states that can be a bridge to helping him stay with such feelings long enough for them to be experienced and digested.

Therapy is of little value if all we do is give him a place to experience what he is already managing. Yes, we must name such behaviours, but if we stop there we are in danger of reinforcing what is a defence for him. He is aggressive and risk-taking because it has felt, or has been, absolutely essential to him to feel he has mastery over adverse circumstances. In being aggressive he defeats a deeper interior sense of being at the mercy of, of being helpless. In taking a risk he revs himself up and feels alive and capable. He overcomes the bleakness by managing adversity and winning out in a business atmosphere that he has made and finds hostile.

When we explore his feelings before drug-taking (and the gambling and women that often accompanies it) we find that he is looking for some kind of enunciation of his humiliated feelings about himself. He doesn't do these things when he feels good. He does them when he feels terrible. He gets stoned to feel bad, goes gambling expecting somewhere to lose, not win, and when he has furtive sexual encounters he feels debased, not stimulated.

What does this mean concretely? In simply naming them as accurately as we can and in suggesting the kind of unease they bring him, as feelings he is uneasy with, they "click" with him and he feels brought into a new or split-off part of himself. He weeps with recognition and relief that something just outside of his reach can be grasped. He's saddened and reflective as this state is acknowledged. Gradually he begins to feel a certain sourness when he finds himself going for the buzz of gambling or drugs. It feels "not right", a behaviour that now emphasizes displacement rather than solving it. He's entering into new emotional territory for himself but he isn't quite there yet and so he's straddling unfamiliarity and newness on the one hand and familiarity and alienation on the other.

This is the process then—he enters into a new idea of a feeling, allows the feeling to emerge: now sadness, now emptiness, now sorrow, now anger, and by allowing such feelings to enter him his emotional core is extended, albeit with a sense of fragility. Along with finding these new feelings some of his habitual responses get folded into his extending emotional repertoire so that he begins to feel more solid. Paradoxically, confronting, engaging, and allowing the vulnerability he has been unable to feel before strengthens and enhances his sense of self rather than diminishing it.

The landscape of feelings that were unexpressed and unacknowledged—helplessness, sadness, grief—because they are thought to be so negative, or difficult, or destabilizing, left him previously depleted, wretched, and inauthentic to himself. By integrating them, or at least knowing about them, he is more inside of himself, less explosive, and more layered. It is a human accomplishment to feel helplessness, sadness, grief, loss, sorrow, disappointment, and so on. These feelings link us to ourselves and when they aren't able to find a place in us because they have never been named or accepted, we can be pretty sure that they will find a translation into other feelings' states. In Paul's case, the activities he engages with provide him with little psychic relief; they simply reinforce his sense of his own inability to deal with distress and his fundamental sense of lack of self-worth.

An examined life

In looking with the patient at feelings in this way we are together drawing a picture of who he is, who he has been and why, and who he might become. We are opening up the possibilities of transformation by enacting them within the therapy relationship. The words we imply, the mental constructs we employ, are designed to help him create a context that will make it possible for him to expand his emotional repertoire and his relationship to himself. In taking him seriously, and his feelings and thoughts, and by being interested and curious in relation to who he is and has become, he too becomes interested in himself, both as an observer and also as a participant in his own emotional and psychic life.

Paul's conscious participation in his own life, bizarre as that sounds (because if he isn't participating who is?), is part of the transformation. He begins to understand his need to merge with his brothers or his need to have a life that has continual threats and emergencies in it—albeit at business—as the attempt to knit together a life in which he has not felt underpinned and supported but instead has had to support and create everything for himself. He has not been able to accept his dependent and needy feelings; they have been split off. As a result he requires constant reassurance that he can't get from anywhere else except himself and he does this by levering himself into positions where he constantly needs to provide emergency first aid to himself in order to remind himself of his existence.

Of course we cannot predict what desires are tucked in behind anyone's particular defence structure and how much of the available behaviours are wanted behaviours. For one person it will be their ambition, for another it might be their shyness and vulnerability, for another their anger and upset, for another, a sense of displacement and not belonging, and so on. What therapy requires of us as therapists is a capacity to sit, to tolerate, to be curious, to understand what frightens us, or where we are inclined to make judgments, and where we need to extend our own emotional vocabulary in order to help the others.

Examining ourselves

Every theme that is an issue for the patient in their life—whether it is dependency issues, fears of helplessness, depression, choosing the wrong partner, affects us too as individuals. It is not only that it has a good chance of coming up in the therapy relationship and between us in the transference–countertransference. It is also that we may have our own hesitancies, strong points, and fears that we need to work on privately so that we don't jump in to solve "an emergency" or confirm in a superficial way someone's existence, or offer a false balm to someone because we are as frightened as they are of their feelings. What we experience in the countertransference is crucial. How we use it is the difference between therapy working and not working.

In looking at the mechanisms within the therapy relationship and the ways in which the therapist sees the process of what she needs to be doing, I have been providing a rather technical view on how psychotherapy works. I hope that when this is read together with the other contributions, we will have conveyed the richness and moving nature of the therapy process for both the patient and the therapist.

References

Aron, L. (1991). The patient's experience of the analysts's subjectivity. In: S. Mitchell & L. Aron (Eds.), *Relational Psychoanalysis: The Emergence of a Tradition* (pp. 243–268). Hillsdale: NJ: The Analytic Press, 1999.

Blomberg, P. M. (1993). Shadow and substance: a relational perspective on clinical process. In: S. Mitchell & L. Aron (Eds.), *Relational Psychoanalysis: The Emergence of a Tradition* (pp. 379–406). Hillsdale, NJ: The Analytic Press, 1999.

Bollas, C. (1987). *The Shadow of the Object: Psychoanalysis of the Unthought Known*. London: Free Association Books.

Casement, P. (1985). *On Learning from the Patient*. London: Tavistock.

Eichenbaum, L., & Orbach, S. (1982). *Outside In Inside Out*. Harmondsworth: Pelican.

Mitchell, S. (1988). *Relational Concepts in Psychoanalysis*. Cambridge, MA: Harvard University Press.

Mitchell, S., & Aron, L. (1999). *Relational Psychoanalysis: The Emergence of a Tradition*. Hillsdale, NJ: The Analytic Press

Orbach, S. (1999). *The Impossibility of Sex*. London: Allen Lane.

Sandler, J. (1976). Countertransference and role resonsiveness. *International Review of Psycho-Analysis*, 3: 43–47.

Schwartz, J. (1999). *Cassandra's Daughter*. London: Allen Lane.

CHAPTER FIVE

Rhythm, reorientation, reversal: deep reorganization of the self in psychotherapy

Roz Carroll

"Life itself is an expression of self-organisation"

(Sardar & Abrams, 1998, p. 77)

What makes psychotherapy work is a question that is both impossible to answer conclusively and yet necessary to address. In this chapter I propose that psychotherapy "works" in the same way that life works (or evolves), only in a more concentrated form by intensifying and containing specific processes that occur in all living developing systems (from cells to individuals, to communities, etc.).

Psychotherapy was once presented to the public as a detective story: clues to the unconscious expertly spotted by the therapist-sleuth leading to a reconstruction of traumatic events in childhood. In this linear account revelation brings catharsis, insight, and healing. Actually this search for a hidden story remains a fairly central feature of psychotherapy, but today's version of therapy encompasses many more nuanced levels of information and interaction that are marked by non-linear cycles of disorganization—reorganization. The emphasis has moved from discovering the origins of neurotic patterns to working directly with relating as a human capacity.[1]

Before attempting to outline some of the intricacies that typify psychotherapeutic work, I want to make a brief comparison between psychotherapy and other life-changing experiences. What else brings about significant lasting constructive change in an individual? A very basic summary might include: relationships of all kinds (falling in love, becoming a parent, friendship, etc.); creativity, sports, spiritual practice, and work. It may also include encounters with phenomena in nature; witnessing or participating in significant social events, including upheaval and mass movements. Any of these might bring about cumulative change, requiring learning, adapting, but *if they to are lead to significant change they will usually include some, or even many, experiences of intensity, of feeling pushed beyond a threshold*, and probably also *phases of enduring uncertainty and even disillusion*. Usually, in order for meaningful change to occur, there will be an assimilation of what has been intense or difficult, and an emergence of a different or expanded sense of oneself.

Psychotherapy is a complex, ambitious, multiplicitous process. A good chat with a friend, priest, or confidante can help to complete an unfinished emotional cycle; it can lead to insight, and life-changing decisions. But psychotherapy goes beyond this by continuing to ask questions and listen for the intangible organizing principles in a person's life. These emerge and are reorganized within the therapeutic relationship via exchanges and insights paralleled by significant shifts in rhythm, perspective, and orientation.

Psychotherapy is also different from the ongoing process of "life" in that it is a specific form in which the practitioner attempts to maximize "openness" in the therapeutic relationship within a set of formal constraints (boundaries of time, space, confidentiality, etc.) which close the system. The structure of the therapy enables a concentration of experience, with an opening out of meaning. This occurs in a non-linear way as trust and mistrust in the client are negotiated. While at times this is characterized by deepening relaxation, at other times the work is intense and unpredictable. Periods (or moments) of assimilation interspersed with crises and transitions lead to more complex and differentiated ways of being (Carroll, 2003).

Psychotherapeutic work rests on and wrestles within the paradox that deep change is spontaneous—it cannot be rationalized, prescribed or controlled (by either client or therapist). Rather it is through *the dialectic of spontaneity and discipline* (with the therapist taking much of the responsibility for discipline) that changes occur in the client that are simultaneously relational, bodily, perceptual, and reflective (Carroll, in press).

In this chapter I want to explore aspects of the developing paradigm of contemporary psychotherapy, which is itself a product of social and cultural change and crisis. I will be focusing on the emergent principles—cutting-edge practice across a number of psychotherapeutic approaches—rather than describing a generic model. Despite the variation between them there are still some noticeably contemporary emphases, such as working with a greater appreciation of difference; a more relational, dialogic style; the use of the countertransference; more cross-fertilization between psychoanalytic and humanistic thinking; and a greater attention to the body (Samuels, 1989).

Complexity, self-organization and feedback

"a theory of everything" (Lewin, quoted in Sardar & Abrams, 1998, p. 85)

It is no coincidence that the shifts in the field of psychotherapy are paralleled by a shift in the overarching scientific paradigm (Carroll, 2003). Chaos, complexity, and field theory have led to a revolution in understanding the principles of living systems and providing a new framework for thinking beyond linear explanations and towards more integrated interdisciplinary holistic ideas. The concept of psychology as the study of "mental" life is gradually giving way to the acceptance of mind as emerging from and encompassing the emotional, bodily, and relational (Damasio, 1999; Panksepp, 1998; Schore, 1994).

Complexity theory overlaps with chaos theory and has been widely applied to self-organizing systems, such as living environments, economies, the weather, and network phenomena such as the Internet.[2] (In this sense "self"-organization doesn't mean a psychological self, merely reflexivity.) A self-organizing system is defined by its complexity, connectivity, and ability to reorganize spontaneously. It exhibits a combination of openness to environmental influence and a capacity to sustain structure, as well as to create new structures and new modes. Science journalist Roger Lewin describes complexity theory as: "the theory of life at the edge of chaos, [it] includes the entire spectrum, from embryological development, evolution, dynamics of ecosystems, complex societies, right up to Gaia—it's a theory of everything" (Lewin, quoted in Sardar & Abrams, 1998, p. 85). Complexity theory is not psychological or philosophical, but it is a theory that looks at how things develop over time when a great many variables are interacting with each other; and especially the behaviour of any kind of system at critical points of instability, change, and crisis.

Complexity and chaos theory have been increasingly relevant in the study of aspects of human functioning, such as consciousness, shifts in emotional states, and the relationship between the nervous system and its environment. Human life is complex because it evolves in the interface between multiple complex systems operating at multiple levels: from the behaviour of cells to the organization of the nervous system, to micro and macro social and historical processes. Complexity theory cannot give us a comprehensive model to explain the specifics of human pathology, instead it embraces what classical science attempted to overcome—*variation and unpredictability*. Diversity, richness, complexity, and creativity are signs of life evolving through the process of self-organization.

Complexity theory uses the term self-organization to describe both the process and effects of change. The original basis of psychotherapy, Freud's technique of free association is structured more as an exchange in many therapies today, but a key principle remains waiting to see what emerges and the nature of its self-organization.[3] The client's assimilation of their own story and its implications is fundamental to psychotherapy, and it is an unfolding, re-working, reorganizing process. Dreams, stories, metaphors, the client's way of communicating with the therapists and so on are all unique self-organizing patterns that gradually become the object of exploration. So, too, are bodily states continually reorganized in an immediate correlation with what is on going on in the therapeutic relationship (Carroll, 2004).

These patterns are explored through various kinds of feedback, upon which all self-organizing systems depend. The function of feedback is to generate a continuous stream of information for assimilation, adaptation, and orientation. Feedback loops enable and trigger spontaneous adjustment to, and interaction with, objects and focal points in the environment, whether it is the Bank of England monitoring interest rates; a monkey learning to crack a nut; or an immune system responding to a virus. Feedback loops are ubiquitous in nature, society, and technology, and the more complex the system, the more elaborate, interrelated, and reciprocal the loops are. In human relationships, feedback loops include subliminal "images in multiple sensory modalities of texture, movement and intensity" (Damasio, 1999, p. 318).

Psychotherapy works by utilizing various kinds of intervention to maximize feedback. The sheer variety of interventions in psychotherapy have in common their aim to stimulate some shift in the client's awareness of themselves. Dialogue and exploration are the core of most approaches, though the style may vary considerably. Interventions include: reflecting back the client's own implicit formulations, challenging the client's expressed perception, discovering new metaphors, formulating questions, hypotheses, and transference interpretation. It may mean exploring and elaborating on symbols and fantasy occurring within the transference relationship and arising from dreams, made and found objects, sand tray, drawing, and claywork (Searle & Streng, 2001). Interventions that emphasize the body may pay attention to the breath, track changes in sensation, or allow and follow spontaneous movements and gestures (Totton, 2003). Some therapies make use of structures and experiments, such as dramatic enactment, visualization or Gestalt "chair work".

Whatever the modality and theoretical model used by the therapist, *the essence of psychotherapy is concentrated feedback, specifically cultivated, and operating in many varying ways.*[4] "Concentrated" feedback means complex, multiplicitous, and spanning a whole range of phenomena; it goes far beyond "mirroring" and is not neutral. This enables the client to acquire a more differentiated experience of life and more elaborated, varied responses to challenge and change.

The psychotherapist of today is often guided by the countertransference to formulate and engage in the relational dynamic, using awareness of their own feelings, sensations and impulses to inform their responses to the client (Carroll, 2005). The discipline required of the therapist is to use their subjective experience (the countertransference) with some degree of objectivity (reflection) and to feed it back into the therapy relationally and in terms of interventions (Orbach, 1999). The countertransference is itself self-organizing: it emerges spontaneously, giving shape to the therapist's necessarily conflicted and complex response to the client. (Soth, in press).

What psychotherapy can offer above and beyond other relationships is that the therapist is dedicated to the task of holding and considering many levels of an interaction. Deep reorganization of the self in psychotherapy occurs through the deepening and expansion of relational capacity in the client (and the therapist). The client experiences a plurality not just of "mental" attitudes but of embodied states in an intricate dance of reciprocal feedback between self and other. In this chapter I want to show how this capacity includes aspects such as rhythm, intensity, orientation, and reversal of perspective (shifts in perception) that embrace both verbal and non-verbal processes.

Rhythm, intensity, and timing

"The magic of a dance, young man, is something purely accidental. The irony of this is that you have to work harder than anyone else for the accident to occur . . ." (McCann, 2003, p. 68)

Rhythm is intrinsic to our lives and permeates every aspect of our self-organization. In the body there are, for example, hormonal, metabolic, and neural cycles, and over fifty ultradian rhythms, such as sleep–waking patterns. In relationships some of these rhythms are more explicitly involved in the dynamic between people: breathing, heart-beat, contraction–flexion of muscles; gait, gesture, eye contact. Rhythm underlies speech (pace, cadence) and conversation (turn-taking, pausing, postural matching, de-synchronization). Other typical rhythms are involved in habits and activities, lifestyle organization and social exchanges, seasons and celebrations.

Rhythm is fundamentally organizing, and it confers a degree of predictability, a structure to follow. It operates at every level in

RHYTHM, REORIENTATION, REVERSAL   91

human engagement embodying nuances of connection, power, desire, and fear. *When we connect to our internal rhythm, we know who we are. How we connect to the rhythm of another defines our relationship with them in that moment.* As much as we need regularity of rhythm, we also need graded differences, surprises, and new movements: and this is the basis for reorganization, a development and expansion of the sense of self.

When a client comes for psychotherapy both parties need to establish a rhythm together—sometimes this is straightforward, perhaps deceptively so; at other times, there is a struggle or intense anxiety that makes for a staccato beginning. Timing and rhythm are generally not in focal awareness or under deliberate control, yet they tell us much about the idiom of the client and the way they are relating to the therapist (Beebe & Lachman, 2002). Some clients find the therapist's silences particularly disconcerting because they struggle with what seems to be an absence of rhythm to adjust to or interact with.

With one client, Fred, the difficulties we had with establishing a rhythm encapsulated the overall difficulties of the therapy. Fred's anxiety to inform me, direct me, and get through to me his history in all its detail meant that it was almost impossible to find a gap in his talking to respond. I felt literally "in the firing line". His talking was usually fast and loud: often volcanic, venomous, steely with contempt. One day, in an effort to get a word in, I implored him "Shut up, Fred!", and he fell at my feet with a salaam. It was a comic moment, both of us were relieved by my interjection and his instant response. War became play, or rather, a temporary truce.

By talking non-stop Fred was literally holding on to himself, avoiding even momentary pauses that carried the risk that I would fail to be there, thus leaving him to drop into an abyss of terror and vulnerability. So, in an attempt to stay with rather than resist the pattern (it was hard not to become defensive in response to this volley), I took to really concentrating on watching his face and body very carefully and started to perceive points at which he seemed to "cohere". These were fleeting but clear moments of repose amidst long sequences of rapid face changes that, observed closely, showed expressions of horror, disgust, hatred, and extreme anguish. My almost exclusive attentiveness to his body, putting aside the attempt to respond to his verbal challenges and exhortations, soothed him and evoked some gratitude. This was a first step in modifying his relentless pace, and allowed for the emergence of other registers, rhythms, and tones: poignant, subtle, clever, passionate, and desperately playful.

Finding the right rhythm with the therapist is reassuring; it gives some shape to emotional intensity. Losing it or letting go of it can be frightening or exciting, and this happens as the client shifts from one state to another. The therapist's work involves attunement to the client's rhythm and awareness of the impact the client's rhythm is making on them. In addition, the therapist needs to consider how their interventions contribute to the shape and direction of the rhythm of the therapy. Synchronizing, counterpointing, emphasizing, pausing, amplifying, and slowing down are finely calibrated aspects of the interaction with the client.

Rigidity or hypermobility in the client's rhythm blocks deeper reorganization and is the hallmark of difficulty with and fear of relating. Insight can lead to more spontaneity; so also can "experiments", following a body process, active imagination with an image or symbol, working through conflicts, and finding unexpected support in the sustained empathy from the therapist. Timing, one of the least written about aspects of psychotherapy, is crucial. Therapists are skilful in gauging the degree of tension in the relationship, the depth of feeling that can be addressed at any given moment, and recognizing defences and their function.

As therapist and client get to know each other the subtlety and complexity of their rhythmic exchange increases. An excerpt from a clinical vignette by the Jungian Schwartz-Salant illustrates the complex dance of the therapeutic alliance. Paula, after years of analysis, starts the session:

> P: I want to be here and stay here today, not wandering in outer thoughts. I need your help.
>
> SS: How can I help?
>
> P: I don't know, I just know I want to stay here. I want to feel the excitement, be with it, not run away.
>
> SS: You are beginning to split now. (I infer this from the intensity with which I find myself fragmenting at this moment.) Your attention is wandering. Try to stay with the excitement. What fantasy arises?

P: (after a long pause) Its difficult to just stay here and not split. The word naughty comes to me—I shouldn't feel this way with father. [Schwartz-Salant, 1986, p. 41, comments in round brackets in original]

Schwartz-Salant explains that the mutual implicit reference point in this dialogue is her father's spanking of her from the ages of six to thirteen and her recollection of fantasies of his sexual arousal. The rhythm and directness of the dialogue reveals the immediate understanding and cooperation, as the two prepare for the emergence of intensity relating to Paula's relationship with her father. Minutes later in the session Paula exclaims "I want to *see* your excitement. I want to undress you, to *see* it." Deeply engaged in the rhythmic feel/field with Paula, Schwartz-Salant allows himself to utter the thought which "forcefully occurs" and thus to identify with the father's emotional state:

SS: What about mother?

P: Fuck her—she doesn't matter. All that matters is us!

SS: I'm scared.

P: I don't believe it. Its incredible. You'd leave me alone in it because you're scared. Well, I'm not! She doesn't count. It doesn't matter what she thinks!

SS: But I'm scared.

P: I feel hate, rage, awe. Disbelief. You're a fucking bastard—you can't leave me in it alone. I feel a fury, chaos, a splitting in my mind. Oh God I don't believe it. I feel like a tornado inside, fragmented, like my insides were just taken out of me, sucked out of me. You are denying your feelings and desires, and since we are merged I have to deny mine, or split them off. I can't trust.

SS: I think that is just what happened to you with your father. [Schwartz-Salant, 1986, p. 45]

There are many aspects to this therapeutic encounter that could be explored (and Schwartz-Salant does) but what I want to highlight is the way that the rhythm changes as the explosive nature of Paula's unconscious feelings bursts through (echoing, perhaps, the rhythm of the spanking). Schwartz-Salant's responses are sufficient both to maintain and then to contain the momentum. The implicit understanding is that they are elaborating transference material "on the edge" with an electric here-and-now experiencing on a bodily level. The point at which Paula as a child had to split in order to survive is revisited in its intensity in the therapy and integrated with a new level of understanding.

This excerpt from Schwartz-Salant exemplifies the mature phase of a psychotherapy and can be likened to a jazz improvization. Like musicians, therapist and client develop the capacity to hold a rhythm together, find a melody, play with another, against another, at a varying pitch and pace. Finding moods, letting them build, climaxing, letting go. Some emotional cycles can last minutes, others can stretch over years and are revisited in the therapy over and over again. Paula's lengthy analysis with other psychoanalysts had failed to release her from perpetual persecutory intensity and acting out. Now the resolution of this wave of intensity, and with it the shift in her inner relationship to men, is reflected in a dream: "Beauty and stillness is all around [. . .] I see a man is swimming in the water next to me. [. . .] He swims gently, carefully with me" (Schwartz-Salant, 1986, p. 51)

Health is the capacity to tolerate, to maintain and to shift between a plurality of states (Bromberg, 1998; Schore, 1997). "Psychological" difficulties of any degree correlate with an incapacity to bear intensity of feelings, or to transition between one feeling state and another, or even to maintain any kind of stable state without it being fragmented by dissociation. Although changes in emotional state are inevitable, when people are depressed, anxious, or traumatized the main experience is that "things stay the same". There is a deadness and dryness and/or overwhelming intensity and chaos, which is experienced as unbearable.

Psychotherapy aims to create the space for deepening the cycles of disorganization–reorganization that can enhance the sense of richness, complexity, and variation in the texture of experience. The length of time involved in psychotherapy is necessary to slow down the frantic rhythms of trauma and stress to allow assimilation of what has happened and what is happening. It also takes time to facilitate the re-emergence of spontaneous rhythms—such as breathing—which have been suppressed in an attempt to control the pain of living and relating (Totton, 1998) Peaks and shifts do occur because of the cyclical nature of bodily rhythms but may not lead to real change unless the wave itself is completed in a meaningful contact with another or with oneself. It is at these peaks—or troughs—that deep reorganization can occur and a new pattern and a new orientation can emerge.

Reorientation

We need to understand why this *movement outwards*, this *movement towards* [. . .] is so fiercely resisted [. . .] *A whole life's orientation is at stake* and the collapse of such an edifice seems like the end of the world. [Symington, 1993, p. 35, my italics]

At the heart of almost any issue that clients bring to psychotherapy is a latent or acute orientation crisis. Where am I going? How can I get out of this mess? What will help? What's the point? Anxiety, depression, and post-traumatic stress are related to loss or failure of orientation. A new-born baby will usually orientate towards its mother by looking at her (even from the other side of the room) and will recognize her voice and the smell of her milk within hours. The rooting reflex (feeding), the Moro reflex (embracing), the grip reflex (holding tight) are all available from birth to enable immediate connection with the source of safety and nourishment. They are the first of many reflexes out of which are elaborated sophisticated embodied processes for sensing direction and orientating in a complex physical and social environment (Frank, 2001; Hartley, 1994).

The acuteness and accuracy of orientating in birds and animals often becomes obscured in humans dealing with complex conflicts around autonomy and dependency. Dreams and other imaginative processes, stimulated through creative arts, movement, free association, have a profound orientating function. Understanding one's place in a family dynamic (for example, between father and mother, or behind an elder brother), a transgenerational pattern (such as Holocaust survival), can reveal powerful unconscious orientations (Hellinger, Weber, & Beaumont, 1998). Orientation is undoubtedly more difficult in the modern, fast-changing world with its vertiginous level of apparent choices. Even in the best of circumstances individuals have a network of interrelated values and orientations that may need work to hold in creative tension, or phases of reorganizing.

Humans have quite a range of reflexes for orientating away from danger and harmful environments and towards goals, resources, and (human) objects in an expressive, receptive, and intentional way (Trevarthen & Aitken, 2001). Feeling states are bound up with posture and subtle movements—movements with, towards, away, around, against another or others. These underpin and are bound up with relating and finding one's way in life—the human need for a home, a vocation, economic survival, a family and friends, creative expression. Body psychotherapists work directly with the bodily expression of orientating impulses, such as birth and feeding reflexes, identifying muscular patterns and their associated affect, and their meaning in the therapeutic context. "The work of therapy," writes Gestalt therapist Ruella Frank, "is to help clients organize their awareness so that they experience themselves as part of, rather than alienated from their environment" (Frank, 2001, p. 70).

Symington articulates the deeply unconscious negative orientation that characterizes the pervasive condition of narcissism, which involves *turning away from life* (relationships and genuinely creative acts). The narcissist remains facing inward essentially, but cut off, and recoils from emotional agency that involves risk. He or she appears to be a participant in life, but actually is operating within a fairly closed system, with fear, envy, and rage barring the entry to relationship. With this also comes anxiety, which occurs when there is a disconnection from basic feelings, leading to a sense of emptiness and disorientation. A capacity to know what one is feeling is vital to finding one's way in the world and therapy works partly on the basis of reawakening genuine curiosity, and persisting in inquiry.

Feelings have a function—to guide us towards actions that enhance survival, meaningful relationships, creative self-expression, and spiritual development (Damasio, 1994) Being able to bear the intensity of feelings depends partly on experiencing them in relation to—being able to orientate towards—an appropriate goal or object. Clients come to therapy because there has been some significant gap or failure of relating by others in early life, or because subsequent experience has disrupted trust in relating. Part of the therapist's role is to stand for different objects (mother, father, lover, friend, sibling) and to help the client identify, negotiate, and shift between different subject positions (including very early infant states and adult and gendered positions).

Detachment, ambivalence, idealizing or denigrating others—any fixed relational responses—blunts the capacity to keep orientating afresh in each moment of a relationship, or in new phases of life. Curiosity is an orientating response, but is not available while in states of intense fear, rage, or loss. People under strain can end up in a state of chronic flight away from their own painful feelings, fixed in keeping going as an act of will. Stopping flight involves feeling the terror and facing what is happening now. Startle reflexes, shaking, trembling, other physical sensations, powerful dreams, and changes in perception can occur during major changes in orientation.

Depression, conflict, breakdown, and hopelessness can be the precursor or indicator of deep reorganization of the self. Outbursts, crying, and confusion are phenomena of transition between states, especially when there is a loss of a protective illusion. The therapeutic relationship has a critical role to play in providing the crucible and testing ground for the spontaneous self-organizing process within the client. This involves the client's suffering—the work involved in feeling and facing that which they would rather not bear—and surrender. The dialetic of these inseparable processes feeds the emergence of something new, a reorientation towards fully living.

In the following case study I want to illustrate how orientation can become deflected in voyeuristic activity and how psychotherapy helped one client, Julian, to tune back into himself and face the ordinary difficulty of being a man trying to find and maintain a relationship.

Julian—etheric space versus relational space

A designer in his late thirties, Julian came to me asking what my success rate with tinnitus was. He was affable and lucid and after initially focusing on the ramifications of the tinnitus, he seemed willing to engage more deeply. He was living with a pervasive half-acknowledged fear and he attributed this to his anxiety about being stuck with this ringing in his ears forever. I suspected that it was linked with abandonment fear. The end of a serious relationship had left him anxious and disorientated. I wondered if the tinnitus echoed like the sound of his own screams coming back to him.

Julian's main theme was the search for a girlfriend and his intense ambivalence towards women. I was struck by the fact that he liked pursuit, but was quick to quit if he anticipated rejection. Reports of his week's encounters were formulated in terms of the woman's age, attractiveness rating, and style. I pointed out to him that these women—he called them girls—were not given names, or real attributes as people. I shared with him my image of him as someone raking through items on a rail in a bargain basement, trying on and discarding possibilities in frantic haste.

Initially there was a bit of a sitcom quality to our interactions: we seemed to be at cross-purposes. He wanted dating advice. I wanted to get behind this bland yet compulsive narrative of the contemporary dating scene of pubs, parties, and text messaging. He would indulge me with explorations of his early life—his parents' divorce when he was two, being brought up by two rather dominating Catholic women (mother and grandmother), and infrequent contact with a narcissistic competitive father. But he could often not feel the connections I made between his way of managing women now and how he had coped as a child.

Then Julian started to tell me about his addiction to Internet porn sites, particularly those involving domination and even fake death scenes. He said that he was aroused by the look of fear on the actresses' faces, but that it was important that it was obviously acted and not real. Although on one level he considered this behaviour shameful, he was also intrigued by its hold on him and was aware that the more he tried to control it, the more compulsive it became. We were both able to recognize that at least one function of visiting these sites was the exploration in a very controlled way of his own feelings of rage, abandonment, hatred, and helplessness. Provocation in real life situations threatened his self-mastery, but via the computer he could click to new extremes.

Julian's symptoms are very much of the twenty-first century: tinnitus indicates an overload of the nervous system; dissociation and addiction are the new neuroses. He did not have as severe and deep rooted a pathology as his fascination with fake death scenes might imply. His obsession with these sites began as he was dealing with the painful feelings stirred up by dating—feeling teased, messed around, rejected. He used the computer for deflection and distraction, a refuge from the real life situation where he felt helpless. But the over-stimulus was also "pumping him up"—excitement, rage, horror, humiliation being triggered via the complex identifications with the on-screen victim and perpetrator.

I was disorientated too—how was this related to being in therapy with me? Was it a test? Was he upping the ante in a battle of the sexes with me? I felt either pinned down and rather helpless, or "on the offensive" regarding his objectification of women. I was held in check by concern that if he felt judged, this key symptom would go underground, or he would leave. I was intrigued—and I think seduced too—by his "controlled experiment" of monitoring his own responses to graded degrees of sadism.

I felt unable to really get to the roots of this, other than by being aware of how being with him produced a passivity in me, a feeling of being slightly suspended and helpless. So I listened for material in his ordinary interactions with others, trying to help him grasp the depth of his responses to rejections and difficulties with the women he met. Gradually we talked more about other relationships, with friends, flat-mates, at work, and other themes—fear of conflict, powerful feelings of rage and shame, betrayal, and disappointment. He remembered himself as a "fat controlling boy" setting his toys on fire once, in evident distress following the departure of his father.

Then Julian was seduced by Mina and suddenly he had a girlfriend— wild, colourful, and childlike, and a highly educated, competent, professional woman. According to him, she was almost out of control, and yet it seemed she was also very much in control. While his feelings of insecurity and jealousy were a closely guarded secret, hers were rampant. Everything he couldn't tolerate in her—her loudness, her possessiveness, her childishness—was in him, and he was trying to keep these under control and *so must she*, he insisted.

One day he came in, on the verge of breaking up with her after another argument. It had errupted when she phoned him on his mobile because he was late. She had started shouting at him, questioning his motives, and he wanted me, now, to support his conviction that "she was wrong". Instead I latched on to his bodily state—his clenched jaw, puffed up chest, the rigidity of his body, the glare in his eyes, and saw the epitome of righteousness. I challenged him to feel what was happening in his body—mirroring his posture back to him—and describing in words what I saw.

Bringing him back to his body subdued his self-righteousness (self-righteousness is a dissociated state), but still Julian wanted me to see she must not behave like that. Aware that I was taking a risk with our relationship and taking sides, I compared the straightforwardness of her outburst to his secret and obsessive use of the Internet and invited him to judge whose was really "the problem". My feeling of losing control and the decision to let go into criticism couched in very ordinary language marked the crystallization of my countertransference. I had contained *my* horror and now it was my turn to be the predator or, indeed, the accuser. This challenge brought out an intensity that paralleled the argument with his girlfriend. The session continued with Julian now trying to get through to me that he was really frightened when she shouted at him, he felt helpless and inadequate. I was moved by the genuineness of his plea and acknowledged his vulnerability in relation to her and to me.

It was a turning point, bringing to a head the theme of abandonment, anger, control, and punishment. Julian continued to struggle with intense feelings of rage, confusion, and despair in relation to Mina. He had met his "match" in her (triple pun intended) and the therapy supported Julian to survive the intensity and chaos and begin to find his feet in the relationship. The therapy, rather than the Internet, acted as a safety valve and they learned to communicate better. Several months later Julian moved cities to live with Mina, and was even contemplating the possibility of marriage and having a child. In our last session together he was a mellowed, bemused man, still mildly toying with the idea that he should be searching for a woman who fitted his ideal image—the long-legged "trophy blonde". He joked that Mina's voice had replaced the tinnitus. There was a lot in this joke—his aggression creatively deflected, and a wry acknowledgement that she was a fundamental part of his life, his latest and most satisfying symptom.

Psychotherapy attempts to maximize the potential of relating by bringing to light how the client is limiting the impact of the other out of fear of what the encounter may or may not bring. The potential and danger of relating is that intensity can be amplified as well as contained through interaction with the therapist. It was precisely this conflict that we were entangled in: the dilemma of how much to reveal, to feel, and the responses each might evoke. In the moment when I challenged him I became the *agent provocateur* in a complex sense: the female judge repelled by his obsession, someone he needed to turn to for support and understanding and the implicit object of his erotic fantasy. Mother, girlfriend, the Internet actresses, are suddenly embodied in me (not just projected, because at this point I have taken sides with them) and he has to face the music. This provokes a strong reorientation, highly charged, complex, and demanding a new relational response.

Countertransference—the therapist's orientating response

Two states differing by imperceptible amounts may eventually evolve into two considerably different states . . . (Lorenz, quoted in Sardar & Abrams, 1998, p. 43)

The use of the countertransference is the hallmark of many contemporary psychotherapies—and its discovery and elaboration have been fuelled because of the way it has been found to catalyse change and reinvigorate therapeutic processes (Bollas, 1997; Orbach, 1999; Schwartz-Salant, 1986). Countertransference may be a refined form of orientating response. The therapist's body becomes an antenna for gathering information from subsumed levels of phenomena. The perception of minute, sometimes fleeting, detail stimulates the cohering of an image, an idea, or an impulse. For example, one day with a client I became aware of the image of collecting eggs and putting them in a basket very gently. The image provides lots of food for thought: the need to be aware of fragility, of gathering pieces, and many associations to the idea of "putting all the eggs in one basket". In this instance the image confirmed my sense that I needed to wait patiently for something to incubate and hatch.

Whatever the motivations holding a pattern of any kind in place, human processes—as with other living systems—will often be cyclic. When a cycle or Gestalt is incomplete, it tends to repeat in the same way, and can become "stuck". New rhythms, waves, or cycles may be inhibited. The therapist's sensitivity to very slight fluctuations that indicate the potential for shifting can enable them to support transitions between states, sensing when to wait, how to intervene, to interpret, or be silent. Sometimes the therapist supports the momentum of spontaneous change and at other times is actively challenging or disrupting certain fixed patterns.

Countertransference is characterized by an extreme sensitivity to relational cues—the therapist has a capacity to resonate to such a degree that quite subtle bodily states can be caught and amplified. Indeed, the therapist allows the client to *evoke* specific modes of relating in them. These may be apprehended by increasing awareness of what is being felt on a bodily level. Paying attention to the range of sensations, images, fantasies, and feelings that occur can help to differentiate emergent patterns in the relationship. These might be patterns organized on the basis of past experience or patterns that are new and creative responses to relationship in the present. The therapist's response accents, highlights, or modifies the client's experience. The therapist may feel compelled to act, intervene, or comment in a striking or dramatic way (as I did with Julian, or Schwartz-Salant with Paula) that is, or comes close to, an enactment of a dynamic in the client's history. Increasingly, in the debate on countertransference, it has been noted that enactment can operate on a fine edge between replaying or re-enacting a traumatic couple (such as parent–child) and transforming it by adding a new depth of holding and awareness (Mitchell & Aron, 1999; Soth, 2005). Such moments become possible, and bear fruit, *when the intensity in the relationship reaches a threshold*, the equivalent of a critical mass, but does not destroy the relationship. Traversing that threshold precipitates a reversal of perspective, position, and/or feeling in the client. This is like a moment of punctuation, which can catalyse a significant reorganization of perception in the client.

Reversal: getting more than you bargained for and other turning points

We wish for a closely fought match containing many satisfying reversals (Mamet, 2000, p. 9)

Bifurcation point: a branch, where there are two distinct choices available to a system (Coveney & Highfield, 1995, p. 424)

A huge body of metapsychological theorizing attempts to account for the recalcitrance of human beings to deep psychological change.

The difficulty of achieving lasting and effective changes in clients and the arguments about the conditions and criteria for that are the subject of wide-ranging debate and conflict (Totton, 2004). It is important to understand that the human propensity to try to maintain equilibrium is not simply "mental" or "psychological" but bodily (neurophysiological) (Carroll, 2001, 2003). It is also the case that cycles of behaviour, feeling, and perception can reach a limit point, which is an opportunity for deep reorganization. In this section I want to elaborate on a basic principle of process, which is that *deep internal structural change occurs when the system is "far from equilibrium"*.

In self-organization theory the threshold for radical change is known as a bifurcation point and occurs as a system is reaching a state "far from equilibrium":

> At this moment of instability, the system may break down and follow an earlier pattern imprinted in its structure (repetition). Or as a result of its exquisite sensitivity to any fluctuation in the environment, it may break through to a new pattern of higher order and complexity. [Capra, 1996, p. 171]

At the bifurcation point the system goes back into a familiar cycle (a regression), or it shifts to a new level of organization, a quantum leap (a progression). One of the trickiest aspects of psychotherapy is the tension between the need for equilibrium (which represents safety and stability, but also entrenched defences) and loss of equilibrium (breakdown, breakthrough, dis-organization). *Much of the time change is facilitated*, and phases of regression may be supported, increasing the client's trust and understanding of their needs. *But at some points a movement to a new pattern is precipitated suddenly*. The tension has been building until an aspect of the client's life, relationship with the therapist, or inner world is far from equilibrium and the client arrives at a crossroads, the all or nothing, sink or swim, now or never. There are many phrases in our language for this bifurcation point because it is such a profound feature of human experience.

In terms of psychotherapy, the bifurcation point is a crisis, perhaps the "make or break", where overwhelming intensity tests the limits of the therapeutic relationship. This can lead to the emergence of something new: a reorganization of perspective (reversal), a more intense contact between client and therapist, the breaking down of barriers. Often it appears things are getting worse. The client may feel abandoned by the therapist, or turned on by them. They may attack or feel attacked. Both clients and therapists desire and fear these heightened, often dramatic, moments. A battleground may get marked out. Does the client need to win, or leave the therapy, to survive or maintain control at this point?

Let's illustrate this "bifurcation point" with vignettes from two brilliant and very different therapists—Joyce McDougall, a psycho-analyst based in Paris for half a century, and Irvin Yalom, an exis-tentialist therapist practising in California. McDougall recounts a session with a patient who spends the session complaining that her analysis has failed to enable her to get a lover, earn enough money to buy a studio apartment, and that even the success of the analy-sis—the alleviation of an old symptom of self-harming—is a nuisance because this had been an effective technique for calming herself down. As she is leaving the consulting room, the patient says, "Well, this weekend I shall commit suicide; there's nothing left for me to live for!" McDougall calls out after her retreating back, "If you do that I'll never speak to you again!" When the patient returns on Monday she confesses that she laughed all weekend and then adds, "Perhaps for the first time I believed you really care for me" (McDougall, 2002, p. 25).

The patient's complaints are a repetition, a familiar way of orga-nizing herself in relation to disappointment. McDougall doesn't analyse the tone of the patient's parting shot—perhaps it contained a nascent self-irony, a sense of her own ridiculousness, but the posi-tive effect of McDougall's response clearly indicates a ripeness for a new pattern, more sophisticated, more relational, more creative. We can also be in little doubt that years of a relationship marked by reliable holding and more typical analytical interventions enable this spontaneous rebellion on McDougall's part to bear fruit. It is a turn-ing point that precipitates a deep reorganization: a reversal (of per-spective, of behaviour); a change of rhythm (the session speeds up at the end with the exchange like a sudden flash of glinting swords) and reorientation (a sudden recognition of the analyst's love).

Laughter, like sobbing, losing one's temper, or a startle reflex, is one of the hallmarks of reorganization. It signals a shift in a fixed relational and situational dynamic. The dynamic intensity of the moment can bring therapist and client into a new level of contact with the other or precipitate recoil from the other. There is a reversal of perspective, a coming together of opposites, as the client glimpses or feels the other side of the story. As Eigen puts it, the client is "enlivened and quickened through the sense of difference" with the presence of the other "no longer taken for granted but appreciated as *coming through*" (Eigen, 1999, p. 8) The antithesis of reversal, in the sense that I am using it, is splitting, which is used to diminish intensity and protect a fragile self from the impact of experience.

Yalom's approach to psychotherapy is quite different from McDougall's—unlike her he makes a point of delivering punchlines and paradoxical interventions. It is hard to distil a vignette from his longish story "Seven advanced lessons in the stages of grief". It has many themes, but the main one is how a very experienced psychiatrist and an expert in bereavement is confronted, challenged, and educated by the patient, Irene, a woman deeply grieving the death of her husband. The tables turn and turn during the lengthy, agonizing, and stormy therapeutic work. In "Lesson 4: the black ooze" he writes about working with her recurring image of black ooze, hideous, acrid, repelling, and threatening to tar anyone who comes near. Its foremost meaning is her grief rage, a feeling that grips her and her therapist with ferocious power.

> After a long stage of agitated suicidal despair, Irene feigns a new stage of acceptance, rather than yearning for what she hasn't got, she will focus on mothering and professional life. When Yalom shows relief at this seeming amelioration, hoping it will provide some respite, she accuses him of betraying her. "What kind of therapist are you? Your caring for me? All pretense! [. . .] You've given up on me!" He is infuriated by this trap and throws down the gauntlet, "I'm sick and tired of your setting tests for me that more often than not I fail. We have too much work to do", he says, taking a line from her dead husband—"we don't have time for this bullshit" (Yalom, 1999, pp. 112–113).

As with McDougall's intervention, Yalom refuses to tolerate this degree of rejection—or misuse—of the relationship that has been developed thus far. The sustained empathy that is such a crucial component of psychotherapy gives way to a new imperative that is effective precisely because it is relationally and contextually acute. In these moments of reversal, the therapists have both "lost the plot" and found it all at once. Suddenly everything is reorganized, and yet the preparation for that exuberant moment has been long and hard. The tension of the old pattern snaps and something more alive is released. Both these moments are products of the countertransference. They are relational responses to—as opposed to interpretations of—a building affective momentum that needs a reformulation.

Reversal occurs at a bifurcation point and manifests as a shift to a more complex, highly organized state that happens when a moment of intensity has been contained.[5] In the sense in which I am using it here, it means a dramatic shift in perception that incorporates and transcends an earlier position. McDougall's client enjoys the simultaneity of being "childish", laughing at herself and feeling assured that her therapist is human and available. Irene realizes that it is not Yalom who is betraying her by welcoming an apparent improvement, but that she is betraying herself by avoiding a real engagement with the work.

Many techniques are used in psychotherapy to help the client identify with all the different parts of themselves. Work with dreams, fantasies, creative arts, or movement—in fact any spontaneous creation of the client—is often used to support the conscious embodiment of a wider sense of self. Gestalt therapy refers to figure–ground reversal—the way attention can be focused on one pattern that seems depict one thing, but a shift in perception reveals another image. The figure–ground reversal may be in the order of seeing everything about someone else that is "different from me" to the shocking recognition that in fact something about the other is "just like me". Jungians have the term "enantiodroma" to describe how this switch to an opposite perception can occur.

These reversals are part of the ongoing reorganization process in psychotherapy. The reversals occur as changes of perspective in the client's awareness of themselves and others, and in different ways of perceiving the therapist. However, I have focused my examples on therapeutic interventions at a climax because the link to loss of equilibrium is crucial for deep reorganization of structure. At a critical point, the therapist's response itself may shift to allow their own temporary loss of equilibrium an honest and realistic place in the relationship There is often an element of shock or at least surprise in this, provoking a moment that precipitates either a regression that may enable the completion of an old cycle, or the emergence of a new pattern. It may be a shift to the other pole in an object-relation, such as from parent to child (as Julian did) or from passive to active, such as seduced to seducer (Paula). This is different from reorientation, which is a reconnection to a directional thrust. *Reversal is the discovery that you have arrived (often quite suddenly) in a different state/place/position/perspective.*

If the therapy does not enable intense feelings to be reworked relationally, it may become stale, and parts of the client remain obscured. When feelings do emerge, the client may be vulnerable to any failure on the therapist's part to miss the rhythm, or trajectory (Schore, 2003b). As the peak in intensity occurs many factors can interrupt, shut down, or amplify the process in the client. The therapist may fail many times to catch the wave or, perhaps, catching it they cannot bear with it. The negotiation is a complex one of timing, understanding, and attending to the somatic detail of the countertransference. Success and failure are sometimes quite close.

Reversal involves both differentiation and integration and is a perceptual shift linked to reorganization of the nervous system. Reaching a threshold of intensity or novelty stimulates a shift between systems, such as between the branches of the autonomic nervous system, or between left and right cortex (Schore, 2003a). In splitting, elements of experience are dissociated and temporarily eradicated (Bromberg, 1998). In contrast, when the intensity is met and contained relationally, more than one dimension of self and other are engaged synergistically and a richer and broader perspective ensues. Reversal in the positive sense that I am using it here manifests in increased structural and functional complexity, where *more parts of the brain and body are used concertively* (Carroll, 2003). This increases the feeling of being fully alive, and although this heightened moment will pass, the encounter supports the opening to a wider range of experience.

Rhythm, reorientation and reversal: contemporary psychotherapy at the cutting edge

Containment is a paradoxical process, a relational dance, in which spontaneity transcends established structures and boundaries only to organise itself into a new contained shape. [Soth, 2004]

The terms "rhythm", "reorientation" and "reversal" are not intended to describe a technique or approach but rather to suggest overarching phenomena that characterize a process of development in psychotherapy. I chose to focus on these functions because they reflect the inseparability of relational, bodily, and perceptual processes. Over a sustained period of therapy, the client's sense of self becomes wider and more differentiated neurophysiologically through the experience of ongoing reorganization. Finding and changing rhythm, reorientating, and surviving and surrendering to reversals becomes a more fluid process. The client experiences more frequent, subtle, tacit body shifts as part of a more spontaneous movement between a connection to themselves and a perception of the other.

Psychotherapy opens things out—undoes knots—in order to mitigate against some of the effects of time-gone-wrong, to allow reorganization where time has stopped a process and encapsulated it. Paradoxically it is also highly concentrated, with elements specifed by the context, which are witnessed, assimilated, and anchored with the help of the therapist. This requires the therapist to maintain the dialectic of spontaneity and discipline that characterizes a relational approach to psychotherapy. Part of the shift in contemporary psychotherapeutic practice stems from the recognition that significant reorganization of understanding is more likely to occur when the client is propelled experientially (and therefore bodily) into a new perspective.

The ideas developed in this chapter draw on a wide range of contemporary psychotherapy theorists, mostly at the more radical end of their field. My sources and influences include authors from body psychotherapy, creative arts therapies, Gestalt therapy, Jungian analysis, relational psychonanalysis, and especially, neuroscience.[6] I have de-emphasized language and insight deliberately in order to highlight the bodily and relational factors that are an essential component of psychotherapeutic change.

Notes

1. For discussion of the development of the relational thread in psychoanalysis, see the Preface of *Relational Psychoanalysis* (Mitchell & Aron,

1999). For a humanistic perspective on the relational going back to Buber and Tillich, see Hycner & Jacobs (1995).

2. Non-linear dynamic systems theory is the overarching term, while chaos, complexity, and self-organization form overlapping branches of theory. Field and information theory are also part of the new scientific paradigm. I have tried to minimize use of technical terms and lengthy explanations of concepts in order not to obscure the emphasis on basic principles. As a non-scientist I followed the descriptions outlined in Coveney & Highfield (1995), Capra (1996), Sardar & Abrams (1998), and for the broadest overview, Wilber (1995)

3. Various writers have made links between chaos theory and psychotherapy, including Field (1996), Scharff & Scharff (1998). Allan Schore's paper on non-linear processes in early development (1997), as well as his discussion of research in psychotherapy using a chaos model (1994: pp. 469–472), was an important influence.

4. For more detailed discussion of negative and positive feedback and the effect of transference as feedback and on feedback, see Carroll, 2003.

5. Unfortunately the term "reversal" has been used in a variety of contexts to mean quite different things. It was used by Aristotle to describe the change of fortune for the protagonist. Reversals remains a principal feature of drama, and all the arts. The playwright David Mamet comments that "aesthetic norms naturally reproduce organic processes of perception or creation" (2000, p. 65). Bion used the term "reversal of perspective" in the opposite sense to describe the patient who appears to take on/in the analyst's perception, but remained fixed internally to the reverse point of view. "Binocular vision" was his term for the capacity to switch from one point of view to another (Bion, 1967).

6. I am grateful to Jon Blend, Michael Soth, Linda Hartley, Graeme Galton, and Ed Mayo for their feedback and help in developing this chapter.

References

Beebe, B., & Lachman, F. (2002). *Infant Research and Adult Treatment: Co-constructing Interactions*. Hillsdale, NJ: Analytic Press.

Bion, W. R. (1967). *Second Thoughts*. London: Heinemann.

Bollas, C. (1997). *Cracking Up: The work of Unconscious Experience*. London: Routledge.

Bromberg, P. M. (1998). *Standing in the Spaces: Essays on Clinical Process, Trauma and Dissociation.* Hillsdale, NJ: Analytic Press.

Capra, F. (1996. *The Web of Life: A New Understanding of Living Systems.* New York: Anchor Books.

Carroll, R. (2001). The autonomic nervous system: baromenter of intensity and internal conflict. http://www.thinkbody.co.uk

Carroll, R. (2003). On the border between chaos and order: neuroscience and psychotherapy. In: J. Corrigal & H. Wilkinson (Eds.), *Revolutionary Connections: Neuroscience and Psychotherapy* (pp. 191–211). London: Karnac.

Carroll, R. (2004). Emotion and embodiment: a new relationship between neuroscience and psychotherapy. Training manual, unpublished.

Carroll, R. (in press). Neuroscience and the "law of the self": the autonomic nervous system updated, remapped and in relationship. In: N. Totton (Ed.), *New Horizons in Body Psychotherapy.* Maidenhead: Open University Press.

Coveney, P., & Highfield, R. (1995). *Frontiers of Complexity.* London: Faber.

Damasio, A. (1994). *Descartes Error: Emotion, Reason, and the Human Brain.* London: Putnam.

Damasio, A. (1999). *The Feeling of What Happens: Body, Emotion and the Making of Consciousness.* London: Heinemann.

Eigen, M. (1999). The area of faith in Winnicott, Lacan and Bion. In: S. Mitchell & L. Aron (Eds.), *Relational Psychoanalysis* (pp. 1–37). Hillsdale, NJ: Analytic Press. Originally published in *International Journal of Psychoanalysis, 62*: 413–433.

Field, N. (1996). *Breakdown and Breakthrough: Psychotherapy in a New Dimension.* London: Routledge.

Frank, R. (2001). *Body of Awareness: A Somatic and Developmental Approach to Psychotherapy.* Cambridge, MA: Gestalt Press.

Hartley, L. (1994). *The Wisdom of the Body Moving.* North Atlantic Books.

Hellinger, B., Weber, G., & Beaumont, B. (1998). *Love's Hidden Symmetry: What Makes Love Work in Relationships.* Phoenix, AZ: Zeig Tucker.

Hycner, R., & Jacobs, L. (1995). *The Healing Relationship in Gestalt: A Dialogic Self-Psychology Approach.* Highland, NY: Gestalt Journal Press.

Mamet, D. (2000). *Three Uses of the Knife: On the Nature and Purpose of Drama.* New York: Random House.

McCann, C. (2003). *Dancer*. London: Phoenix.

McDougall, J. (2002). Concluding remarks. In J Raphael-Leff (Ed.), *Between Sessions and Beyond the Couch*. Colchester: CPS.

Mitchell, S., & Aron, L. (1999). Relational Psychoanalysis: *The Emergence of a Tradition*. Hillsdale, NJ: Analytic Press.

Orbach, S. (1999). *The Impossibility of Sex*. Harmondsworth: Penguin.

Panksepp, J. (1998). *Affective Neuroscience: The Foundations of Human and Animal Emotions*. Oxford: Oxford University Press.

Samuels, S. (1989). *The Plural Psyche*. London: Routledge.

Sardar, S., & Abrams, I. (1998). *Introducing Chaos*. Duxford: Icon.

Scharff, J. S., & Scharff, D. E. (1998). *Object Relations Individual Therapy*. London: Karnac.

Schore, A. (1994). *Affect Regulation and the Origin of the Self*. Hove: Lawrence Erlbaum.

Schore, A. (1997). Early organisation of the non-linear right brain and development of a predisposition to psychiatric disorders. *Development and Psychopathology*, 9: 595–631.

Schore, A. (2003a). *Affect Regulation and the Repair of the Self*. New York: Norton.

Schore, A. (2003b). *Affect Dysregulation and Disorders of the Self*. Hove: Lawrence Erlbaum.

Schwartz-Salant, N. (1986). On the subtle body concept in clinical practice. In: N. Schwartz-Salant & M. Stein (Eds.), *The Body in Analysis*. Chiron Publication.

Searle, Y., & Streng, I. (2001). *Where Analysis Meets the Arts: the Integration of the Arts Therapies with Psychoanalytic Theory*. London: Karnac.

Soth, M. (2004), Chiron Staff Training Paper, unpublished.

Soth, M. (in press). Embodied countertransference. In: N. Totton (Ed.), *New Dimensions in Body Psychotherapy*. Maidenhead: Open University Press.

Symington, N. (1993). *Narcissism: A New Theory*. London: Karnac.

Totton, N. (1998). *The Water in the Glass: Body and Mind in Psychoanalysis*. London: Rebus Press.

Totton, N. (2003). *Body Psychotherapy: An Introduction*. Maidenhead: Open University Press.

Totton, N. (2004). Both/and. *The Psycotherapist*, 22: 11.

Trevarthen, C., & Aitken, K. J. (2001). Infant intersubjectivity: research, theory and clinical application. *Journal of Child Psychology and Psychiatry*, 42(1): 3–48.

Wilber, K. (1995). *Sex, Ecology and Spirituality*. London: Shambala, London.

Yalom, I. (1999). *Momma and the Meaning of Life: Tales of Psychiatry*. London: Piaktus.

CHAPTER SIX

When thought is not enough

Nicola Diamond

Introduction: the relational approach and attachment

I n this chapter I will explore a form of relational psychoanalysis, which is particularly influenced by attachment theory and related contemporary developments. The emphasis here is on the centrality of relations with others, in the context of developing a body and a sense of subjectivity. From this perspective, disturbed relations with others in early and ongoing development give rise to emotional problems that can lead to psychosomatic dysfunction and problems with the sense of "self".

In this theoretical context, the understanding of relationships involves the view that organism and environment are interdependent. The baby's physiological and neurological functions require facilitating relationships with key attachment figures for their optimal development. The internal world is inseparable from interactions with others. Relationships with others inform the content and form of the world of the developing individual, which is renegotiated and reorganized in later relations in an ongoing way.

In therapy, the relationship with the analyst becomes the setting in which the key relationships that form the "self" are relived in the transference and have the opportunity of being reorganized over time. In attachment theory the sense of the "self" that we carry around inside us is understood to be made up of the self and other (key attachment figure(s)) and these are called "internal model(s) of self and other". These are derived from relations with others. Such models of self–other are brought to awareness in analysis. Deep-seated beliefs about the self, derived from past interactions with others, are elicited and then challenged as given realities. These models can then be updated in the light of new experiences of self with others, in particular in the light of the emotionally "corrective" relationship with the analyst.

For Bowlby, who first formulated attachment theory, internal working models are dynamic scripts or maps that an individual has about him/herself as a unique embodied being and his/her significant others. These maps have emotional connotations and can range from elementary constructs to complex organizations. I am suggesting that these working models are rooted in bodily interpersonal action-based memory, which will be referred to throughout this chapter as "procedural memory".

The term *internal working model* has several advantages when considering how psychotherapy works. The concept of *"working"* refers to the dynamic nature of the model, while the term *"model"* implies construction and hence development towards more complex working models as the person, through analysis, identifies and alters current models of self–other and generates new interpretations of the present, which can also involve giving fresh meaning to other people's behaviour and re-evaluation of one's own responses.

Internal working models begin to be formed in the early months of life. However, they continue to be construed and reshaped in later years and throughout the life cycle. The importance of the earliest models is that they are likely to influence the way the child will subsequently experience the world and, hence, the construction of later models. Working models are not static structures. They are very stable, yet they can gradually change under certain conditions, such as therapy.

Because of the fact that internal working models are relationally based, the developing working models of self and other are, by definition, mutually complementary. A key feature of the experience of the other as part of the working model is the availability of the other, how much they can be trusted, and how sensitively they are likely to respond when needed. A key feature in the development of the internal working model of oneself is how acceptable or unac-ceptable, how lovable, one is in the eyes of one's attachment figures (see Diamond & Marrone, 2003, pp. 41—69).

In my conception of the therapeutic process, the role of inter-pretation includes the exploration and understanding of the links between current feeling states, somatic experiences and attachment history. In this way, the patient is helped to make fresh sense out of these connections. These connections are crucial to the therapeutic work and assist the person to contextualize his/her experience and realize that current states and experiences are rooted in real past events and a relational context.

The emotional understanding derived from a reconstruction of the individual's attachment history, and the transmission of affect that takes place across generations, help the analyst and analysand build together the emotional links that make sense out of experi-ence. In this context, the role of historical reconstruction is seen as central to the analysis. It is viewed as a retrospective and creative process, where the analyst and analysand produce together a narra-tive, which redefines the past in the light of the present. (Diamond & Marrone, 2003, pp. 153–184).

The retelling of the attachment history as an activity between analyst and analysand has been termed co-thinking (Diamond & Marrone, 2003, pp. 125–152). Co-thinking is relational thinking, where sharing and dialogue facilitates the processing of somatic affect (embodied emotion) into meaning. It is an interpersonal process or—properly speaking—"intersubjective". The analyst has the specific role of facilitator, to use him/herself for the project of another, to bear the other's feelings, to attune with the other, and to aid in metabolizing emotional experience by deeply respecting the other.

Thinking revisited: the importance of procedural interpersonal knowing

Traditionally in psychoanalysis the capacity to emotionally think and alter one's experience has been aligned with verbal speech and the word. In this formulation there are a number of assumptions at work. The body is seen to be made up of somatic states and raw feeling that exist apart from the capacity to emotionally symbolize and think. Following Melanie Klein's seminal paper on the importance of symbol formation and the development in the ego (1930), a plethora of articles were published in which the primacy of symbolic thinking was considered to be the road to cure. Here, symbolic thought was understood as the processing of raw feeling and somatic affects by articulating them in thought and finding words for emotion. In doing this, a person contains his/her affective states in thought, thus creating the mental space for reflection. I argue that this notion of symbolic thinking is not enough on its own for therapeutic change; that the notion of thought as cognitive and word-bound is limited.

Analysis can be said to go "beyond interpretation" because it rarely rests upon a clever insight that the analyst makes about the patient's psychic functioning and content of the psyche, nor simply upon a process of finding words for hidden thoughts. It is more fundamentally dependent upon an affective communication of attunement, in which the analysand comes to feel understood. What I would like to propose is that this non-verbal basis of communication is very important to tap into for therapeutic change. Words need not be spoken in this process, and if they are, what makes them effective is the emotional non-verbal network of interaction that has made possible a moment of meeting. Stern and members of the Boston Change Process Study Group, which has been influenced by attachment theory, originally formulated this idea (Stern et al., 1998).

A person in analysis can present with a capacity to be emotionally thoughtful and reflective, but find that this does not help them to change their emotional suffering and life situation. There is the possibility of pseudo reflective capacity, which may even fool the analyst, and this can happen in cases of "normopathy" where there is an over-adaptive self reliant on extreme splitting so that there is no sign of the part that is entirely split off. There can be complex rationalizations of pathogenic functioning, which are disguised in a psychoanalytical friendly form. I would argue that to "mentalize emotion", that is, to commit it to thought and to give it a name, may not bring about change in deeply felt sensory-feeling states. Hence, the development of a bodily basis for emotional thinking requires an elaborated explanation and language.

It might be useful here to incorporate insights from developmental psychology. Colwyn Trevarthen (1979, 1993), in his exploration of infant development, examines theories of language and thinking. He observes that emergent linguistic and thought-linked skills are built upon established shared emotional and body-based communications, found in the non-verbal interaction between mother and baby. He adds that the sharing and exchange of feeling states between mother and baby are directly communicated through sensory modes of expression such as touch. The development of emotional understanding takes place through looking, facial and bodily gesture, as well as intonation in vocalization.

The work of Trevarthen (1978, 1979), other developmentalists such as Stern (1977, 1985, 1998), data obtained through academic and attachment research in neuroscience (Schore, 1994), and studies on the function of memory all contribute to clarification of issues that psychoanalysts have been struggling to understand. Today we have more information than ever before to begin to understand the exchange between infant and caretaker. In this exchange, the tuned-in shared bodily modes of communication are built over time into an interpersonal know-how of emotional understanding and meanings that are stored as bodily memory (procedural memory) predominantly in the right hemisphere of the brain.

Contemporary neuroscience emphasizes the importance of brain–body processes and their role in non-verbal interpersonal understanding (Schore, 1994, 2003). The brain is rooted in the body, the sensory–motor system, involving a complex bi-directional processing, and the body is in direct contact with a world from which the sensory information derives.

Allan Schore describes how the sharing of affect that is expressed in facial and bodily communication stimulates the production of neurones in the baby's brain, the creation of neural networks in the baby's and the mother's brain, as well as biological processes, genes, hormones, and rhythmic patterning. These early interactions determine what we can call "co-regulating and deregulating emotional–somatic processes".

Procedural memory is bodily memory, a mode in which we remember embodied acts like driving a car, typing, dancing, and, most importantly, bodily interaction with another in its performance. Such memory becomes an unconscious pre-reflective "know-how", where states of emotional–somatic attunement with another, states of sharing and exchange, are stored and revivified as action and somatic memory (see Diamond & Marrone, 2003, pp. 153–166).

It is this biological–emotional basis of procedural interpersonal know-how that is so important for emotional and somatic integrity, over and above any linguistic acquisition. We need to understand the specific mode of linking the raw feeling–somatic affects of the baby with the emotional communication that takes place in a relationship with the caretaker. We need to understand the emotional links between soma—the body of the baby—and the relationship with the caretaker, as well as how bringing the body into relational shared meaning is so necessary for emotional thinking. In my definition, emotional thinking is embodied and relational; this representational area of being has to be changed in the therapeutic process.

The emotional and meaningful quality of the relationship is important. If there are disturbances in this linkage between body and relationship, then there are emotional disturbances. When the parent fails to affectively and somatically tune in to the baby, fails to share feelings and build them into meaning, and fails to tolerate and process the baby's emotion, then the result will be emotional and symbolic disturbances. A failure to integrate affect and soma into meaning and relationships will be reflected in the linguistic arena. Words will fail to couple with an expression of feeling and integrated somatic function; instead there will be a rift between feelings/somatic states and the use of verbal language. One example of this failure is *alexithymia*, which is a name for a psychosomatic condition where the person somatizes feelings and is unable to link them to a relational context. Words are used, but are dislocated from emotional expression and somatic integration.

The aim of the psychotherapeutic cure, in my view, is to engage the non-verbal emotional somatic experience with the therapeutic relationship, so that early interactive failures can be restructured to achieve greater somatic and affective integration with interpersonal understanding and meaning. In other words, the process of working through involves making links between somatic, feeling, and belief states as well as the reconstruction/construction of attachment history and current interactions with others. Hence, the focus no longer privileges the mental as reflective, since this area of functioning is seen as the tip of the iceberg. This is the major shift in thinking and has implications for theory and technique.

The redefinition of thinking: embodied relational being

Within developments of post-Kleinian thinking, Wilfred Bion's theory of the transformation of *beta* into *alpha elements* has been influential. Partially stemming from Bion's ideas, Peter Fonagy (2002), whose position is strongly rooted in attachment theory, has placed emphasis on his concepts of "mentalization" and "reflective function", a notion "mentalization" derived from the French psychosomatic school of Pierre Marty (1976, 1990). Joyce McDougall (1980) has integrated both post-Kleinian thinking and the work of Marty in her definition of symbolic thought and her explanation of psychosomatic conditions and thought dysfunction. In such formulations the *beta elements* (that is to say the raw undigested somatic–affective states of the infant) are transformed into *alpha elements*, that is, into processed thoughts.

In Bion's explanation, importance is placed on the other—the maternal function. The maternal other is present, tolerating and being with the infant's affective states. The transformation of these somatic–feeling states into a contained, thoughtful, and reflective *alpha mode* takes place thanks to the mother's capacity to process her own affective responses in the realm of thinking. She then gives back to the baby metabolized emotion with meaning, in a digestible form, and this acts as a mental container. The infant can later incorporate this function for itself.

This model should not be viewed as dualistic, based on a division between the body (beta) and the mind (alpha). I argue that we need an integrated brain–body model. All thinking is physical. The brain's synaptic links make up neural networks, the production of which result in qualitative states that we may refer to as subjective experience, consciousness, perception, and so on.

There are not "raw somatic states". Instead there are socialized feeling–soma states, in a soma that has an "interpersonal know-how". This interpersonal feeling–soma is the outcome of the processing of *beta function*. This link between soma and relationship has to be in place for an integrated emotional and linguistic function. Problems are rooted in a failure of this soma and relationship linkage, leading to affective deregulation, confusion, unprocessed feelings expressed as somatizations, as well as inability to contact feelings and express them in words.

The "maternal function" in Bion's account was noted as crucial to the question of processing sensory affect into meaning and relationality. Anyone who plays the role of primary carer would perform this function, and indeed later the role of others—whether a schoolteacher who forges a relationship with the child, an important relative or friend, lover or partner; they can all adopt a form of maternal function, facilitating the processing of affect into sense and a discriminate relational understanding.

I would say that that this "function of the other" informs the analyst's function with the analysand, and although the analyst cannot be the mother as such (he/she is not working with an infant, and cannot go through such fundamental experiences), the model of "maternal function" does have validity. For the analyst is often working with analysands who suffered developmental deficits in this sphere and is facilitating the processing of feeling through a more dialogic mode of creative co-thinking. Here, the analyst's capacity to emotionally tune in to the client's frequently non-verbalized feeling states and to bear the sharing of these affective states is a central part of the process. The therapist facilitates the making of links between the feeling states and the attachment history, helping the analysand to reflect on the attachment styles at work that restrict the capacity to explore new possibilities for living and being.

Co-thinking partly involves an unconscious processing that engages in the relational organization of bodily feeling states, which are components of internal working models. Therapy has to establish an engagement with procedural experience (bodily interpersonal memory) for change to take place. It is the processing of the soma and this mode of feeling that psychotherapy has to contact. The therapist contributes to this process through his/her co-thinking abilities.

This is not to deny or ignore the importance of verbal dialogue, or the acquisition of linguistic skills, that of course bring additional abilities. I am trying to highlight that such capacities come "on line" developmentally later and are informed by and based on the procedural (embodied and action-based) understanding and know-how that became established in the baby–caretaker relationship. In therapy the verbal dialogue relies on the affective procedural connections that have been forged at the heart of the therapeutic relationship. It is not a matter of reversing the hierarchy by privileging the procedural (bodily memory) over the linguistic, but understanding that development is ongoing and that it is not about a separation of soma from linguistic function, but the integration of the body into the language of speech and words, an integration that takes place in the cortex of the brain.

People often ask the question: how are patterns of behaviour and the established internal working models reworked when a style of relating has become so ingrained that it is hard-wired, so to speak? It is true that patterns of behaviour, the repeated activation of certain neurological networks, do get deeply ingrained. This is particularly the case in traumatic patterning of attachment behaviour that leaves their legacy in dissociative states and repetition. When this is the case, and it is not simply a matter of getting rid of engrained neural patterns, but of producing new neural networks that are superimposed upon the former. There is plasticity, which permits development and change, for the constant shift between disorganization–organization, and reorganization that takes place throughout the life cycle. New patterns emerge out of the analytic relationship.

From withdrawal to relatedness: a clinical illustration

I am now going to demonstrate these points in relation to therapeutic work with a woman in her late thirties whom I will call Melanie. On entering therapy my patient presented as a woman who had withdrawn into herself, focusing on her own body as an object of preoccupation. She suffered severe headaches and nausea. Her fear was that she would suffer an aneurysm. When this anxiety increased she felt like fainting. This was so intense and concrete that she often swooned and would lose balance and collapse. She had been tested for organic conditions, including a brain scan for tumour or lesions and middle ear problems but nothing was found.

As we shall explore later, it could be said that at the beginning of her therapy Melanie had alexithymic features in so far as she could not identify her feeling states or link them with meaning. Instead, she tended to express feelings directly in the form of disturbing body symptoms.

During the course of therapy, Melanie moved from the state of withdrawal into herself and her body to a relationship with her emotional self, thereby becoming able to link her feelings with experiences in human relationships. After eighteen months she was almost free of her bodily symptoms as the therapeutic work had helped her move towards a greater state of relatedness with others.

The body speaks

Melanie's symptoms became manifest at the age of twenty in the transitional period between leaving home and renting a flat, when she experienced violent head pains while looking for new accommodation.

The patient described her mother as knowing best and controlling, her father as unavailable, always at work overseas, and she spoke of a younger sister, five years her junior. The sister was born with multiple handicaps, including severe head trauma that resulted in migraines, dizziness, difficulty in breathing and walking. The sister nearly died as a child, so the family were all under the strain of death being potentially imminent.

Melanie would always begin the session with a description of her somatic state. She would tell me of the headaches, fear of fainting, the tightening and tensing of her body all over. She had little recollection of the feelings she experienced in childhood. She also could not describe those she had in the present or those associated with her somatic state. She would simply repeat a description of the physical states.

Within the first months of treatment Melanie's symptoms got worse. She developed severe head pains and dizziness, which would happen just before she fell asleep, thus effectively waking her up. It was one of her most frightening symptoms; she really felt she was about to die. This symptom would often occur the night before a session.

Melanie then started to bring her symptoms into the sessions,. She would tense all over, have full-blown migraines, make jerky movements on the couch and suddenly sit upright.

I did not interpret or explore the feelings in a psychological language, which would have been experienced as abstract and somewhat alien. I was simply with her, bearing and sharing the somatic feelings. I wondered if she might fear that therapy would make her worse or if she might become unconscious in the sessions, or share something unknown with someone that she could not trust. What kind of parent did she fear in me—someone who would do something bad to her unless she was vigilantly alert? I tried to convey my understanding, my style of being, in facilitating responses and intonation of voice, bearing and sharing her experience, and communicating an empathic state of being-with.

The vividness of her symptoms in the sessions may have suggested a worsening of Melanie's state, but she was, in fact, bringing her pain and anxiety into the sessions, into the very heart of the therapeutic relationship. Melanie was telling me with her body how awful she felt. Her symptoms were a communication in the only medium she had. This was her way of being emotionally alive in the room and in relation to me. In this way she made me a witness to her pain, hardship, and discomfort, to her alarm and terror. In this sense she entrusted me with the possibility of hearing and validating her experience. Her body was speaking on her behalf. She was unable to note the possible meanings of her feelings. Instead, she was telling me her story in a doing way, in non-relational terms as she had no emotional understanding of the relational context as yet. At this point I was two contradictory transference figures, a potentially feared other, who could make the symptoms worse, bring on an explosion of migraine that could annihilate the self, while simultaneously I was entrusted with the role of witness, with the possibility of hearing what she was expressing and validating her communications as another who understood and knew that they were true. We could say that I was taking on the initial role of "maternal function" but in the context of being an analyst with a now adult analysand. I was bearing with and sharing her feelings and somatic states through atunement. I was doing the work that had not yet been done (signpost of a developmental deficit). It was very important that at this stage I did not verbalize in an interpretive mode, as Melanie in her fragility would have felt taken over by another rather than being allowed the space to exist. As her story unfolds we will find an experience of a mother who impinged.

Bringing body speak into a relational familial context

From the state of bodily attacks came aggression. Melanie came early in the mornings for her sessions. One morning the doorbell was not working, I did not know. It was only when I heard a bang on the door that I opened the door with the buzzer.

She lay on the couch, remained silent for some minutes and then initiated the following exchange:

M: It's not okay. I got here on time and then you're late. I get so angry waiting. It reminds me of the waiting I did for Dad and Mum while they got Judith ready. I always had to be patient.

T: You have to put your needs on the back burner while others are being attended to!

Another silence; then

M: It's really good that I can say I'm angry. That's the kind of thing I could never say!

Through my mistake I had for that moment become the neglectful parent and this had activated hurt. The memory became emotionally relived in the transferential present. Now, due to active engagement of the analysand's historical experience, it was the time to begin a reconstruction–construction of the attachment history.

A couple of weeks later Melanie came some minutes early for the session and had to wait in the waiting room. When we started the session, it became quite clear that she had not noticed she had arrived early, but had assumed it had been my mistake again:

M: I feel you don't care about me, that you are preoccupied with other things. My rational mind said it doesn't matter, but I feel like it does!

This interaction confirmed that I had become the neglectful parent who was not keeping her in "mind". Melanie painfully lived her feeling of being unimportant and not valued by her parents or me. She was telling me how she felt her parents had let her down. This communication had begun in the first sequence of exchange and had continued into the second interchange. Melanie had unconsciously "used" my "mistake" to represent her experience of earlier environmental failure (Casement, 1990, p. 11; Winnicott, 1965, p. 258). She was still expressing her feelings in action, but the expression of anger was now to an external object. She had released her body from self attack by communicating to me her attachment disturbance through a transference relational re-enactment.

Winnicott (1965) notes:

> The patient uses the analyst's failures, often quite small ones, perhaps manoeuvred by the patient. The operative factor is that the patient now hates the analyst for the failure that originally came as an environmental failure outside the infant's omnipotent control, but this is now staged in the transference. So in the end we succeed by failing. [p. 258]

Casement (1990) clarifies Winnicott's point by explaining that patients can unconsciously use the analyst's "mistakes" to help the analyst understand the patient's experience of environmental failure and earlier trauma. The analyst "succeeds by failing", by enabling the analysand to unconsciously communicate earlier trauma, to relive it in the transference and thus begin to work through it. When Melanie found herself waiting for me the second time, she "manoeuvred" the situation so it again was my failure and the experience of earlier parental failure could be represented and staged in the transference. This communication is unconscious and, in being enacted in the new situation with the analyst, it is pre-reflective, emotional reliving. It is important that the analyst is conscious of the transference and resists the pull of enacting a parental role of being neglectful and irritated by a demand, but rather offers a response of empathic understanding. This process is necessary for working through.

> Melanie became able to express the aggression that she felt towards me. She found the emotional space for these angry feelings to be openly expressed rather than stifled. Having no relational mode of communicating she had felt physically stifled from within.
>
> The final transformation came when Melanie could think, "I believed my parents loved my sister and not me, but now I understand and know that they loved us both but had become so worried about Judith that they had not realised that I was missing out."
>
> She was then able to make the difference between feeling "I am unloved, I am unlovable", to "I felt unloved, but that was the feeling at

the time, I now understand why, I now know that I can be lovable". Even when there has been a fundamental failure in being loved, the reflexive stance can shift. This capacity to reflect in thought is reliant on the procedural shifts (bodily-based memory relived in action) in somatic and feeling experience. Meanwhile, the headaches were no longer taking place in the sessions and Melanie had stopped focusing on them as the sole issue.

And then this exchange occurred:

M: I never expressed any negative feelings towards Judith. I could never physically play with her. I always felt I had to protect her body. Her body was so weak; she couldn't dance or go for walks or anything. Even now, if someone does something she does not like, she becomes angry.

T: So Judith can express anger and all that she doesn't like and you feel inhibited. I can't help thinking about your sister's frail, damaged body and how you with your severe headaches and fear of bringing on an aneurysm cannot exert yourself in any way, and of how you feel you are living in a damaged body. It's as if you swapped your healthy body with your sister's.

Melanie, like her sister, had (in her symptom) a body so tortured and potentially fragile that she could not play or do any physical exercise. She feared exertion in case it increased her blood pressure and fainting and precipitated an aneurysm. By becoming her sister's body Melanie could disown her angry feelings. She became the victim and not the aggressor. In particular, she could punish herself for the competitive and jealous feelings she had towards her sister. This was complicated because she could avoid bearing the emotional guilt of these feelings by becoming the sufferer herself and yet pay the physical price as punishment. At the same time, paradoxically, by becoming like her sister, she could receive the same sort of attention she had got and have her pain taken seriously.

Bowlby, in supervision, always encouraged the therapist to ask questions about the detailed nature of particular past experiences with significant others. For instance, if the patient had hinted that the parents rowed, Bowlby would ask for a detailed account: where and when did it happen, how did you feel, what exactly were they saying to each other?

Now when I asked Melanie questions about her relationship with her sister, memories flowed. Judith had the seizures and was allowed to get her own way, whereas Melanie was the quiet compliant child. In identifying with her sister Melanie could associate herself with her sister's more demonstrative and demanding behaviour. In this family, being an able-bodied person meant that Melanie had nothing to complain about. In the transference, Melanie's bodily pain was also a way of calling out for help from me.

I did not make such further interpretations to Melanie, as she was not ready for them in this form. I think she would have experienced them as accusations and criticism rather than as a source of insight. The fact that something was implicitly understood between us was enough. Melanie had assumed her sister's state of damaged body and then took it up to express her own conflicts. Entering the therapeutic relationship helped Melanie's symptoms to partake in a relational and meaningful process. Melanie was communicating to someone (me) about something; hence her symptom became anchored in an interpersonal experience and interaction. This was the beginning of a repair of the developmental deficit, because Melanie had not had the opportunity before to properly express her anger and other negative feelings to someone who had the capacity to listen and tried to attune; nor had she been able to make links between her feeling states and the relational context in which they had emerged; nor had she perceived how this had resulted in an embedded structure that had become part of the embodied self.

Melanie told me in more detail what happened. What was revealed was that family life revolving around the sick child played a significant role in Melanie's formative years. Melanie felt that she ought to keep her demands for care and affection at a lower level, since the one who really required being looked after was Judith. In this context, she could not openly express her "bad" feelings, such as those of neediness, competitiveness, and resentment

From Melanie's description, Judith was seriously handicapped, having a potentially life-threatening illness. Consequently, mother stopped working and devoted herself to looking after the child. Melanie felt displaced. Parental attention was focused on Judith. Implicit in Melanie's description was a picture of a parental couple that could not openly recognize the fear of a child's death. Intense anxieties were present in the family but were left unprocessed. It is plausible to think there is a historical and associative connection between the inhibited but high anxiety in the household and the later development of Melanie's high level of tensions, the headaches and the anticipatory fear of death.

Melanie, now in the therapy for the first time, could really complain about things that her mother and father always thought she could cope with. In therapy she could show her vulnerability and neediness. She got a great sense of relief out of the fact that I could listen and understand. Her affective states were being contained in the context of the therapeutic relationship. Having found her feelings, she then found a voice. Her somatic–affective enactments (that were linked to past relationships and meaning) were then explored in the context the therapeutic relationship.

As Melanie began to get in touch with her feelings in relation to her key family relations, her headaches resolved. We could say she replaced her feelings in their right and full context. Instead, as I was talking about this and that, having started (at this stage in the work) to express what I was gathering about her interpersonal situation, a quiet feeling filled the room and snoring emanated from the couch. Melanie had fallen asleep. As soon as I noticed this I stopped speaking and sat quietly until the end of the session. I felt like a mother watching over her child as she slept, making things safe and calm.

Melanie had told me that she had been a precocious reader and how she had read to herself as a child and lulled herself to sleep. She told me how she had wished for a parent to read to her and sit by her bedside as her sister would have had, watching over her for her life. I became the parent that had not been there and was now watching over her by the bedside. As Melanie woke just before the end of the session, she spoke of feeling very relaxed and calm. I thought of how she felt safe enough with me; she entrusted her unprotected unconscious sleep state to me.

In childhood, with no calming attentive mother, there had been no internalization of a caring other that made things safe and could be incorporated into an internalized form of self-care. Instead, Melanie felt unsafe in her own body (it could do anything to her, go out of control, deregulate and go off the rails). She was open to all her fears, anxieties, and malevolent forces. Indeed, it was no coincidence that a major fear was that her body would go out of control and into death. Her sister's body was such a body and, as noted, the smell of pending death filled the house. Her parents' uncontained anxieties about her sister affected Melanie.

Missteps in the dance

Melanie saw her mother as always thinking she "knew best". "I would respond in the way she wanted me to . . . She was always full of her theories". In response, she would get confused; "I did not really know if it was mum's theory or true for me". The following vignette illustrates this point:

M: Mother always said that we were a family where no one expressed emotion and this is why Judith and I have problems.

T: That's mum's interpretation. Do you think that?

M: Mum's got so many books on human motivation, as many as you have here. Sometimes I think psychologically but that is not the same as feeling things.

T: I think your more negative feelings about mum are in the room here and felt in relation to me. You are looking at all the psychology books in front of you (a bookshelf facing Melanie lying on the couch). I, like your mum, have lots of books, theories, and interpretations. You're not sure (like with your mum) if what I say is just intellectual. You're not sure if I am really relating to your feelings.

M: That's right, I don't know if mum's interpretations are mine. And I do get annoyed with you when you don't get it right.

Melanie reacted in the most spontaneous and alive way when she felt disappointed with me, or when I failed to understand her. It appeared that the mishaps and the mismatches, which occurred between us, were of primary importance. When Melanie re-experienced the failure to be heard and the imposition of Mum's thoughts on her, we seemed to be re-enacting the disturbance in the mother–daughter relationship,

In the transference Melanie seemed to be showing me that she could not find a space for her feelings with her mother. Instead she told me how she got entangled in mother's ideas that are not in contact with her feelings. She demonstrated how she struggles to find her true thoughts.

We repeated the "missteps in the dance" (Stern, 1977, p. 109) with a difference, because there was a working through of the maternal transference. While reliving the exchange we were also able to forge a space to voice what was happening and thus reflect upon it. I became like Melanie's mother and at the same time was not like her mother, I was the object of transference and at the same time—by showing sensitivity and being attentive—I was also a therapist who did not treat her as she expected to be treated. As Winnicott notes "the practising of a good psycho-analytic technique may in itself be a corrective experience, and for instance in analysis the patient may for the first time get full attention from another person" (1965, p. 258).

One of the most helpful things seemed to have been the way I did not always have to be right and the fact that Melanie could tell me I was wrong. This happened when, in Melanie's words, "I pressed the wrong buttons", or when I used the wrong word, or— best of all—when she experienced what I said as a mistake (and when I was able to acknowledge this). Then, there was movement forward in the session; there was a shift towards a greater capacity for dialogue. In other words, I did not have to be the mother who was always right, as she had experienced her own mother. The being wrong and being okay about it got us into the action-based therapy—it was necessary to enact the missteps in the dance with a difference to reorganize Melanie's somatic–affective procedural working model of self in relation to other.

However, as Winnicott reminds us, "Corrective experience is not enough" (1965, p. 258). Again we can understand the way the patient made use of what she saw as my "mistakes" to represent earlier parental failure and work it through in the transference. When, in Melanie's eyes, I failed her and yet, at the same time, could listen and understand her view, she then experienced me as someone who could hear her. This "use" by the analysand is evidence that she has understood something; the active re-enactment is a procedural knowledge of the communication.

Narcissism: from mono-logic to dialogic dialogue

It was Freud who simply defined narcissism and the body symptom as the withdrawal of emotional investment back from the world and on to the body as an object of cathexis. It was understood to be the move out of this narcissism and towards a reinvestment in the world that was the necessary developmental step. In more recent theory the original formulation of a primary narcissism is questioned, since it is implausible to pose the infant as initially objectless. It is now agreed (Fairbairn put this very clearly) that the infant is born object-relating from the first and already object-seeking. I am in whole agreement with Laplanche and Pontalis when they say, "narcissism—and even 'primary narcissism'—is no longer seen as a state independent of any intersubjective relationship" (1973, p. 256). Narcissism, in this light from our perspective, is understood as a disturbance in intersubjective relating rooted in attachment experience.

Melanie would complain if I did not use the right word, which implied the same word as she would have chosen. Melanie's idea of me being attuned to her at times meant that she wanted me to be the perfect reflection of herself, like a mirror image, so that there was no trace of me as another person in the room. We could say Melanie would show utter irritation and intolerance if I had not able to meet her expectations. At these moments a dialogue was not possible because only one person was allowed to exist. Melanie wanted a mother, who could offer what she considered a perfect response. This response had to fit so exactly with Melanie's own feelings and thoughts that I disappeared as a different human being. The demand on the therapist was to offer a perfect mirroring experience.

Melanie would treat me as she felt she had been treated, depriving me of emotional space by negating my presence as another in the room. She had felt that her mother gave her no space. Now I knew what it felt like. When Melanie insisted that she was right and I was wrong, she became the self-righteous mother. Pearl King (1978) calls this process a "reversal of transference roles", which is a form of identification with the aggressor. In doing this, the patient communicates to the analyst what it feels like to be in the vulnerable position (see also Casement, 1990, p. 8).

At these times, analytic work was a struggle. My feelings would range between boredom and anger. When Melanie expected the perfect maternal response and could not tolerate a different point of view, I would experience Melanie in monologue with herself.

I would get sleepy, and at moments find myself drifting into a state of limbo, neither quite in the room with her nor outside the room either. I let myself be in this state but I also tried to understand what this emotional response could tell me. When Melanie's indifference to my existence felt like a negation of me I did feel angry and this gave me insight into what it was like for Melanie to feel ignored and not seen. Through countertransference feelings I tried to further my understanding of Melanie's procedural communications.

At times in the work it felt as if we were at an impasse. The following vignette illustrates an interaction in which we experienced some breakthrough. Melanie reacted to a remark I made with an outburst of anger. She told me that I was completely wrong and I replied:

> *T*: Because I did not capture what you felt in the way you wanted me to, you then feel I got it all wrong. I am just imposing my theories on you rather than understanding you.
>
> *M*: I realize that what you said was not totally wrong, but because it was a bit wrong I felt you were all wrong.
>
> *T*: It seems it is a matter of either/or. You tell me what you think or I tell you what I think. There is no space for sharing. Or for me to respond to your feelings. There can be no space for an exchange between us, none for negotiation. It seems impossible to think that a picture can be created out of our work together.
>
> *M*: I had never imagined that before.

The patient had never imagined before that there could be a space for sharing feelings and thoughts. When Melanie said, "I had never imagined that before", she was making a very important statement. In this context she found she could risk some exchange of views and her feelings of self would not be robbed from her. Hence, I was not conforming to her belief that I would be acting as a mother who would impinge on her experience and appropriate it for my own purpose.

Conclusion

The discussion and analysis offered here is an attempt to address the question "How does therapy work?" I have mentioned some key areas to consider, but I wish to emphasize that this is just a partial exploration; it is meant to be suggestive—open to more discussion and debate—and in no way portends to be exhaustive. Much has been left out of the account, indeed, the focus has been on attachment and particular somatic–affective states, Gender and sexuality have not even been broached and, of course, are central concerns for a fuller exploration and understanding.

I have argued that the therapist has to tune in to the procedural mode of being, that is where the somatic and affective life is based, and be with—to witness, understand, share, and process. Process in this context largely means making affective–somatic links with the relational experience of being with others—the attachment history, so that body and relationship are integrated. As seen from the case study, the initial and important basis for the therapeutic relationship and the key emotional shifts that took place were not reducible to verbal exchanges or interpretations but were rather fundamentally rooted in the analysand's enactments as a mode of communication—the action basis of procedural being. The more wordy reflective interchanges came later, and there success was based in the hook-up, and reorganization of procedural mode was already under way between therapist and analysand.

"Corrective" therapy is a very unfortunate term, and one that does not capture the unconscious and procedural mode of reliving with a difference. Nevertheless, with this new definition in mind, we can say that "corrective" therapy plays a role, so the re-enactment of the disturbances in the attachment relationships is met with the difference in the analyst's response. This permits a new working model of relationship to be generated, and new and more innovative patterns of relating and experiencing the world are made possible.

References

Bion, W. (1962a). A theory of thinking. In: Bion, W. R. *Second Thoughts*. London: Heinemann, 1967.

Bion, W. (1962b). *Learning from Experience*. London Heinemann.

Bowlby, J. (1988). *A Secure Base*. London: Routledge.

Casement, P. (1985). *On Learning from the Patient*. London: Routledge.

Casement, P. (1990). *Further Learning From the Patient*. London: Routledge.

Diamond, N., & Marrone, M. (2003). *Attachment and Intersubjectivity*. Whurr Publishers

Fonagy, P., & Target, M. (1997). Attachment and reflective function: their role in self organisation. *Development and Psychopathology, 9*: 679–700.

134   HOW DOES PSYCHOTHERAPY WORK?

Fonagy, P., Gergely, G., Jurist, E. L., & Target, M. (2002). *Affect Regulation, Mentalisation and the Development of the Self.* New York: Other Press.

King, P. (1978). Assertive response of the analyst to the patients' communications. *International Journal of Psychoanalysis, 59*: 329–334.

Klein, M. (1930). The importance of symbol formation and the development of the ego. In: J. Mitchell (Ed.), *The Selected Melanie Klein* (pp. 95–111). Harmondsworth: Penguin, 1986.

Laplanche, J., & Pontalis, J. (1973). *Dictionary of Psycho-Analysis.* London: Hogarth Press.

Marty, P. (1976). *Les Mouvements Individuels de vie et de mort.* Paris: Payot.

Marty, P. (1990). *La Psychosomatique l'Adulte.* Paris: Presses Universitaires de France.

McDougall, J. (1980). *Plea for a Measure of Abnormality.* New York: International Universities Press.

Panksepp, J. (1998). *Affective Neuroscience.* New York: Oxford University Press.

Schore, A. (1994). *Affect Regulation and the Origin of the Self.* Hillsdale, NJ: Lawrence Erlbaum.

Schore, A. (2003). *Affect Dysregulation and Disorders of the Self.* New York Publishers.

Stern, D. (1977). *The First Relationship.* Cambridge, MA: Harvard University Press.

Stern, D. (1985). *The Interpersonal World of the Infant.* New York: Basic Books.

Stern, D., Sander, L., Nathum, J., Harrison, A., Lyons-Ruth, K., Morgan, A., Bruschweiler-Stern, N., & Tronick, E. Z. (1998). Non-interpretive mechanisms in psychoanalytic therapy: The "something more" than interpretation. *International Journal of Psychoanalysis, 79*: 9003–9021.

Trevarthen, C. (1978). Secondary intersubjectivity: confidence, confiding and acts of meaning in the first year. In: A Locke (Ed.), *Action Gesture and Symbol, The Emergence of Language,* London: Academic Press.

Trevarthen, C. (1979). Communication and co-operation in early infancy: a description of primary intersubjectivity. In: M Bullara (Ed.), *Before Speech: The Beginning of Human Comunication.* London: Cambridge University Press.

Trevarthen, C. (1993). The self born in intersubjectivity: the psychology of an infant communicating. In: U. Neisser (Ed.), *The Perceived Self:*

Ecological and Interpersonal Sources of Self Knowledge. New York: Cambridge University Press.

Winnicott, D. W. (1958). *From Paediatrics to Psychoanalysis.* New York: Basic Books.

Winnicott, D. W. (1965). *The Maturational Process and the Facilitating Environment.* London: Hogarth Press.

CHAPTER SEVEN

Primal psychotherapy

Susan Cowan-Jenssen

P rimal psychotherapy is a development of Arthur Janov's cathartic primal therapy, which flowered rather dramatically in America in the 1970s and 1980s. In this chapter I look at what was significant and useful in Janov's contribution to psychotherapy, what were its weaknesses, and how primal psychotherapy evolved. As I began to write on the background of primal therapy it struck me that catharsis, or abreaction, i.e., emotional release, has an interesting history in psychotherapy since it gets discovered and then rediscovered with rather monotonous regularity. But first: what is meant by the word "primal"?

The Oxford English Dictionary defines "primal" as "Belonging to the first age or earliest stage; original; primitive; primeval". Freud was to use the expression "primal scene" to describe the impact of a child witnessing parental intercourse. Arthur Janov (1970) used the expression "primal pains" to describe the "original, early hurts upon which later neurosis is built". For Janov, neurosis was not necessarily sexual in origin or necessarily linked to the trauma of one event, but is the culmination of hurts that result from the unmet needs of the infant and child:

> We are all creatures of need. We are born needing, and the vast majority of us die after a lifetime of struggle with many of our needs unfulfilled. These needs are not excessive—to be fed, kept warm and dry, to grow and develop at our own pace, to be held, caressed and to be stimulated. These Primal needs are the central reality of the infant. The neurotic process begins when these needs go unmet for any length of time. . . . [Janov, 1970, p. 22]

For Janov, a loved child is a child whose natural needs are fulfilled and who is accepted for what he or she is. If too many needs are unmet it is unbearable for the child and what results is the repression of the pain from consciousness. Rather than feel that it is the much-needed parents who are at fault, the child will blame him or herself. Fairbairn described precisely this phenomenon when he wrote that for the child, "it is better to be a sinner in a world ruled by God than to live in a world ruled by the Devil" (1943, p. 331).

It was Freud who introduced the notion of repression and the unconscious, but for Freud what had to be repressed were incestuous, murderous, and libidinal impulses. Janov's unconscious is the pain of failed attachments and unmet needs, and as such it is a relational unconscious. Primal therapy was enormously popular in the 1970s and it was popularized in the music of John Lennon, who was Janov's most famous patient. It captured the *zeitgeist* of the period. Feelings had to be "felt", not just talked about. For Janov, the essential component of therapy was in the re-experiencing of the repressed emotion and connecting it to the original hurt. In fact, he distinguished between "abreaction", which was emoting in order to release tension, and "primalling", which was the reliving of earlier emotions and connecting them with understanding. However, understanding or insight could only come from *feeling the feeling* and not just *knowing* about the pain; "Because we are psychophysical entities, I believe that any approach that separates that unity cannot succeed" (Janov, 1970, p. 42).

The interesting question is why, when he wrote his book in 1970, the idea of crying and screaming in therapy should appear so radical. Primalling, or the re-experiencing of past traumas, is as old as psychotherapy itself. The re-experiencing of early traumatic memory, call it catharsis, abreaction, or primalling, has a fascinating history because it is constantly being rediscovered. Like the tide it comes in, then eventually goes out only to come in again, yet, unlike the tide, each time it reappears it takes a somewhat different form.

It is commonly believed that it was Freud and Breuer who discovered the use of catharsis in treating hysterical symptoms. In their paper 'On the psychical mechanism of hysterical phenomena' (1893a) they described how traumatic memories, which, unlike other past memories, "are not at the patient's disposal", can be retrieved through hypnosis and, once retrieved, the hysterical symptoms can be resolved. They also describe the phenomenon of "splitting of consciousness", the tendency to dissociate the memory from the painful feelings. In fact, both Freud and Breuer cited the earlier work of the now almost forgotten Pierre Janet, who hypothesized that painful memories underlay hysterical symptoms (1887, 1889). Janet was Charcot's protégé in Paris and was considered to be Freud's great rival. Interestingly, it was Janet who first used the word "subconscious" (Ellenberger, 1970). In his essay "The aetiology of hysteria" (1896c), Freud believed that the most significant factor in the development of hysterical symptoms were memories of sexual abuse that had been lost to consciousness. But nine years later, in the "Three essays on the theory of sexuality" (1905d), Freud abandoned his belief in the reality of sexual abuse and instead he substituted a belief that seduction memories were in fact fantasies linked to unconscious longings. There are different theories as to why Freud should have given up believing his patients' experiences, but one factor seems to have been that he wasn't having too much success in treating this group of highly disturbed clients. He wrote of his frustration to his friend Fleiss, mentioning "the continual disappointment in my efforts to bring any analysis to a real conclusion" (Freud, 1897, quoted in Masson, 1984, pp. 108–109).

Freud abandoned the use of catharsis but although it fell out of vogue it didn't go away completely. Usually it was to prove a poisoned chalice for whoever picked it up, because with its use came professional scorn and ridicule. Sandor Ferenczi, one of Freud's closest disciples, came again to believe in the reality of trauma. Ferenczi uses the words "primal trauma" to indicate not a sexual trauma but a trauma relating to an early disturbed relationship with mother:

The question arises whether the primal trauma is not always to be sought in the primal relationship with the mother, and whether the traumata of a somewhat later epoch, already complicated by the appearance of the father, could have such an effect without the existence of such a pre-primal-trauma mother–child scar. [Ferenczi, 1932, p. 83]

In other words, would the oedipal drama be so significant if there was not an original failure in the mother–child relationship? Given the stern child-rearing practices among late nineteenth century upper and middle classes, the group that would have sought psychoanalysis, this was a pretty acute observation. In their book *The Legacy of Sandor Ferenczi* (1993), Lewis Aron and Adrienne Harris point out how Ferenczi became increasingly interested in the quality of the parental care. He considered that while it was accepted that the child should adapt itself to the family, the need for the family to adapt itself to the child was often ignored. For Ferenczi, the patient's experience was more meaningful than their insight, and the quality of the therapist's empathy more important than their interpretations.

It definitely looks as if one could never reach any real convictions at all through logical insight alone; one needs to have lived through an affective experience, to have so to speak felt it in one's body, in order to gain . . . conviction. [Ferenczi, 1912, p. 194]

Ferenczi experimented with touching his patients, holding them, extending the boundaries of the therapeutic hour, and with mutual analysis of therapist by patient and patient by therapist. He constantly thought about technique and how best to help his clients. Ferenczi wrote much of what Arthur Janov later claimed for himself, although it isn't clear if Janov knew of Ferenczi's work when he wrote *The Primal Scream*.

For example, in Janov's primal therapy the defences are regarded as inevitably unhealthy, developed to protect the individual from the pain of earlier hurts. One of the goals of therapy would be to challenge the defences. Patients would be discouraged from "acting out" in order for them to reach the pain. Smokers would be told to stop smoking, those that were isolated would be encouraged to socialize, and the extraverts would be encouraged to spend more

PRIMAL PSYCHOTHERAPY   141

time alone. Ferenczi advocated something similar in his paper delivered at the Sixth International Congress of Psycho-Analysis at The Hague in 1920. It was called "The further development of an active therapy in psycho-analysis". He encouraged patients to try to control activities such as "onanistic stimulation of the genitals, stereotypies, and the tic-like twitches or stimulation of other parts of the body . . . the result was that new memories became accessible and the progress of analysis was visibly accelerated". He encouraged patients who had a fear of singing to sing in front of him. Such a practice would put the patient into what Janov calls the "primal zone". This is the space where the patient is open and able to access the emotion. If the defences are too few, the patient will be overwhelmed and if the defences are too many, then the patient will stay shut off from him or herself. For Janov, it is the role of the therapist to lead the patient into the "Primal Zone".

> The importance of the Primal Zone is that until one falls into that zone, healing doesn't occur. It is in the Primal Zone that feelings are accepted and *integrated*. It is, for the neurotic, the doorway to the repressed areas of the real self. [Janov, 1980, p. 55]

Ferenczi also used another concept, which Janov developed and called the "dialectic". Ferenczi wrote that the "principle of frustration and indulgence should govern our technique" (1929). Patients who have been deprived do not benefit from an excessively austere therapist. They need kindness and warmth. It is the contrast between the past and the present that opens up the therapeutic space. He wrote about a patient who had severe parents, and while she identified Ferenczi with her harsh parents the therapy did not progress well.

> But when I deprived her of all occasion for this attitude, she began to discriminate the present from the past and, after some hysterical outbreaks of emotions, to remember the psychic shocks of her childhood. *We see then that, while the similarity of the analytic to the infantile situation impels patients to repetition, the contrast between the two encourages recollection.* [Ferenczi, 1929, p. 124]

Janov discussed something similar and called it the "dialectic" of therapy. "The dialectic means the interpenetration of opposites forming ever-new syntheses . . . We must always keep in mind the dialectic when considering psychotherapy. We do not treat repression with more repression and hope to solve anything" (Janov & Holden, 1977, p. 229).

Ferenczi's use of catharsis and regression led to him being isolated from the psychoanalytic movement and his contributions sidelined. However, the work of Balint, Bowlby, and Winnicott in the UK continued to look at the importance of early childhood experiences and their impact on the adult psyche. Michael Balint, a disciple of Ferenczi and fellow Hungarian, worked with regression and identified two types, which he labelled "benign" and "malignant" (1968). These distinctions are enormously useful and help explain why for some people the re-experiencing the pain of the early memories is hugely beneficial while for others it is an endless cycle of pain and despair. Malignant regression is "regression aimed at gratification". The patient will demand that the therapist be a better parent and refuse to accept that the past is really over. The frustrations of the therapy situation are unbearable and the patient demands care that is not available. With benign regression, the patient accepts the limitations of the therapeutic relationship and needs the therapist to be there, accepting, and a "witness" to the process. Thus, what distinguishes between a regression that leads to further disintegration and a regression that heals is the ability to mourn the past and accept that what was lost cannot be regained.

I cannot write about the use of emotional release in psychotherapy without mentioning Wilhelm Reich, to whom Janov owed a huge, if largely unacknowledged, debt. Nichols and Zax wrote: "It was Wilhelm Reich, a contemporary of Freud's who made the transition from concern with talking about feelings (cognitive catharsis) to physical discharge of emotions (somatic emotional catharsis)" (1977).

As early as 1927, Reich was interested in going beyond talking about feelings to exploring the physical expression of those feelings. By 1934 he was dropped from the International Psychoanalytic Association, his views, like Ferenczi's, deemed too radical. Reich came to believe that suppressed emotions were experienced in the body as physical tension. Emotions could be released by working physically on the "body-armour". Reich's recognition of how our psychology can be physically embodied was a major contribution to psychotherapy and is the core of today's body-work psychotherapies.

Reich held strong social and political views and was a member of the Communist Party until he was expelled in 1933. He blamed a sexually repressive society for many symptoms of neurosis and, for him, a healthy adult was one who had full orgasmic potential. Janov did not place the same emphasis on the damage created by sexual repression, but argued that society's institutions, such as schools and hospitals, often hurt the children in their care.

This is a theme that was developed by Dr Alice Miller, a Swiss psychoanalyst, who broke ranks and attacked her therapy colleagues for their refusal to accept the reality of childhood trauma. Her first book, *The Drama of the Gifted Child*, published in 1982, was a huge best-seller. She describes, as Janov did before her, the price a child will pay to be loved, how much cruelty there was and still is towards children in our society, and how we tolerate and perpetuate it. She also came to advocate a primal technique developed by a Swiss therapist called J. Konrad Stettbacher. Stettbacher (1991) promised cures for illnesses, both emotional and physical, and catharsis was popular once more. At one point he had thousands of patients on his waiting list, yet within a few years, after numerous complaints from patients, Alice Miller denounced him and again the promise of emotional reliving failed to deliver.

Looking at the story of the role of catharsis in psychotherapy we can see that it has a traumatic history all of its own. The therapy community has been slow to acknowledge the reality of their patients' early experiences at the hands of those who are supposed to care for and love them, and all too often there is a backlash against those therapists who do take these painful memories seriously. The area of sexual abuse of children illustrates this very clearly. No sooner than the experience of sexual abuse of children becomes believed than there are attacks on therapists for creating false memories. So how do we think about forgotten memory that emerges during therapy?

Whatever their orientation, it is essential for therapists to understand the nature of memory and reality. Steven Rose points out the distinction between two different types of truth, the historic truth of what actually occurred and the narrative truth, which is the person's account of their remembered experience.

If human memories were like computer memories, neatly filed somewhere on a disc and waiting to be called up, the two might be identical. Indeed, this is what some of the theorists of recovered memory seem to believe. But our memories are not like this; they are biological, labile and dynamic . . . Patterns of connections are labile and change over time; memories are not localized in particular brain regions but distributed and represented in the brain by fluctuating patterns of neural activity. This means that remembering is not a passive process of simply reactivating circuits, but requires real work—it is, literally, re-membering. [Rose, 1998, pp. 123–124]

Daniel Schacter in his book *The Seven Deadly Sins of Memory: How The Mind Forgets and Remembers* says something similar.

We now know that we do not record our experiences the way a camera records them. Our memories work differently. We extract key elements from our experiences and store them. We then recreate or reconstruct our experiences rather than retrieve copies of them. Sometimes, in the process of reconstructing we add on feelings, beliefs, or even knowledge we obtained after the experience. In other words, we bias our memories of the past by attributing to them emotions or knowledge we acquired after the event. [Schacter, 2001, p. 9]

What this means for the therapist is that the material recalled in the consulting room is constantly being constructed and interpreted. So how would we understand something like sexual abuse, or indeed birth trauma, which has played such a large part in Janovian primal therapy? I will first look at birth trauma, which is in some ways, legally at least, a less controversial area than childhood sexual abuse. What is happening when the body "relives" a birth experience? Is there an imprint at a cellular level, which can be reactivated, a body memory? Many psychotherapists would agree that early painful experiences are imprinted and affect our later behaviour and physiological development. But this is not photographic, cognitive recall. Memories from a pre-verbal level cannot be retrieved verbally or indeed known consciously in the normal sense, but they can be understood implicitly from behaviours. This is called "enactive" or "implicit" memory, and is often used in work with children. Piontelli (1988) described her work with a two-year-old disturbed child who, in her therapy sessions, wrapped a chain around her neck, tied herself tightly in the curtain, and pressed an object against her navel. This child had stopped moving at five months old in the womb and was born with the umbilical cord around her neck. How are we to understand the idea of a physical memory from a pre-natal or birth experience? The work done in this area is still highly speculative. Dr Candace Pert, a professor at Georgetown University, writes of how the mind and the body communicate through chemicals called peptides. Peptides are found in the brain and all the major organs. In her view it would be possible for body memory to be accessed through the peptide–receptor network (Pert, 1998).

A study in Sweden (Jacobson *et al.*, 1987) also indicates the possibility that birth experiences will be unconsciously re-enacted later in life. The birth records of 412 alcoholics, drug addicts, and suicides were compared with the records of 2,901 controls. The results of this study certainly bear out Janov's hypothesis that the manner of our birth is highly significant for our future development (Janov, 1970, 1980, 1983, 1990, 2000; Janov & Holden, 1977). The study found that suicides involving asphyxiation were closely associated with asphyxia at birth. Suicide by mechanical means was associated with mechanical trauma at birth, while drug addiction correlated with the administration of opiates or barbiturates during the mother's labour. "This possibility of implicit affective, sensory or procedural memory, established at birth and driving towards some kind of compulsion to repeat in later life clearly requires further study before definite conclusions can be drawn" (Mollon, 2002, p. 69). Compare this with Janov's writing on suicide,

It seems like an incredible idea that people attempt suicide because something went wrong with their birth process, but I hope to show how this may be so . . . With specific regard to the problem of suicide, I believe that, by and large, death as a solution to current Pain stems from a prototypic trauma—usually around the time of birth—in which death *was* the only solution. The notion of death as the *only* way out then becomes fixated in the system as an unconscious memory, shaping the way a person thinks about solutions to overwhelming problems later on. [Janov & Holden, 1977, p. 273]

It is important to think about and acknowledge what impact a birth trauma or very early childhood experience might have in an individual's life and to give that patient the freedom and space to explore this if and when it is appropriate. But given that our memories are permeable and open to outside influences, it is equally important that the therapist in no way pushes or gives these trauma a privileged position in the therapy. Actions like holding heads or suffocating people under cushions, which can happen in rebirthing groups or sessions, are clearly telling the patient what is expected of him or her and it is not surprising if the patient then produces what is required in the way of "birth memories".

The idea of re-experiencing birth might seem extreme to many therapists but compared with the furore around recovered memories of early sexual abuse, it tends to pass relatively unnoticed. Allegations of sexual abuse have huge emotional and legal consequences for families and in this area it is especially important that the therapist doesn't leap to conclusions or encourage a patient to leap, when there was previously no memory of abuse. Lists of symptoms such as those produced by Bass and Davis (1991) in answer to the question "How do I know if I was sexually abused?" are not, I believe, helpful. Not understanding why one feels the way one does is painful, and answers can bring immediate relief, but if they are reached too quickly they can also be very wrong. There is no doubt that actual sexual abuse occurs with much greater frequency than we would want to believe. There is also good evidence that memories of these traumas can be forgotten. A study by Williams (1994) looked at the records of 206 girls aged between ten months and twelve years who had been taken to hospital in the early 1970s in connection with sexual abuse. When a group of the victims was interviewed in the early 1990s, some 38% did not recall the abuse. Older children were included in this group and so the "forgetting" was not simply a result of the age at which the abuse occurred.

However, actual sexual contact is not the only way a child's boundaries can feel violated. The French psychoanalyst Laplanche (1999) described a form of adult unconscious communication that emanated from the sexual sphere and which he called the "enigmatic signifier". It is impossible for the child to comprehend this "enigmatic" communication since it is generated from an adult sexuality that the child doesn't share or understand. These messages are not necessarily verbal, but can be gestural, visual, or tonal. An example of this might be a father who cannot be tender with his young daughter because of his own sexual feelings for her. A relationship with such a father might well evoke confusion, anxiety, and shame in the daughter at the receiving end of his powerful, unconscious feelings. It isn't hard to see that in later years the daughter might come to understand her own "inexplicable" feelings of discomfort as proof of an actual seduction. I use this example to show that recovered memories of abuse can be real and they can also be symbolic of a different form of sexual disturbance. It is clear that since these enigmatic communications occurred implicitly rather than explicitly they do not readily lend themselves to easy or quick interpretations. Since it is within a relationship that these messages were passed then it is within a different sort of relationship with a sensitive therapist that these messages can be disentangled.

Janov, like Freud before him, was always fascinated by the role of neurobiology in our emotional development. Many of the hypotheses he put forward have since been proven with the development of the technology to map brain activity. Memory might not be registered cognitively like a video, but it seems to be registered chemically. As Janov predicted, this has implications not only for birth and the early years of development but also for the foetus in the womb. Smoking, drinking, or excessive stress have all been shown to be detrimental to the development of a healthy foetus. He developed the idea of the three levels of consciousness, with memory being represented on all three levels: the thinking, feeling, and self-regulating visceral level. The "first line" or visceral level involves the anatomic midline, gastric, respiratory, bladder and bowel functions. These functions are controlled by the inner portion of the brain that is practically fully functional at and before birth; this is the visceral level of consciousness. The "second level" is the affective–expressive level and it becomes operational some six months after birth as the limbic system develops and the infant becomes more aware of his/her environment and relationships. The baby is capable of feeling physical and emotional pain. It is only some years later, however, that the "third line", cortical, thinking brain will be fully functional. The three levels of consciousness are used by Janov as a diagnostic tool. Thus, physical symptoms such as stomach complaints, colitis, high blood pressure, and even cancer would be understood by Janov as caused by very early childhood pain that has been imprinted biochemically. While this assumption has not been proven, much of what Janov hypothesized has turned out to be prescient. The work of neurobiologists like Allan Schore (1994) confirms that emotional deprivation in the first two years of life will change the brain structure and chemistry in ways that will affect the ability of the infant to cope with the stresses and emotions of later life. The brain of a child deprived of love is measurably different from the brain of a child that has received love and care. Early trauma is registered neurologically. There is now no doubt that feelings and thoughts are registered in different areas of the brain and therefore a therapy that deals solely with ideas will not be sufficient to resolve underlying traumatic feelings. In 1994, Bessel van der Kolk published his well known paper "The body keeps the score", which looked at how trauma disrupts the stress hormone system, the nervous system, and prevents people from processing traumatic memories into conscious narrative memory. So current scientific work is generally favourable to some of Janov's core assumptions but, for reasons that I will explain, Janov's primal therapy has not really benefited from these developments.

Science has shown that we are our bodies and our experiences, but it is a huge jump to claim, as Janov does, that all mental illness, homosexuality, and cancer are the result of early life experiences and that reliving these experiences will cure them. He claims that "homosexuality gets started so early, it *seems* genetic" (2000, my italics). He can provide no evidence for this claim. Likewise, our understanding of cancer is that it is a hugely complex illness that develops from a variety of factors and we do not yet know what, if any, impact early life experiences have on its aetiology. By overstating the claims for catharsis, it seems that much of what is really useful and important gets lost. The history of openly expressive therapies has been very chequered and yet there is the core of truth at the heart of these therapies that will not go away. In fact, even the cognitive–behavioural school of psychotherapy has its own expressive branch, which uses regression in a very specific way for post traumatic stress disorders. This is the eye movement desensitization and reprocessing technique (EMDR) developed by Francine Shapiro (1995), which has proved to be highly successful in the treatment of post traumatic stress. It is extremely well researched and validated but is still considered controversial.

However, the greatest weakness of the Janovian model of therapy has been the failure to appreciate the work of fellow psychotherapists and the central importance of the therapeutic relationship and the clinical setting. It is ironic that, while Janov was so prescient about the impact of the early years for our well being later in life, he failed to pick up the significance for psychotherapy of one of the central messages of the work of neurobiologists like Allan Schore. What we have learned is that human infants are, above all, relational; our connections, both emotional and physical, make us human and it is the quality of our connections that will make us or break us. Our attachment history profoundly affects our biology. This has huge implications for psychotherapy, of course, and the role of the therapeutic relationship. Indeed, current research shows it is not the method *per se* that is "curative"; rather, it is the quality of that therapeutic relationship, a secure setting for the therapy, a sense of direction or action and a narrative that makes sense of the experience (Frank & Frank, 1993). Janov spares very few words on this and is dismissive of transference issues. His therapist is empathic, yes, but above all he or she is a technician who must get the patient to the appropriate feelings. It is in the area of clinical practice that primal psychotherapy has moved most radically away from the Janovian model.

Over the past twenty years primal psychotherapy has developed against a background of deep distrust of cathartic therapy, and it has been an ongoing process involving attempts to address the dangers and weaknesses of catharsis without throwing the baby out with the bathwater. It should be said that the past ten years have seen a real change in the psychotherapy movement itself, with much more acceptance of the power of childhood suffering and the effect of this suffering over our behaviours.

So, what are the core principles that need to be held in mind when working as a primal psychotherapist, or indeed a psychotherapist of any persuasion? I cannot improve on the list written by Fiona Palmer Barnes in the publication *Mindfield: Therapy on the Couch* (1999). The point of therapy is

- To provide a service within an ethical and theoretical framework
- To offer a therapeutic relationship which aims to aid increased self-understanding

- To help patients to gain greater understanding of both current and past experiences
- To provide an appropriate environment in which patients can identify, clarify and explore their difficulties.

The therapeutic process can involve one or more of the following objectives:

- To alleviate conflict, distress and mental suffering
- To enhance self-esteem and self-acceptance
- To increase personal effectiveness
- To expand the capacity to develop positive relationships with others
- To explore alternatives and make choices
- To act with greater spontaneity and autonomy
- To bring about continuing change, growth and self-development
- To enjoy a better quality of living
- To tolerate states of unhappiness.

The setting is crucially important for whether a therapy will be successful. It is not just about providing a room that is private, soundproof, and safe, although these are necessary. It is also about providing an environment that is non-judgemental, non-pressured, and where the patient's own experiences and pace are acceptable. If the therapist has an agenda such as birth, sexual abuse or, indeed, oedipal conflicts, then the patient might feel pressured to produce what he or she feels is required. If "feeling" is what is considered curative, those who cry or "primal" easily achieve a certain status. This is especially true in group therapy. Accounts of patients in primal type groups recall that unless you have "birth" feelings you are not really *getting* anywhere. Likewise groups of incest survivors can also develop the similar dynamic of a higher status going to the most abused member of the group. Since memory is fragile and open to interpretation it is easy to see that certain experiences can be seen through the lens of "birth" or "abuse". It is thus essential that *not* knowing and uncertainty can be tolerated by the therapist in order to allow the patient's experiences to unfold at their own rate. Answers can bring relief but they might not be the right answers.

The danger of calling a therapy "primal psychotherapy" is that patients have a view of what might be expected of them. The therapist genuinely needs to feel that each journey is unique for each patient and that tears are not an essential requirement. Too many patients have felt they failed in expressive therapies because they couldn't cry or cry deeply enough. Also, all too often patients in many therapies have been blamed for therapeutic "failures", rather than the therapist questioning if they are the right therapist for a particular patient. I especially liked Ferenczi's approach to his occasional failures in that he attributed them to his own lack of skill rather than to the patient's "narcissism", incurability, defensiveness, and unanalysability (1931). All therapists know that it is the work with "difficult" clients that develops our thinking and understanding of both patient and ourselves, and it is this process that will develop our work and bring it forward. If you take seriously that it is the connection between two people that will be of crucial importance in therapy, then you have to take seriously the possibility that two people will not always successfully work together. There does need to be a realistic assessment of the person seeking help in order to ascertain whether the therapy and therapist that are on offer are the most appropriate, and this is part of providing an ethical framework. This is especially important when working with deeply damaged patients who are desperate for relief. Not all methods or all therapists suit all patients, and this has to be acknowledged. Above all, there is no one cure-all that will solve all problems.

The role of catharsis in psychotherapy is still one that provokes heated debate. For Janov's primal therapy it is the central plank, without which there can be no "cure". Yet he does not really address the problems and difficulties of regression that undoubtedly occur and that need to be considered if catharsis in psychotherapy is to be as useful as it could be. Unfortunately, Janov, in his eagerness to sell his cause, underestimated the problems that can result from regression if great care is not placed on assessing the patient and the quality of the clinical setting. In developing primal psychotherapy it soon became clear that the importance of the therapeutic relationship was greatly underestimated by Janov. The Janovian model, with its three-week intensive phase, followed up with group work and some individual work if necessary, was simply inadequate to the task. People were left overwhelmed by feelings and not able to cope. Janov has nothing to say about the need for consistency in therapy. If your understanding of a therapist is simply as a technician who gets you into the feelings then it is not seen as a problem if you have to change therapists. Unfortunately, this overlooks the fact that many people who seek therapy have had difficult, if not catastrophic, early attachment histories. If a patient is not to be retraumatized then he or she would need a therapist to be at the very least consistent, honest, and empathic. While the therapist cannot be the hoped-for parent, he/she should offer sufficient security and help in working with and through the most difficult of feelings. What is on offer is "quality not quantity" as a colleague puts it.[1] Within the boundaries of the relationship, the therapist should provide the empathy, understanding and emotional availability that is needed for good therapy work. This is what is meant by "quality", not "quantity", or the promise of endless care. Therapy is not a process that can be shared around. It requires one therapist who is willing to engage fully in this process. Trivializing the relationship with the therapist also flies in the face of current research. As mentioned before, there is good evidence that it is this "therapeutic alliance" that is the key to a successful therapy. Chris Mace, in his article "Psychotherapy and neuroscience" (2004, p. 72) points out that "there are increasing grounds too for thinking that non-verbal processes based on very rapid, mutual tuning of behavioural interaction, are important to therapeutic success". Thus in order to understand what is going on in a highly interactive and interdependent therapy situation, the changes in the nervous system of the therapist would need to be measured along with those of the patient. (There are fascinating echoes here of Ferenczi's ideas on mutual analysis.)

If you understand that humans are always raised within a relationship, then it goes without saying that the interactions within relationship are crucial. It was Winnicott who, in 1965, coined the famous phrase "there is no such thing as an infant", emphasizing that the baby can only be understood in relation to mother. The relational systems approach in psychotherapy has developed this further, understanding that the individual only exists within the context of their interpersonal relationships (Beebe, Knoblauch, Rustin, & Sorter, 2003). There are always two people in the therapy

PRIMAL PSYCHOTHERAPY   153

room, and what passes between them is surely one of the richest areas of research and debate in psychotherapy.

Primal psychotherapists have also been concerned to ensure that patients are able to manage their emotions once they leave their session. The history of cathartic therapies is littered with patients who have regressed in therapy and have not been able to manage themselves outside of the therapy hour. They could cry and "primal" endlessly, but their lives were in complete disarray. Therefore it is essential that the pace of the therapy process be very carefully monitored indeed. Defences have developed to protect us from what we experience as unmanageable, be they longings, terrors, or a sense of disintegration. These feelings have to be worked with gently and respectfully. Babette Rothschild in her book *The Body Remembers* (2003) uses the helpful expression "putting on the brakes". You need to have the ability to help the patient keep part of themselves in the present so that they don't lose contact with reality. There is a variety of techniques for this, but essentially they all emphasize that the past reality and the present reality are different. The patient might have felt helpless against the pain as a child, but as an adult they do have choices *even if they don't feel that they have*. The emotions that patients experience can be totally overwhelming and ultimately are the core of the therapy work, but they need to be worked with in a setting and a structure that makes them bearable and resolvable. I give an example of this in the following vignette. The pace of the work is slower than would be expected in traditional primal therapy. This is especially important where there has been a betrayal of trust, as in sexual abuse. Time is needed to establish a strong, respectful relationship in which it is safe to explore the traumas. For the sake of confidentiality I have not used the experience of one person, but a clinical composite inspired by a number of actual examples.

> Judy was in her late thirties when she first came for therapy. She was a yoga teacher and had a successful practice. She had been married for eighteen years when her husband announced he was leaving her for another woman who was pregnant with his child. Judy felt utterly abandoned and humiliated, and experienced a severe depression with thoughts of suicide.
>
> What was striking when I first met Judy was how crushed she appeared and how depleted. She talked in a monotone and blamed

herself for the breakdown of the marriage. She knew she *should* feel angry but didn't; all she could experience was desolation and despair. She had wanted children but an untreated severe pelvic infection meant that she was childless. The end of the marriage also seemed an end to all hopes of motherhood. The fact that her partner had fathered a child with someone else was too much to bear.

Judy's childhood was seriously unhappy. She was the eldest child of three sisters. Her parents were both alcoholic but maintained a middle-class life style. However, all the children were beaten badly, often for the slightest misdemeanour and apparently without cause. When Judy was eight, her mother went away to dry out and Judy went to a boarding school run by nuns. Her sisters went to stay with an aunt. Judy stayed at the school for a year and it was a terrible experience. She was frightened by the nuns and by their seemingly endless stories of sin, heaven, and hell. She was lonely, missed her sisters terribly, and found it difficult to make friends.

After her first term at the school she formed a close attachment to one of the younger nuns who taught English. This was Judy's favourite subject and she excelled in it. The teacher gave Judy books to read and they would go on walks together. It was while they were out that the teacher made a sexual move on Judy, kissing her and fondling her genitals. Julie was shocked, frightened, and totally confused. On the one hand she liked this teacher, she yearned for warmth, but she was horrified by what was being done to her. The teacher explained to Judy that if she told anyone what happened, the teacher would lose her job and it would be Judy's fault. Moreover, since it was a mortal sin, they would both go to hell. The abuse carried on for the rest of Judy's stay at the school. She tried different strategies to get away from this teacher but to no avail. The teacher terrified Judy with her sexual demands and obsessive rantings on sex, hell, and damnation. Judy never told anyone what had happened to her.

Her teen years were marred by bulimia and she had periods of deep depression with episodes of cutting her thighs and stomach. When she was in her twenties, Judy discovered meditation and yoga and found both to be extremely helpful to her. The bulimia and the cutting stopped and she felt much calmer. She met her husband at this time and fell deeply in love with him. He seemed her saviour; kind, thoughtful, and loving.

My sense of Judy was that she was immensely fragile and that she was now in a place where her resources and reserves were utterly depleted.

She felt once again like an abandoned child in a hostile world, having lost all her coping skills. She knew her childhood had been grim but couldn't really remember many of the feelings. Likewise, she remembered the sexual abuse by her teacher but had lost touch with its impact on her. The first year we proceeded very gently and when she brought up the abuse I worked with it cognitively. By that I mean that I helped her understand that she was in a terrible situation that was utterly confusing; she was being taken advantage of and the shame was not hers. While she could start to see this reality, she didn't fully believe it. There were times when Judy came to her sessions utterly exhausted. She was teaching yoga and it was enormously demanding of her when she felt so low. She wanted to lie quietly and not move, not make an effort. At these times the room was filled with a sadness that moved both of us. One day she asked me to take her hand and I did so. She wept and wept. For several sessions after that she sat quietly, just holding my hand.

Touch is a very powerful tool and, like catharsis, has a difficult history within psychotherapy that has led to its being frowned upon as liable to encourage the libidinous needs of the patient. I would argue that while many cathartic and bodywork therapies have not paid sufficient attention to the seductive aspects of touch, the analytic therapies have not paid sufficient attention to its nurturing power. Pamela Geib (1998) discussed the research that has been done on the use of touch in therapy, which confirmed the potentially positive role of therapeutic touch but with important provisos. Touch can be containing, providing a link to the external world that is solid compared to a sense of internal chaos. But it can also be perceived as intrusive, invasive, and a breaking of psychic and physical boundaries. Undoubtedly, it has the possibility of encouraging a malignant regression and a sexualized response from the patient. However, studies have shown that a patient's positive evaluation of touch in therapy is associated with its congruence, the patient's sense of control, and the ability to speak freely about it with the therapist. An unexpected discovery of some of the studies was the usefulness of touch with patients who had been sexually abused. This is the patient group where touch is open to every meaning and interpretation. The negative interpretations are obvious, but the reported answers from sexually abused patients showed that respectful touch carries two crucial messages. First, it communicates that you are touchable, worthy of respectful touch. Second, respectful touch has the ability to communicate appropriate boundaries.

> After she had taken my hand over a few sessions, I asked Judy what holding my hand meant to her. The following exchange ensued:
>
> *Judy*: It stops the mad feeling in my head. I can breathe more freely even though it makes me feel tearful.
>
> *SC-J*: I was concerned that it might remind you of Sister Agnes (the abusing nun).
>
> *Judy*: I wondered too. But it is such a relief to know that I can be touched and it be OK. You're not going to do anything I don't want. You know, it makes me realize how I never knew a touch that was easy. They were either beating me up or touching me up. Just having my hand held nicely makes me weep, isn't that *appalling*? (Judy's voice rose here and her anger became palpable.)
>
> In experiencing the contrast between the past and the present, the feelings of rage began to come to the surface and Judy started to be much more aware of her intense rage towards the adults who had betrayed her. In the sessions that followed she talked out loud to her parents and to Sister Agnes, expressing her thoughts and her feelings. She shouted, she wept; the feelings about the abuse became accessible. Slowly she could feel real understanding for the little girl who was without protection, so vulnerable to abuse, and in need of much more love and care than she received. Judy's therapy was not a speedy or easy one and there were many hiccups along the way. She had suffered much loss, both in the past and in the present, but gradually she began to feel more alive and more hopeful. What she felt was important was that I had let her proceed at her own pace. She needed a long time to feel safe and respected, and she was not pushed to feel things she couldn't handle. Having to respond to her therapist's agenda, rather than her own, would have been very detrimental. It was Judy who asked for touch; she could feel some sense of agency, authority in our work together. She could appreciate her successes and feel that despite everything she was glad to be alive.

Much has been written about the dangers of false memories being encouraged in therapy. In my experience it is far, far more common for people to have painful conscious memories but to have lost touch with the feelings connected with those memories. I think that one of the most healing aspects of any therapy is the reconnection between knowing and feeling, as the vignette with Judy illustrates. Only once the emotional impact is understood can you really comprehend the impact and the power of trauma on the rest of your life.

What is difficult about working with traumatic memories, is knowing *if* and *when* it might be appropriate to explore the feelings. The *how* of emotional work is less complicated. A therapist needs to know their patient and have a good sense of how much they can manage emotionally. They need to have a therapeutic relationship that is strong enough to bear what emerges, especially in the transference. A patient with disassociative tendencies needs to be treated with the greatest care, and the therapist must be able to recognize when a patient needs to stop and reorientate. They need to know when the patient is ready, and not hurry the process along. With very fragile, disassociative patients, this can take a number of years. It is very important that the patient is not retraumatized by the experience of remembering the emotions of the trauma. If the client has been sexually abused, then they will know what it is to feel utterly powerless, betrayed, confused, and guilty. It is very important that, while these feelings and others will emerge in the memories and in the therapy transference, there is sufficient understanding that in the present things are *not the same even if they feel the same*. The patient does have choices, can say no, *even though he or she might not feel that it is possible*. If the patient is not to be retraumatized, the distinction between the past and the present day reality must always be held in mind and emphasized. Without this distinction, the past cannot be left behind.

There is also the question of secondary gain and "malignant" regression. If the patient senses that what the therapist is *really* interested in are the "feelings", or if the therapy culture glamorizes "catharsis" or "primals", then it is easy to see that regression becomes an end in itself. Regression for gain is a malignant process because it stops the work of mourning. The mourning process has to acknowledge that something really is over, what happened did happen, and there was no rescue. So often children have to hold their real feelings back in the hope that if they are "good" then bad things won't happen. The child might think "If I don't complain, I won't be beaten or if I am good, then Mum won't drink". The fury, disappointment, and despair get locked away. The only goal of re-experience can be the working through of the experiences so that their impact on the present is reduced; the past can never be changed and no amount of tears, catharsis, or primals will change that.

The retrieval of memories is in itself not very complicated if the memory is near the surface. I might ask if a patient feels some emotion when talking about a painful past situation. If there are feelings attached to the memory then it might be the moment to pursue those feelings. Memories are laid down in different areas of the brain and also involve different senses. First, asking about the detail of a scene is very helpful. In the following vignette you will see that this is what the therapist does first. The more information, the more connections are being made. So asking the patient to describe the room, setting, clothes being worn, food being eaten, is part of setting the scene. The more detail the better, no matter how trivial. Then the therapist might ask what it is that the patient was feeling and thinking at that time. All too often we assume that thought and feeling are the same, but they are not. Memory is also registered physically and it is important to ask the patient where in the body they experience sensation when they are thinking about the memory. Thus, the essence of the work is to identify what was felt cognitively, emotionally, and physically. This is also the stategy used very successfully in EMDR therapy (see above) when working with post-traumatic stress. Clearly there is no guarantee that the emotional connection will be made, for the timing might not be right, but it is a helpful template. A therapist might work with this template in a variety of ways as the following vignette illustrates.

John came to therapy, having suffered from depression. He was in his early thirties, was married and had a young son that he adored. His childhood had been marred by the psychiatric illness and alcoholism of his father. He had painful and shameful memories of having to fetch his father from the pub and walk him home. His father would be shouting and yelling, and the entire neighbourhood seemed to witness it.

John could recall the scene, the shame, the upset, and his sense of failure, but he could not really empathize with himself as a child. Somehow he felt he should have been able to manage it and he wanted to keep a distance from the humiliated child that he felt himself to be.

He told me that he didn't think it was such a big deal. In such a situation, where the patient cannot relate to his or her own past experiences, it can be helpful to back away and help the patient to see the scene through the eyes of another.

SC-J: Would you want your son to have to do such a thing, get you out of the pub, drunk and shouting?

John: [Looked as if I had slapped him.] God no, never, never, never. I would never let that happen to him.

SC-J: But it did happen to you.

John: I know. [At this point he looks very sad and the atmosphere in the room has filled with sadness.]

SC-J: Was it manageable?

John: No, no it wasn't.

[We sit quietly with this for a while.]

SC-J: Can you picture yourself as a child?

John: Yes, I think so.

SC-J: What do you look like?

John: About eight years old, light brown hair that isn't tidy, wearing shorts, looking lost.

SC-J: Is there anything you would want to say to you as the child that was you, that would be helpful?

John: I'm sorry, I'm so sorry this had to happen, you didn't deserve it.

Here John could really be in touch with the memory of the experience and the loss of so much of his childhood. With or without tears, what was helpful to John was the realization that the situation with his father was really beyond him and was not his fault. Instead of contempt for himself for not managing better, he could begin to have real understanding of his plight. He could begin to really grasp that there really isn't one rule for himself as a child and another rule for all the other children. He was as helpless in the situation as any child would be.

This sort of work is not about demonizing parents and blaming them endlessly, which, unfortunately, was a hallmark of Janovian primal therapy and many cathartic therapies. John did become very angry with his father, but eventually he also came to appreciate that his father was trying to manage his own mental breakdowns at a time when there was little support and understanding. He had been sailor in the North Atlantic during the war, was on a vessel that was sunk, and he saw terrible things. Nowdays he would have been identified as suffering from post traumatic stress disorder. As John's sense of contempt lessened for himself, so it lessened for his father. A fellow therapist once said that therapy was not about blame but about widening the sense of tragedy.

I hope that in this chapter I have given the reader a better sense of what primal psychotherapy is and how it has developed from a primal therapy that placed almost total emphasis on the release of emotion. Catharsis is powerful and it can be extraordinarily healing, but only when used appropriately, respectfully, and within a trusting therapeutic alliance. Not all patients want or feel comfortable with open emotional expression. Each therapist and ideally each patient chooses the model of therapy that they feel most comfortable with and which makes the most sense for them. Human beings and their relationships are immensely complicated and it seems to me obvious that there is not going to be a single approach that will be helpful in every circumstance. I would like to think that, as therapists, we have a range of approaches that we can reflect on and use, so that we can offer our patients the therapy that is right for them.

Note

1. In conversation with fellow psychotherapist, Einar Jenssen, one of the co-founders of the London Association of Primal Psychotherapists.

References

Aron, L., & Harris, A. (Eds.) (1993). *The Legacy of Sandor Ferenczi*. New York: Analytic Press.
Balint, M. (1968). *The Basic Fault*. London: Tavistock.
Bass, F., & Davis, L. (1991). *The Courage to Heal: A Guide for Women Survivors of Child Sexual Abuse*. London. Heinemann.

Beebe, B., Knoblauch, S., Rustin, J., & Sorter, D. (2003). Symposium on intersubjectivity in infant research and its implications for adult treatment. Part I. *Psychoanalytic Dialogues, 13*(6): 743–775.

Breuer, J., & Freud, S. (1893a). On the psychical mechanism of hysterical phenomena: preliminary communication. In: Studies on hysteria (1893–5). *S.E., 2*: 1–251. London: Hogarth Press.

Ellenberger, H. F. (1970). *The Discovery of the Unconscious*. New York: Basic Books.

Fairbairn, W. R. D. (1943). The repression and return of bad objects (with special reference to the "war neuroses"). *British Journal of Medical Psychology, 19*(3, 4): 327–342.

Ferenczi, S. (1912). Transitory symptom-constructions during the analysis (E. Mosbacher, Trans.). In: M. Balint (Ed.), *First Contributions to Psycho-Analysis* (pp. 193–212). London: Karnac, 1980.

Ferenczi, S. (1920). The further development of an active therapy in psycho-analysis (J. Suttie, Trans.). In: J. Rickman (Ed.), *Further Contributions to the Theory and Technique of Psychoananlysis*. London: Hogarth Press, 1950 [reprinted London: Karnac, 1980, pp. 198–217].

Ferenczi, S. (1929). The principle of relaxation and neocatharsis. (E. Mosbacher, Trans.). In: M. Balint (Ed.), *Final Contributions to the Problems and Methods of Psycho-Analysis*. London: Hogarth Press, 1955 [reprinted London: Karnac, 1980, pp. 108–125].

Ferenczi, S. (1931). Child analysis in the analysis of adults (E. Mosbacher, Trans.). In: M. Balint (Ed.), *Final Contributions to the Problems and Methods of Psycho-Analysis*. London: Karnac, 1980, pp. 126–142.

Ferenczi, S. (1932). *The Clinical Diary of Sandor Ferenczi*. J. Dupon (Ed.), M. Balint & N. Z. Jackson, Trans.). Cambridge, MA: Harvard University Press, 1988.

Frank, J., & Frank, J. (1993). *Persuasion and Healing: A Comparative Sudy of Psychotherapy*. Baltimore: Johns Hopkins University Press.

Freud, S. (1896c). The aetiology of hysteria. *S.E., 3*: 189–221. London: Hogarth Press.

Freud, S. (1905d). Three essays on the theory of sexuality. *S.E., 7*: 125–245. London: Hogarth Press.

Geib, P. (1998). The experience of nonerotic physical contact in traditional psychotherapy. In: E. Smith, P. Clance, & S. Imes (Eds.), *Touch In Psychotherapy: Theory, Research and Practice* (pp. 109–126). New York: The Guildford Press.

Jacobson, B., Eklund, G., Hamberger, L., Linnarsson, D., Sedvall, G., & Valverius, M. (1987). Perinatal origin of adult self-destructive behaviour. *Acta Psychiatrica Scandinavia, 76*: 364–371.

Janet, P. (1887). L'anesthésie systematisée et la dissociation des phénomènes psychologiques. *Review Philosophique*, 23: 449–472.

Janet, P. (1889). *L'automatisme psychologique*. Paris: Alcan.

Janov, A. (1970). *The Primal Scream*. London: Abacus.

Janov, A., & Holden, E. M. (1977). *Primal Man: The New Consciousness*. London: Abacus.

Janov, A. (1980). *Prisoner of Pain; Unlocking the Power of the Mind to End Suffering*. New York: Anchor Press.

Janov, A. (1983). *Imprints: The Lifelong Effects of the Birth Experience*. New York: Putnam.

Janov, A. (1990). *The New Primal Scream*. London: Abacus.

Janov, A. (2000). *The Biology of Love*. New York: Prometheus.

LaPlanche, J. (1999). *Essays on Otherness*. New York: Routledge.

Masson, J. M (1984). *The Assault on Truth: Freud's Suppression of the Seduction Theory*. Harmondsworth: Penguin.

Mace, C. (2004). Psychotherapy and neuroscience: how close can they get? In: J. Corrigall & H. Wilkinson (Eds.), *Revolutionary Connections* (pp. 163–175). London: Karnac.

Miller, A. (1982). *The Drama of the Gifted Child*. New York: Basic Books.

Mollon, P. (1999). Memories are made of . . . what? In: S. Greenberg (Ed.), *Mindfield: Therapy on the Couch* (pp. 89–98). London: Camden Press.

Mollon, P. (2002). *Remembering Trauma: A Psychotherapist's Guide to Memory and Illusion* (2nd edn). London: Whurr.

Nichols, M., & Zax, M. (1977). *Catharsis in Psychotherapy*. New York: Gardner Press.

Palmer Barnes, F. (1999). The point of therapy. In: S. Greenberg (Ed.), *Mindfield: Therapy on the Couch* (pp. 76–81). London: Camden Press

Pert, C. (1998). *The Molecules of Emotion*. New York: Simon & Schuster.

Piontelli, A. (1989). Pre-natal life and birth as reflected in the life of a two-year-old psychotic girl. *International Review of Psychoanalysis*, 15: 73–81.

Rose, S. (1998). Syndromitis. In: V. Sinason (Ed.), *Memory in Dispute*. London: Karnac.

Rothschild, B. (2003). *The Body Remembers—Casebook*. London: W. W.Norton.

Schacter, D. (2001). *The Seven Deadly Sins of Memory: How The Mind Forgets and Remembers*. New York: Houghton Mifflin.

Schore, A. (1994). *Affect Regulation and the Origin of the Self*. New Jersey: Laurence Erlbaum.

Shapiro, F. (1995). *Eye Movement Densentisation and Reprocessing. Basic Principles Protocols and Procedures*. New York. Guilford Press.

Stettbacher, J. K. (1991). *Making Sense of Suffering: The Healing Confrontation With Your Own Past*. USA: Penguin.

Van der Kolk, B. A. (1994). The body keeps the score: memory and the emerging psychobiology of post traumatic stress. *Harvard Review of Psychiatry, 1*: 253–265.

Williams, L. M. (1994). Recall of childhood trauma: a prospective study of women's memories of child sexual abuse. *Journal of Consulting and Clinical Psychology, 62*(6): 1167–1176.

Winnicott, D. W. (1965). *Maturational Processes and the Facilitating Environment*. New York: International Universities Press.

CHAPTER EIGHT

Containment: the technical and the tacit in successful psychotherapy

Robert M. Young

I don't know how psychotherapy works. However, I don't find that very odd. I have some ideas, but to tell the truth I think of them as a way of comforting myself while I get on with doing psychotherapy, something I do more than thirty hours a week and think about for quite a lot more hours as I teach, write, edit, and talk to colleagues. What I propose to do in this paper is share those ideas and to look behind them to other ideas that I believe to be more helpful in explaining what I do.

First, of course, psychotherapists, at least ones of my persuasion, make interpretations. I was taught only to make transference interpretations, but after I stopped having supervisions, i.e., after a decade of training and postgraduate training, I slowly moved on to making any interpretation I thought might help my patients. Then one day a patient asked me what was the relationship between my interpretations and therapeutic benefit. There was a time I'd interpret the question, but I thought it a reasonable one, and this patient was not prone to use theory as a place to hide. The answer I had been taught was that a truthful or accurate interpretation of a patient's unconscious motivations, the more primitive the better, and after being worked through, reduces primitive anxieties. This, in turn, makes the patient less trapped in his or her neurotic patterns. The emphasis was on the accuracy of the interpretation.

However, an image came into my mind, and after pondering it, I decided it was what I believed, so I spoke it. I said, "Do you know what a pedalo is?" "Yes", she said, "a sort of bicycle boat." "Imagine us on a pedalo in the ocean. We have to go on pedalling, sometimes fast and furiously, sometimes in a more leisurely way. At the bottom of the ocean there are large plates like the ones that we are told move with infinite slowness to reshape the earth's crust. The pedalling is what we say to each other, especially my interpretations. The movement of the plates is the therapeutic benefits from our work. If we don't pedal, the plates don't move. If we do, they do move or are very likely to. What goes on in the huge depth of water between the pedalo and the plates no one knows." I grant that this is an inelegant picture. Its main attractions are to draw attention to the very large gap in understanding, symbolized by the depth of the water, between the therapeutic discourse and the psychic change in the inner world of the patient. This is in sharp contrast to the cinema rendition of psychotherapy, where the therapist figures out the moment of trauma and, hey presto!, the patient is cured. I am thinking, for example of how Ingrid Bergman cured Gregory Peck in *Spellbound* or how Sean Connery cured his wife in *Mandy*. This is the cathartic model: remove the block and life flows again.

Actually, we do know a thing or two about what happens between the pedalo and the plates, but I'm not confident about it, and the longer I practise, the more I think what I say is diminishing in relative importance compared to how I say it and how I am. However, I am confident about two things that are essential for psychotherapy to work. They are the role of the analytic frame and the fact that what we interpret is not the patient's material but our own countertransference to that material. I'll discuss each of these topics.

First, the analytic frame, of which abstinence is a central aspect. Marion Milner, who coined the phrase "analytic frame", wrote about an analogy between providing boundaries for the analytic situation and a picture frame:

> The frame marks off the different kind of reality that is within it from that which is outside it; but a temporal spatial frame also

marks off the special kind of reality of a psychoanalytic session. And in psychoanalysis it is the existence of this frame that makes possible the full development of that creative illusion that analysts call the transference. Also the central idea underlying psychoanalytic technique is that it is by means of this illusion that a better adaptation to the world outside is ultimately developed. [Milner, 1952a, p. 183; see also 1952b]

Some years later José Bleger wrote,

Winnicott (1956) defines "setting" as "the summation of all the details of management". I suggest that we should apply the term "psychoanalytic situation" to the totality of the phenomena included in the therapeutic relationship between the analyst and the patient. This situation comprises phenomena which constitute a *process* that is studied, analysed, and interpreted; but it also includes a *frame*, that is to say, a "non-process", in the sense that it is made up of constants within whose bounds the process takes place. [Bleger, 1967, p. 511]

There are many elements of the analytic frame. It is a room—a physical setting. It is a set of conventions about how one behaves. It is a state of mind—a mental space. It is all of these at once and something more, something ineffable. It has been described as a facilitating environment and as a container. It needs to be a safe enough place for psychotherapeutic work to occur, a place where the patient can allow herself or himself to speak about things that are too painful or taboo or embarrassing to speak about elsewhere. The essence of the safety of the space is that the patient can project things into the therapist that are contained by the therapist, detoxified, and given back in due course in a form that can be used as food for thought.

If I listed all the factors making up the analytic frame, I would still miss out some things and not capture its essence. The things I will spell out are, therefore, examples, designed to set you thinking. The point is that the frame should make the analytic space that it bounds a suitable place for analytic work. It should be quiet. No interruptions, phone calls, or answering the doorbell. It should not have very personal pictures in sight or other mementoes that reveal personal matters or relationships. It should be pleasant and comfortable. It should, as far as possible, remain the same.

In part, the analytic frame takes the form of a contract about what the patient can expect and what the therapist will and will not do, will or will not allow, what can and cannot be expected. In this sense it includes the ground rules, implicit and explicit, of the analytic relationship (Langs & Searles, 1980, pp. 43–45), a basic framework, customs, and practices that have developed over the history of psychoanalysis and psychotherapy. Their overall purpose is to minimize uncertainty and ambiguity and to make a big contribution to containment.

There are a number of desiderata about the therapist's behaviour and demeanour. She or he should answer the door promptly and begin and end the session on time. Most agree that she should not give out personal details, although some believe that there are occasional circumstances when this may be appropriate, though only when it contributes to the patient's understanding, i.e., never gratuitously or self-indulgently. The bill should be presented at the same session every month (i.e., regularly). Sessions should not be changed unless necessary and, when they are changed, maximum notice should be given. Information about breaks or fee changes should be given well in advance. Occasions for differing over sessions, breaks, fees, or any matter concerning the frame should be minimized. Bleger stresses that the frame "should be neither ambiguous nor changeable nor altered" (1967, p. 518). Robert Langs argues that when the frame is broken a misalliance pathological symbiosis exists between therapist and patient until it is mended and until the break is understood and interpreted (Langs & Searles, 1980, pp. 44, 127).

The frame holds something in. It defines a border or limit. Confidentiality is guaranteed, but it is judiciously breached in training cases, when case material is taken to supervision, which is why it is unethical not to mention that one is a trainee. The law also specifies some exceptions to absolute confidentiality—certain criminal acts. Boundary maintenance is another way of conveying what containment means. The patient is being helped to hold himself together, to feel held, neither too tightly nor too loosely, as one holds a baby in distress, imparting a sense of care, taking in and not reprojecting anxiety.

It has been argued by Bleger that the analytic frame is the place where the madness is held so that the therapist and patient can have a space to think and feel about matters felt with a degree of intensity that is painful but still bearable. It keeps overwhelming distress at bay, while allowing something short of that to be thought about. "The frame as an institution is the receiver of the psychotic part of the personality, i.e., of the undifferentiated and non-solved parts of the primitive symbiotic links" (Bleger, 1967, p. 518). It contains "the most regressive, psychotic part of the patient" (p. 516). The implication is that when the frame is breached, these forces are likely to be let loose.

Having conveyed some basics, I must now say that there are exceptions to practically everything I have said. For example, the analytic frame is not confined to the room where the therapy is done. Ideally, it is tacitly in the minds of both therapist and patient all the time. It is there when you open the door or speak on the phone. It is carried with the patient (or not) between sessions: it is internalized. It is conveyed by the therapist's demeanour, tone of voice, pauses, silences, grunts, the wording of any note or letter that it is appropriate to send to the patient. It is evident in pauses. It is all aspects of analytic space. To maintain the frame is to maintain the analytic relationship. As I said, its essence is containment.

Acting out is breaking the analytic frame. (There is also a concept of "acting in", whereby the transgression occurs inside the therapy room, but I do not find this idea useful and will not employ it.) Acting out is not defined by what the patient does. Rather, it is characterized by the motive—to break the frame. For example, if the therapist and patient meet by chance outside the consulting room, e.g., at a party or at the cinema, the frame has been broken, and it is important to interpret the encounter, but it is possible that no one has acted out. It could be argued that every act which is characterized as acting out could occur for other reasons. If the patient is late, the reason may be a stoppage on public transport or a traffic jam. If the patient is persistently late, she is acting out. There is, however, another level of meaning here. The patient may have a perfectly good story about being late, even including events out of her control, but she may also unconsciously relate to that explanation in a way that involves acting out.

There are many fairly routine examples of acting out: not coming to sessions, unnecessarily phoning the therapist, bringing gifts, not paying the bill or doing so in a way which invalidates the payment (cheque unsigned, wrongly dated, numbers and words not the same, even the payee's name incorrect), refusing to speak, flooding with speech, coming early, reluctant or even refusing to leave at the end of the session, shouting, screaming, preventing the therapist from speaking, dressing provocatively, acting seductively, lying, bringing inappropriate things to the session (e.g., mobile phone, tape recorder), taking a holiday before or after an analytic break (thus extending the break). I had a patient who was usually on the couch but came into a session and turned the upright chair away and sat down with her back to me. I only wish I had made the interpretation that there was something she could not face. Another stood on the threshold of the therapy room and would not come in. After a long time it occurred to me to say that he wanted me to feel the panic of being on the edge that he felt. He then came in and sat down and began work.

Acting out is a substitute for verbal expression. It is expressive, symbolic communication, but it is not reflective. The patient is acting rather than reflecting. Where acting out is, thought cannot be.

One feature of acting out is that the therapist is usually put under pressure to do something he would not otherwise do—to go after the patient in some way, e.g., to write to the patient or phone, to reveal something, to move, to change a session, to press the patient, to relent about a decision or take a firm line, even to lose his temper.

Many believe that a good therapist is less likely to have patients act out, but I am not so sure. If you want to take account of the purist position in these matters, read the writings of Robert Langs or perhaps Carol Holmes (1998), a follower of his "communicative" approach. It is also true that acting out always has a meaning, just as a dream or a parapraxis does. It conveys a message, and the therapist's job is to interpret it—to get the message and convey that one has got it. Some say that the patient acts out because he cannot find any other way of conveying that message. As the example of my patient who stood on the threshold of the therapy room shows, the way to deal with acting out is to make the appropriate interpretation, one that hits the spot, reduces the primitive anxiety, and allows the patient to re-enter the analytic space on the agreed terms, i.e., that he remain on the couch (or in the chair) and take part in a talking therapy. I did not make the appropriate interpretation to the woman who turned the chair around and sat in it with her back to me, and she left therapy abruptly.

Persistent acting out indicates a deeper, untouched or unresolved conflict. I have a patient who always comes late and another who used to come very late. The first is indicating an ambivalence about coming at all, so he comes but always late. The other offered two explanations. First, she could not bear the thought of being kept waiting but felt that if she came late, I would always be there and come quickly to the door. The baby would not be left crying, unattended to. She also had low self-esteem and felt she wasn't a full person and did not have enough to say to fill a whole session, so she came twenty minutes late, believing that she could just about fill three-fifths of a session. She offered a different rationalization every day about what had delayed her, but the coming late stayed the same. Then we changed her session time to one she had before, and thereafter she came on time. It emerged that she had felt displaced and when she got back the original slot, she felt she had been given back her "own rightful time".

I had another patient who acts out frequently over money matters. She was highly reactive and stormed out and held out until I made contact and drew her back into coming to her sessions. She came from a family in which money matters were fraught to the point of involving the law, and she was particularly jumpy about them, often accusing me of holding views about her that were demeaning and of acting in an unfair way. At one time she was so defensive about paying me that she would give me the monthly payment before I gave her the bill. Matters of fees and payment were frequently the occasion for an outburst and sometimes a threat or short-term decision to leave therapy.

Another way of referring to these matters is the concept of abstinence. The therapist is supposed to abstain from doing various things that would perhaps be natural in a social situation. He should not speak to the patient while walking from the door to the therapy room or after the session ends. He should not lightly offer opinions or advice or make moral judgements about the patient's material (although tacitly conveying such opinions and judgements seems to me inevitable). Some say he should never ask questions. That is not my position. He should concentrate on interpreting the unconscious. I think this degree of abstinence is practically impossible to maintain, but it is the goal. This is not the same as saying that the therapist should be cold and too formal, just that she should not chat or exchange opinions. If, as I believe, what we do is to interpret our countertransference, it is essential that this be done in a temperate, civil, and level way. To do otherwise is to reproject the patient's transference projections and to act out in the countertransference. There are those who believe in a judicious "expressive use of the countertransference" (Bollas, 1987), in which the patient is carefully told what response she elicits in the therapist. I think this is a dangerous practice, but it has its advocates.

Psychoanalytic psychotherapists are almost all agreed that one should not have social relations with patients. Most agree that the transference never ends and that the patient may need to return, so social relations with ex-patients are also contraindicated. The same taboos apply to physical contact between therapist and patient and ex-patients. I learned about this the hard way. My analyst, an elderly and rather formal man, shook hands with me at the end of each term. I took up this end-of-term gesture when I began my own practice but soon abandoned it. One female patient with a strong sexual transference, who also had severe fertility problems, missed her next three periods. Another, a woman in her late fifties with a particularly intense romantic transference, went straight to a shop from having her hand shaken at the end of her first term of therapy with me, bought a red dress and told the people in the shop that she was having a baby. A supervisee who had been in the habit of hugging a patient gave up this practice under my guidance, and the patient came to feel that this abstinence from physical comforting allowed a greater degree of intimacy in the verbal realm. This supervisee, who was initially unconfident about what she had to offer, also sometimes let sessions run over time, until the patient told her that this made her anxious that the therapist could not handle (contain) her distress. These examples show that abstinence and boundaries are important for the patient and help her to feel safe and contained. This approach is characteristic of orthodox psychoanalytic psychotherapy. Some therapies that have derived their identity by breaking away from some of these forms of abstinence have involved various forms of "the laying on of hands". I am convinced that not touching leads to greater intimacy.

The most important and charged area of abstinence and of potential acting out is that of sexual relations between therapist and patient. There are various estimates of how often this happens. Somewhere between two and ten per cent of male therapists have sexual relations with their patients, and about two or three per cent of female therapists do (Bates & Brodsky, 1989; Ciardiello, 1996; Russell, 1993; Rutter, 1990). The analytic space is an oedipal space, and the analytic frame keeps incest at bay. The analytic relationship involves continually offering incest and continually declining it in the name of analytic abstinence and the hope of a relationship that transcends or goes beyond incestuous desires. Breaking the analytic frame in this way invariably involves the risk of child abuse, and sleeping with patients or ex-patients is precisely that.

Martin Bergmann puts some of these points very nicely in his essay on transference love. He says,

> In the analytic situation, the early images are made conscious and thereby deprived of their energising potential. In analysis, the uncovering of the incestuous fixation behind transference love loosens the incestuous ties and prepares the way for a future love free from the need to repeat oedipal triangulation. Under conditions of health the infantile prototypes merely energize the new falling in love while in neurosis they also evoke the incest taboo and needs for new triangulation that repeat the triangle of the oedipal state. [Bergmann, 1987, p. 220]

With respect to patients who get involved with therapists or ex-therapists, he says that they claim that " 'unlike the rest of humanity I am entitled to disobey the incest taboo, circumventing the work of mourning, and possess my parent sexually. I am entitled to do so because I suffered so much or simply because I am an exception' " (ibid., p. 222). Such sexual relations may seem a triumph to the patient, but, as Freud eloquently observed,

> If the patient's advances were returned it would be a great triumph for her, but a complete defeat for the treatment. She would have succeeded in what all patients strive for in analysis—she would have succeeded in acting out, in repeating in real life, what she ought only to have remembered, to have reproduced as psychical material and to have kept within the sphere of psychical events. In

the further course of the love-relationship she would bring out all the inhibitions and pathological reactions of her erotic life, without there being any possibility of correcting them; and the distressing episode would end in remorse and a great strengthening of her propensity to repression. The love-relationship in fact destroys the patient's susceptibility to influence from analytic treatment. A combination of the two would be an impossibility.

It is, therefore, just as disastrous for the analysis if the patient's craving for love is gratified as if it is suppressed. The course the analyst must pursue is neither of these; it is one for which there is no model in real life. He must take care not to steer away from the transference-love, or to repulse it or to make it distasteful to the patient; but he must just as resolutely withhold any response to it. He must keep firm hold of the transference-love, but treat it as something unreal, as a situation which has to be gone through in the treatment and traced back to its unconscious origins and must assist in bringing all that is most deeply hidden in the patient's erotic life into her consciousness and therefore under her control. The more plainly the analyst lets it be seen that he is proof against every temptation, the more readily will he be able to extract from the situation its analytic content. The patient, whose sexual repression is of course not yet removed but merely pushed into the background, will then feel safe enough to allow all her preconditions for loving, all the fantasies springing from her sexual desires, all the detailed characteristics of her state of being in love, to come to light; and from these she will open the way to the infantile roots of her love. [Freud, 1915a, p. 166]

From the therapist's point of view, "When the transference relationship becomes a sexual one, it represents symbolically and unconsciously the fulfilment of the wish that the infantile love object will not be given up and that incestuous love can be refound in reality" (Bergmann, 1987, p. 223). This is a variant on the Pygmalion theme. The analytic relationship works only to the extent that the therapist shows, in Freud's words quoted above, "that he is proof against every temptation" (Freud, 1915, p. 166). Langs puts this very well when he says that "the therapist's appropriate love is expressed by maintaining the boundaries" (Langs & Searles, 1980, p. 130).

Nevertheless, as I have indicated, alarmingly many therapists do sleep with their patients. If the motives for abstinence are not sufficiently strong, the situation is perfect. There is opportunity in the therapy hour and on the analytic couch. There is no fear of interruption. The patient has placed herself in the therapist's hands, under his care, trusted him to look after her. In their omnipotent and incestuous way of seeing things, what could be a more tender and intimate way of doing so? When the transgression is discovered (usually when the therapist belatedly finds himself), the matter is frequently brought before a professional ethical committee, and the therapist is struck off, suspended and/or required to undergo further therapy. I know of a case where this was done twice between a training therapist and supervisor, who took up the practice again and finally had to be permanently removed from the professional organization.

Turning now to my second large topic, the countertransference, I begin by saying that what happens inside the analytic frame is that the patient talks—or not—and does some other things. We make responses; most significantly, we make interpretations. I have heard it said that we really make only one basic interpretation. "You are speaking as if I was your mother/father" or whatever internal object the patient is projecting into you, the therapist. That is, patients' problems stem from inappropriately transferring the untoward feelings that they have about significant persons on to us, and we point out that they are mistaken and that life would be better if they'd stop making these false accusations and take life more as it comes and give it an even chance rather than prejudging things, distorting them, and repeating self-limiting patterns learned in infancy and childhood.

I know I am making it sound awfully simplistic, so let me try to enrich the model. Patients behave toward us in neurotic ways, i.e., they react to us as if we were the problematic people in their inner worlds. We'd like to shift their internal objects so that they are less caught up in repetition compulsions, delusions, and other reactions that are making them unhappy, unfulfilled, sexually hung up or whatever. In classical psychoanalysis the therapist was thought of as observing the patient, spotting their distortions and pointing out the mistaken attributions, the transferential material. The therapist was considered to be objective. In so far as the therapist was not objective, he or she was considered to be incompletely analysed. You could tell this if they reacted inappropriately towards the patient as a result of an unconscious reaction to the patient's material. This was called countertransference, i.e., a reprojection. A conscientious therapist would spot this reaction, keep it to themselves and reflect upon it or get some further analysis. However, in the period just after the Second World War, a number of people here and in the USA had second thoughts about the countertransference and thought it would be a good idea to pay some attention to it. Donald Winnicott (1947) and Margaret Little (1985), among the Independents, thought this, and Roger Money-Kyrle, a Kleinian, did, too (1956). What Money-Kyrle said was that when your unanalysed countertransference leads you to make a wonky interpretation, the patient senses that you are in trouble and relates to you as a damaged object. Getting back into a good therapeutic alliance takes some work. Paula Heimann, who shifted allegiance from the Kleinians to the Independents, wrote two influential papers on learning from the countertransference (1949–1950, 1959–1960), but her recommendation was that you should listen to it in order to reduce the likelihood of its occurrence. Harold Searles, a greatly gifted American analyst of no particular school, went further and advocated being in constant touch with your countertransference and making your efforts to decipher such reactions the basis of your interpretations. British Kleinians took the same line, though independently, and ended up arguing that what we do is not make objective observations of our patients' material. On the contrary, we take in their projections, attend to them, detoxify them in our own inner worlds and make interpretations based on our ruminations which, hopefully, will be of use (Searles, 1949, 1979). Two features of this changed perspective are important. First, we attend to the total situation of the patient (Joseph, 1983) and what his or her material evokes in us. We are not, as it were, looking objectively at the patient through an optical instrument. Instead, we are resonating in our deepest subjectivity to what they put into us and what it evokes in our unconscious. This means that we should keep our own counsel until we have made sense of our countertransference. I remember one of my supervisors offering the following good advice: "Sometimes all you can do is hold on to the arms of your chair."

I'll give you an example from my recent work. I have a patient who always comes in looking angry. She rarely begins talking without prompting, and her first utterance is often that she wonders if she should stop coming or whether the therapy is doing her any good. In the course of the session we almost invariably climb out of this slough of despond and get somewhere. She leaves in a better frame of mind, often with a thank you, only to return with the same negative anticipations. I found myself over time not looking forward to the beginnings of our sessions and bracing myself for her expressions of disappointment. One day, however, I found myself saying, after she had told me a particularly poignant story about her father's distressingly superficial reaction to something important and painful she had said to him, that with a father like that and a mother who was preoccupied with her own self-pity, it's not surprising that she comes to me anticipating not being heard, taken in, or supported and angry about it before she got to the door. I linked this to other situations in her work and home life where she had a hair trigger and lost her temper very early in situations where it was not at all obvious to me that they would end as badly as her outbursts led them to do. I was led to this interpretation by how she made me feel. She did not expect the objects of her feelings to hold, contain, and draw the hurt from her painful experiences in life. Her premature outbursts ensured that she would be disappointed. She creates what she expects, what she fears, and, of course, she gets back from life the echoes of her own anxieties.

A paper by Irma Brenman Pick takes the normality of countertransference to its logical extreme, without a trace of seeing it as something to be got rid of. She carefully considers it as the basis of understanding throughout the session: "Constant projecting by the patient into the analyst is the essence of analysis; every interpretation aims at a move from the paranoid–schizoid to the depressive position" (Brenman Pick, 1985, p. 158). By this she means that we are constantly trying to shift the patient's thinking from an approach dominated by extreme splits, concrete thinking, and punitive guilt to a frame of mind in which life is a continuum, where there is a whole range of options other than the two extremes—where there is a middle ground. We strive to encourage thought that is not persecutory but, rather, shows concern for the object, and guilt is not punitive but leads us to repair the object rather than thinking in terms of attack and counter-attack.

Brenman Pick makes great play of the tone, the mood, and the resonances of the process: "I think that the extent to which we

succeed or fail in this task will be reflected not only in the words
we choose, but in our voice and other demeanour in the act of
giving an interpretation ..." (*ibid.*, p. 161). Most importantly,
she emphasizes the power of the projections and what they evoke
countertransferentially:

> I have been trying to show that the issue is not a simple one; the
> patient does not just project into an analyst, but instead patients are
> quite skilled at projecting into particular aspects of the analyst.
> Thus, I have tried to show, for example, that the patient projects
> into the analyst's wish to be a mother, the wish to be all-knowing
> or to deny unpleasant knowledge, into the analyst's instinctual
> sadism, or into his defences against it. And above all, he projects
> into the analyst's guilt, or into the analyst's internal objects.
>
> Thus, patients touch off in the analyst deep issues and anxieties
> related to the need to be loved and the fear of catastrophic conse-
> quences in the face of defects, i.e., primitive persecutory or super-
> ego anxiety. [*ibid.*]

As I see it, the approach adopted by Brenman Pick takes it as read
and as normal that these powerful feelings are moving from patient
to analyst and back again, through the processes of projection,
evocation, reflection, interpretation, and assimilation. Moving on
from the more limited formulations of an earlier period in the writings of Winnicott, Heimann, and even Money-Kyrle, these feelings
are all normal, as it were, in the processes of analysis. More than
that, as she puts it, they are the essence.

As I said earlier, Kleinians have not always taken this view of
countertransference. Klein had begged Heimann not to deliver her
first paper on countertransference and told Tom Hayley in the late
1950s that she thought countertransference interferes with analysis
and should be the subject of lightning self-analysis (Grosskurth,
1986, p. 378). According to Elizabeth Spillius, "Klein thought that
such extension would open the door to claims by analysts that their
own deficiencies were caused by their patients" (Spillius, 1992,
p. 61). Having said this, it is important not to be too literal about
the use of the term "countertransference". Klein's subtle interpretations of her patients' inner worlds—especially their preverbal feelings and ideas—only make sense in the light of her ability to be

resonant with their most primitive feelings, and Wilfred Bion's injunction to "abandon memory and desire" is made in the name of countertransference, whatever term we attach to the process. Indeed, it can be said that his writings are about little else.

Implicit in the phenomena of countertransference is a model for knowledge—that the way we really learn is from the other's response to what we convey. We learn by evoking and provoking. We do not learn by imparting but by re-experiencing what we have projected and has then been passed through another human being (though that person may be held in imagination). We learn by putting something out and finding out what comes back. Our relationship with the world is a phenomenological "I–thou", not a scientistic "I–it". It is evocative knowledge.

In the analytic relationship, it turns out that the real justification for the free-floating attention that is characteristic of psychoanalysis is that it makes our minds available for the patient's projections and facilitates their search for the resonances in us for what they feel. Freud said, "He should simply listen, and not bother about whether he is keeping anything in mind" (Freud, 1912a, p. 112). Bion put it poetically in his injunction that the analyst should "impose upon himself the positive discipline of eschewing memory and desire. I do not mean that 'forgetting' is enough: what is required is a positive act of refraining from memory and desire" (Bion, 1970, p. 31).

If this sounds a bit mystical, so be it. The Argentinian analyst Heinrich Racker shares an appropriately Oriental parable: one day an old Chinese sage lost his pearls.

> He therefore sent his eyes to search for his pearls, but his eyes did not find them. Next he sent his ears to search for the pearls, but his ears did not find them either. Then he sent his hands to search for the pearls, but neither did his hands find them. And so he sent all of his senses to search for his pearls but none found them. Finally he sent his *not-search* to look for his pearls. *And his not-search found them.* [Racker, 1968, p. 17]

Once one is in this state, one is open to the patient's unconscious and to the injunction that "Constant projecting by the patient into the analyst is the essence of analysis" (Brenman Pick, 1985, p. 158).

And at the other end of the analysis lies the ability of the patient to take back his or her projections. This is an important criterion of improvement. Bearing projections is the whole basis of containment: the therapist can bear to take in and contain the projections, to hold them and give them back, in due course, in the form of accessible interpretations. I am suggesting that countertransference—as an aspect of projective identification—is not only the basis for analytic work but is central to the basic process in all human communication and knowing. We only know what is happening because we are moved from within by what we have taken in and responded to from our own deep feelings. The space between people is filled—when it is and to the extent it is—by what we evoke in one another.

I have two concluding thoughts. First, in my announcement for this talk, written months ago before I had thought much about it, I said I would review various theories of how psychotherapy works. There are forty-five papers in the main psychoanalytic journals on the nature of the therapeutic action of psychoanalysis. I have read many and perused more, beginning with James Strachey in the 1930s, moving on to Hans Loewald in 1960, as well as innumerable workshops and critiques, including a very interesting one by Herbert Rosenfeld (1972). These are available on the CD-ROM of Psychoanalytic Electronic Publishing of those journals. Having reviewed this literature, I do not have anything to draw from it that, in my opinion, is as helpful as what I have been telling you.

In closing, I want to draw your attention to the writings of R. D. Hinshelwood, whose *Dictionary of Kleinian Thought* (1991) is a very valuable resource for understanding the therapeutic process. In particular, he writes very helpfully about containment and the work of Bion. He argues that the concepts of container and contained offer the key terms of reference for how we relate to our own minds, to the minds of others, and to groups and institutions. Containment is the essence of what we do with our patients' projections, which we metabolize, detoxify and give back in the form of an interpretation which—if we do our job—is potentially helpful in allowing them to take back their projections and bear the vicissitudes and pain that are inescapable features of the lives of mature people and which we have vainly tried to evade with our neurotic symptoms.

References

Bates, C. M., & Brodsky, A. M. (1989). *Sex in the Therapy Hour: A Case of Professional Incest*. London: Guilford.

Bergmann, M. S. (1986). Transference love and love in real life. *International Journal of Psychoanalytic Psychotherapy*, 11: 27–45; reprinted in Bergmann, M. S. *The Anatomy of Loving* (pp. 213–28). New York: Columbia, 1987.

Bion, W. R. (1970). *Attention and Interpretation*. London: Tavistock.

Bleger, J. (1967). Psychoanalysis of the psycho-analytic frame. *International Journal of Psychoanalysis*, 48: 511–519.

Bollas, C. (1987). Expressive uses of the counter-transference. In: *The Shadow of the Object: Psychoanalysis of the Unthought Known* (pp. 200–235). London: Free Association Books.

Brenman Pick, I. (1985). Working through in the counter-transference. *International Journal of Psychoanalysis*, 66: 157–166; reprinted in E. B. Spillius (Ed.), *Melanie Klein Today* vol. 2 (pp. 34–47) London: Routledge, 1988.

Ciardiello, J. (1996). Therapist–patient sexual contact. *Psychoanalytical Review*, 83: 761–775.

Freud, S. (1912a). Recommendations to physicians practising psycho-analysis. *S.E.*, 12: 109–120. London: Hogarth.

Freud, S. (1915). Observations on transference-love (Further recommendations on the technique of psychoanalysis III). *S.E.*, 12: 159–171. London: Hogarth.

Grosskurth, P. (1986). *Melanie Klein: Her World and Her Work*. Hodder and Stoughton.

Heimann, P. (1949–1950). On counter-transference. In Heimann, P., *About Children and Children No Longer: The Work of Paula Heimann* (pp. 73–79). London: Routledge, 1990.

Heimann, P. (1959–1960). Counter-transference. In Heimann, P., *About Children and Children No Longer: The Work of Paula Heimann* (pp. 151–160). London: Routledge, 1990.

Hinshelwood, R. D. (1991). *A Dictionary of Kleinian Thought*, 2nd edn. London: Free Association Books.

Holmes, C. (1998). *There is No Such Thing as a Therapist: An Introduction to the Therapeutic Process*. London: Karnac.

Joseph, B. (1983). Transference: the total situation. In: *Psychic Equilibrium and Psychic Change: Selected Papers* (pp. 156–67). London: Routledge, 1989.

Langs, R., & Searles, H. (1980). *Intrapsychic and Interpersonal Dimensions of Treatment: A Clinical Dialogue.* London: Aronson.

Little, M. (1985). Winnicott working in areas where psychotic anxieties predominate. *Free Associations,* 3: 9–42.

Milner, M. (1952a). Aspects of symbolism and comprehension of the not-self. *International Journal of Psychoanalysis,* 33: 181–185; reprinted in expanded form in Milner, M. *The Suppressed Madness of Sane Men: Forty-four Years of Exploring Psychoanalysis* (pp. 83–113). London: Routledge, 1987.

Milner, M. (1952b) The framed gap. In Milner, M. *The Suppressed Madness of Sane Men: Forty-four Years of Exploring Psychoanalysis* (pp. 79–82). London: Routledge, 1987.

Money-Kyrle, R. (1956). Normal counter-transference and some of its deviations. *International Journal of Psycho-Analysis,* 37:360–366; reprinted in *The Collected Papers of Roger Money-Kyrle* (pp. 330–342). Strath Tay, Perthshire: Clunie Press, 1978, and E. B. Spillius (Ed.), *Melanie Klein Today,* vol. 2 (pp. 22–33). London: Routledge, 1988.

Racker, H. (1968). *Transference and Countertransference.* London: Hogarth [reprinted London: Maresfield Reprints, 1982].

Rosenfeld, H. (1972). A critical appreciation of James Strachey's paper on the nature of the therapeutic action of psychoanalysis. *International Journal of Psychoanalysis,* 53: 455–461.

Russell, J. (1993). *Out of Bounds: Sexual Exploitation in Counselling and Therapy.* London: Sage.

Rutter, P. (1990). *Sex in the Forbidden Zone.* London: Unwin.

Searles, H. (1949)[1978–1979]. Concerning transference and counter-transference. *Journal of Psychoanalytic Psychotherapy,* 7: 165–188.

Searles, H. (1979). *Countertransference and Related Subjects.* Madison, CT: International Universities Press.

Spillius, E. B. (1992). Clinical experiences of projective identification. In: R. Anderson (Ed.), *Clinical Lectures on Klein and Bion* (pp. 59–73). London: Routledge.

Strachey, J. (1934). The nature of the therapeutic action of psycho-analysis. *International Journal of Pschoanalysis,* 15: 127–159; reprinted in *International Journal of Psychoanalysis,* 50: 275–292.

Winnicott, D. W. (1947). Hate in the countertransference. In: Winnicott, D. W., *Through Paediatrics to Psycho-Analysis* (pp. 194–203). London: Hogarth, 1975.

Further reading

(* recommended, ** highly recommended)
On *the analytic frame* the best single source is:

**Blejer, J. (1967). Psychoanalysis of the psycho-analytic frame. *International Journal of Psychoanalysis, 48*: 511–519.

Standard sources are:

Stone, L. (1961). *The Analytic Situation*. International Universities Press.
Gabbard, G. O., & Lester, E. P. (1995). *Boundaries and Boundary Violations in Psychoanalysis*. New York: Basic.
Langs, R. (1977). Psychoanalytic situation: the framework. In: B. Wolman (Ed.), *International Encyclopedia of Psychiatry, Psychology, Psychoanalysis, and Neurology* (pp. 220–222). Aesculapius.

More accessible is his paperback:

*Langs, R. (1992). *A Clinical Workbook for Psychotherapists*. London: Karnac. See index entry: "ground rules" [frame].

Langs writes a lot about this matter in his weighty tomes on theory and technique. I prefer to follow the continuing thread about this topic running through

**Langs, R., & Searles, H. (1980). *Intrapsychic and Interpersonal Dimensions of Treatment: A Clinical Dialogue*. London: Aronson. See index for specific passages, but the whole book is a feast, not least because of their contrasting characters and styles.

For a succinct account, have a look at the comprehensive volume:

*Etchegoyen, R. H. (1991). *The Fundamentals of Psychoanalytic Technique*. London: Karnac, Chapters 36–38, 43, 52–54 on the analytic situation and setting, container–contained and acting out.

See also

Meissner, W. W., SJ (1998). Neutrality, abstinence and the therapeutic alliance. *Journal of the American Psychoanalytical Association, 46*: 1089–1128.

There is a useful chapter by

Thomä, H., & Cachelë, H. (1987). Rules. In: *Psychoanalytic Practice*, Vol. 1 (pp. 215–52). London: Springer-Verlag/Aronson.

See index entries on "frame", "boundaries", and "space, analytic" in

Casement, P. (1985). *On Learning from the Patient*. London: Routledge.
Casement, P. (1991). *Further Learning from the Patient: The Analytic Space and Process*. Routledge.

The concept of the analytic frame broadens out and has been written about by a number of interesting people. Have a look at

Davies, M., & Wallbridge, D. (1981). *Boundary and Space*. London: Karnac.
Gray, A. (1994). *An Introduction to the Therapeutic Frame*. London: Routledge.
Milner, M. (1987). *The Suppressed Madness of Sane Men*. London: Routledge—see index re: framed gap, boundaries.

Perhaps the most general approach to the topic is W. R. Bion's concept of containment. A good place to begin with this is

**Hinshelwood, R. D. (1991). Containing. In: *A Dictionary of Kleinian Thought*, revised edn. (pp. 246–253). London: Free Association Books.

On *acting out*, start with

*Laplanche, J., & Pontalis, J.-B. (1983). *The Language of Psychoanalysis*. London: Hogarth [reprinted Maresfield].

There is a useful introduction in

Sandler, J. *et al.* (1979). *The Patient and the Analyst* (Chapter 9). London: Maresfield.

On the subtler debates about acting out, see

Boesky, D. (1982). Acting out: a reconsideration of the concept. *International Journal of Psychoanalysis*, *63*: 39–55.
Gaddini, E. (1982). Acting out in the psychoanalytic session. *International Journal of Psychoanalysis*, *63*: 57–64.

There is a symposium on acting out, with several articles, commentaries, and a discussion in volume 49 (1968) of *International Journal of Psychoanalysis*.

The discussions I have found most helpful are in Etchegoyen, *op. cit.*, Chapters 52–54.

For *personal accounts of failure to maintain boundaries*, see

Hill, J. (1993). Am I a Kleinian? Is anyone?. *British Journal of Psychotherapy*, *9*: 463–475—a candid account of three Kleinian analysts' very idiosyncratic behaviour about boundaries.

Fox, R. P. (1984). The principle of abstinence reconsidered. *International Journal of Psycho-Analysis*, 11: 227–235.

*Little, M. (1985). Winnicott working in areas where psychotic anxieties predominate. *Free Associations*, 3: 9–42—where Winnicott does.

Carotenuto, A. (1984). *A Secret Symmetry: Sabina Spielrein between Jung and Freud*. London: Routledge—about one of Jung's patients who fell in love with him.

Masson, J. (1991). *Final Analysis*. London: HarperCollins—in which the notorious apostate describes a training analysis with practically no boundaries.

There are well-known accounts of rule-breaking which the authors believed to be beneficial:

*Coltart, N. (1986). "Slouching towards Bethlehem" . . . or thinking the unthinkable in psychoanalysis. In: G. Kohon (Ed.), *The British School of Psychoanalysis: The Independent Tradition* (pp. 185–199). London: Free Association Books [reprinted in *Slouching Toward Bethlehem . . .* (pp. 1–14). London: Free Association Books, 1992].

Symington, N. (1986). The analyst's act of freedom as agent of therapeutic change. In: G. Kohon (Ed.), *The British School of Psychoanalysis: The Independent Tradition* (pp. 253–270). London: Free Association Books.

There is a useful brief discussion of these issues about self-revelation and 'expressive uses of the countertransference' in

Rayner, E. (1990). *The Independent Mind in British Psychoanalysis* (pp. 289–296). London: Free Association Books.

On boundaries in the analytic and post-analytic relationship, see

Blomfield, O. H. D. (1985). Psychoanalytic supervision—an overview. *International Review of Psychoanalysis*, 12: 401–409.

Crick, P. (1991). Good supervision: on the experience of being supervised. *Psychoanalytic Psychotherapy*, 5: 235–245.

Limintani, A. (1989). The training analyst and the difficulties associated with psychoanalytic training. In: *Between Freud and Klein: The Psychoanalytic Quest for Knowledge and Truth* (pp. 73–87). London: Free Association Books.

Norman, H. F. *et al.* (1976). The fate of the transference neurosis after termination of a satisfactory analysis. *Journal of the American Psychoanalytic Association*, 24: 471–498.

Wallerstein, R. S. (Ed.) (1981). *Becoming a Psychoanalyst: A Study of Psychoanalytic Supervision*. New York: International Universities Press.

*Schachter, J. (1990). Post-termination patient–analyst contact: I. Analyst's attitudes and experience, II. Impact on patients. *International Journal of Psychoanalysis, 71*: 475–486.

*Schachter, J. (1992). Concepts of termination and post-termination patient–analyst contact. *International Journal of Psychoanalysis, 73*: 137–154.

Grinberg, L. (1990). Theoretical and clinical aspects of supervision. Part Four of *The Goals of Psychoanalysis: Identification, Identity and Supervision* (pp. 289–369). London: Karnac.

Peddar, J. R. (1986). Reflections on the theory and practice of supervision. *Psychoanalytic Psychotherapy, 2*: 1–12.

CHAPTER NINE

The value of attachment theory in understanding how psychotherapy works

James Pollard

T he conceptual and procedural problems in assessment of the effectiveness of psychotherapy are daunting. It is not possible here to review the many approaches that have been offered. Each approach raises its own technical issues and reflects a particular value base. The problems are so great that many psychotherapists have retreated from the problem altogether or become content to theorize the impossibility of the task.

In the public sector the profession faces demands for "evidence based practice" and measurements of outcomes on the model of the randomized clinical trial. Many individuals report that they have found psychotherapy to have been helpful to them. This individual experience is so persuasive that psychotherapy flourishes in the private sector. Psychotherapists owe it to those who finance their own psychotherapy, as much as to public sector managers, to remain committed to the task of developing and supporting an account of how and why psychotherapy works. Not least psychotherapists owe it to their patients to offer an account of what they mean by "psychotherapy works".

This presupposes that psychotherapy is meant to work in some sense. If there is any sense at all in a distinction between psychotherapy and psychoanalysis it is here that it lies. Bion suggested that psychoanalysis is an encounter in which two people meet to explore how one of them has learned from experience. From this point of view, to be concerned about outcomes would interfere with the analysis. Bion wrote:

> Even psycho-analysis is tainted with ideas of cure that imply a better state. I think it is "better" to know the truth about one's self and the universe in which I exist. . . . Whether it is "better" is a matter of opinion which each individual has to arrive at for himself: his opinion and *only his*. [Bion, 1977, Introduction, original italics]

Bion's description could apply to psychotherapy also—certainly to psychoanalytic psychotherapy—but the term "therapy" does suggest a healing intent, and the form of this has to be clearly articulated and established. The danger of failing to address this is that a circular argument is established. The patient turns up to the sessions because psychotherapy works. The fact that the patient turns up for the sessions shows that psychotherapy works. Attachment theory developed, in part, as a response to this problem.

This is important not only because of its significance for the future of psychotherapy as a profession. It is crucial because it has such a powerful bearing on how people understand the science of human relationships and development. Our wisdom-traditions now have to take account of academic psychology, human biology, in particular neuro-biology and social and political changes towards a culture that is less deferential and less accepting of traditional wisdoms and the power relations embedded within them. In particular, psychotherapists have much to say about how we treat children and need to find effective ways to express this.

Any approach to this task requires a theory, and psychotherapy abounds in theories. It probably suffers from a surfeit of theories, which have been developed as psychotherapists seek to make sense of their clinical work. In contrast to many other professions this requires the creation of a language to articulate inner experience. This gives rise to a profusion of languages. The many literary productions that form a great part of the published research in psychotherapy are very valuable. Attachment theory is less literary—and less attractive to some psychotherapists as a consequence.

It has been developed because it allows the learning that there has been from psychotherapy to be relocated so that new questions can be asked in new ways. In particular, attachment theory creates a bridge between psychoanalysis and academic empirical psychology.

It is over thirty years since the publication of *Attachment*, the first volume of John Bowlby's trilogy: *Attachment, Separation and Loss*. Originally, Bowlby saw attachment theory as a means of developing psychoanalysis (which he approached primarily from the standpoint of object relations theory) and a way of placing it on a firmer ground. To achieve this he was willing to accept much greater limitations in the elaboration of theory than was common in psychoanalytic thinking and adopted a much more cautious approach to making claims for the explanatory power of the available theories. Attachment theory is not an all-embracing theory of the personality; it implies the need to theorise other aspects of the personality and to consider the relationship between them. A key concept is exploration: secure attachment opens the way to the exploration through which other aspects of the personality develop.

Reviewing the first volume of *Attachment and Loss* in 1971 for the *International Journal of Psychoanalysis* Matte Blanco wrote, "It would not be surprising if it met with strong opposition. Once the problems it raises and the objections that will be made to it are discussed and assimilated, however, it will give rise, I believe, to fruitful developments". The difficulties envisaged by Matte Blanco were perhaps greater than even he foresaw. Not only has the process of discussion and assimilation of problems and objections been slow and difficult over the intervening thirty years, but attachment theory quickly took on a life of its own. In the following years it provided the foundation for a major research effort that was substantially independent of psychoanalysis. This effort was carried forward by researchers who valued the more specific, but necessarily more confined, framework of the new theory.

Psychotherapy draws on wisdom traditions—philosophical, religious, and literary—and on a practice of internal reflection. The strength of psychotherapeutic practice has not resided in the salience of any one particular element of theory but in a thoughtful approach to relationships and an immensely flexible approach to metaphor. In psychotherapy the focus on the inner world is allied with a willingness to use metaphors fluidly in the pursuit of an understanding of a complex and elusive psychic reality.

This flexibility with language, symbols, and metaphor, which is valuable in clinical practice and to the enquiry into the internal world, sat uneasily with Bowlby's positivist approach. It was not that Bowlby was unaware of the problem. He wrote of "the large, difficult, and profound questions of how a child gradually builds up his own 'inner world'". He referred to "matters . . . that raise too many giant problems (and giant controversies)" and concluded "systematic research has only just begun and little that is firm is yet known" (Bowlby, 1969). It is out of his attempt to understand psychotherapy in his own positivist terms that Bowlby shaped a theory that can assist psychotherapists to understand key aspects of what they do in these terms and to explain this to essentially positivist, scientific, and managerial communities.

The aim of this paper is to consider the value of attachment theory to understanding what works in the clinical practice of psychotherapy. The emphasis is not on the wide-ranging research findings under the umbrella of attachment theory but on the elements of attachment theory that relate directly to the work of the individual psychotherapist and the individual patient—the particular clinical experience.

The place of cognitive psychology

Bowlby made a clear statement about what he was seeking to achieve:

> By framing the processes in terms of cognitive psychology, I believe, much greater precision becomes possible and hypotheses regarding the causative role of different sorts of childhood experience, through the persistence of representational models of attachment figures and self at an unconscious level, can be formulated in testable form. [Bowlby, 1979]

This was written with reference to psychoanalysis. The concepts of "representational models of attachment figures and self" is both less colourful and more precise than the model of "internalised object". However, psychoanalysis was only one reference point for attachment theory. Its benefits include a stronger approach to three key problems.

First, the strong focus on individuals in psychotherapy is linked to confusion about individual responsibility. In a culture that emphasizes individualism there is a strong emphasis on the need for individuals to take responsibility for their problems. However, this is often falsely read backwards into a preference for causal explanations of an individual's difficulties that emphasize his or her individual responsibility for those difficulties. This is partly a product of a common difficulty in tolerating feelings of guilt and partly a result of a desire to locate the need to change in the other. Attachment theory includes an account of the inter-generational transmission of attachment patterns that is not simplistically genetic but is sufficiently carefully framed to be distanced from a cultural preoccupation with guilt.

This is linked to the second issue, which is the widespread preference for physical and genetic explanations and the bias towards pharmaceutical interventions. What is at issue here is an ideological preference that operates independently of the scientific evidence, or lack of it. The best conceptualization available is that genetic material is necessarily generated in an environmental context and that this process is immensely complicated and poorly understood. It is essential to develop improved frameworks for understanding environmental impact to run alongside and to contribute to the investigation of organic development that is now taking place.

A third concern is the widespread reluctance in scientific work to focus on emotional or dynamic aspects of human experience. Attachment theory brings together emotional and dynamic processes and cognitive and behavioural dimensions in a new way that is particularly significant in addressing the cognitive and behavioural bias of positivist science. As we will see, the cognitive processes that Bowlby refers to are not neutral. The representational models of self and other are not abstract concepts but are emotionally charged. Attachment theory proposes an interconnection between attachment security (or insecurity) and the development of the capacity to think. Not only does secure attachment promote the exploration required to develop reflective function but reflective function also promotes attachment security as events experienced as threats to attachment security can be better understood.

Secure attachment

Attachment theory formulates a link between relationships and cognitive processes. At the heart of this link are the feelings of security, anxiety, and the confidence to explore and to overcome negative experiences. A central image in attachment theory is the secure base. This is an image that links the experience and practice of parenting with the experience and practice of psychotherapy. The notion that the therapist offers a secure base from which the patient explores is very problematic and liable to misunderstanding.

There is a model of cognitive processes that suggests that development represents a series of moves from global undifferentiated experience to a state of increasing differentiation. There is much debate about the full extent of the early lack of differentiation and about the speed with which greater differentiation is established. The process of differentiation is accompanied by the development of patterns of association. These patterns of association are then, to a greater or lesser degree, integrated and schematized. This process produces mental structures. The study of the link between these mental structures and physiological structures is in its infancy. It is itself poorly distinguished and only the most tentative associations are possible.

The move from association to structure offers cognitive economy. Once complex phenomena are differentiated and then formed into structures, which are then treated as whole, thought processes proceed more swiftly and lightly. Without these structures the burden of remembering becomes too heavy. A limited or impaired ability to develop such structures creates major problems in carrying out ordinary daily functions. However, the process of differentiation is often resisted and the resistance is not solely defensive. Attachment as a term has been criticized as an avoidance of the term love. The emotional appeal of a relatively undifferentiated concept like love is very different from the appeal of a relatively differentiated concept like attachment. There is a tension between undifferentiated experience and the differentiated and structured experience.

However, this cognitive economy is only achieved at the expense of discrimination of the particular. This is so whether cognitive economy is being achieved at the level of "fish" or "bicycle" or "happy childhood" or "sworn enemy". The balance of the usefulness of the economic gain and the discriminatory loss depends upon categorical incisiveness. That is to say, it depends upon how well the differentiations, associations, and structures correspond to an ultimately unknowable reality. This categorical incisiveness is critical. If, as a result of environmental threats or failures, schemas are developed that are excessively defensive, the loss of categorical incisiveness may be very high. The ability to develop structures at all will also be affected.

Many factors may promote the defensive exclusion of experiences from the schemas that are developed. These may include association with painful affect or the need to protect the mental structure of relationships with attachment figures. Even if the loss of incisiveness is considerable, the schemas will often continue to have high value because the memorial burden is so heavy without them. One familiar expression of this is the power of habit.

This is an important cause of resistance to the dissolution of existing structures. Self-esteem is strongly linked to the development of a capacity to differentiate, structure, and organize. These structures, once achieved, generate a sense of competence. This is reflected in the dislike of being wrong about something. This common characteristic has been something of a problem in the development of our own field—although it is a feature of all scientific inquiry. And it is possible to be wrong even in a field as value based as psychotherapy. Not all differentiations and structures have equal categorical incisiveness.

It is important to appreciate that the feeling of self-esteem derived from established mental structures is not the same as self-image but is based on the experience of the burden of processing unstructured experience and the sense of the ease that comes with the organizing and structuring of experience. This leads patients to be generally reluctant to suspend the established structuring of their thoughts. Free association, which was Freud's original formulation of what is required in psychotherapy, is difficult. It also requires high levels of trust. Trust has to be present both in the self and in the other. The trust in the self is in the capacity both to tolerate the loss of structure and to recreate functioning structures when required. The trust in the other is a trust not only in the specific present other but also in the environment more generally.

To relinquish the organization and structure of thought is a form of regression and one of the most powerful of the factors that push the patient into a dependent relationship with the psychotherapist. Michael Balint pointed out that there are many factors which push the patient into a dependent relationship.

> This is inevitable, and the only question is how much dependence is desirable. . . . The real question is how much dependence consti-tutes a good starting-point for a successful therapy and when does it turn into an obstacle. [Balint, 1964, p. 248]

Psychic change

The extent to which psychic structures have to be loosened to allow particular problematic structures to be given up—or at least to operate less powerfully—is a major source of debate in psychother-apy. There are also important differences over the extent to which the aim of any particular course of treatment is the modification of a particular problematic psychic structure or a more extensive reshaping of psychic development. From this latter perspective it becomes clear that psychotherapy is as much an educational as a health-related project.

The dissolution of familiar psychic structures is very difficult, but the continuing unacceptability of memories or desires and feel-ings such as rage, guilt, and shame associated with them are crucial factors. These give the internal working models much greater force than their familiarity. They are dynamic structures. It is the function of the therapist to allow dynamic structures to come into view but to contain them as feelings and thoughts and carefully limit their development within the psychotherapy into actions.

These dynamic structures may come into view as a result of observing and listening to the patient individually or in a group. A vital element of this is what comes into view in the relationship between the patient and the psychotherapist. In psychoanalytic terms this second process (allowing the dynamic structures to appear in the patient–psychotherapist relationship) is the establishment of the transference. The question of how—including how far and how rapidly—to allow the transference to develop is a key problem. It is a problem over which the psychotherapist has only limited influence. The psychotherapist's management of the countertransference can also only ever be imperfect. Apart from the careful management of the extent to which the dynamic structures are acted upon in the psychotherapeutic relationship, there is no simple rule as to how to work with the transference. The nature of the transference will always depend upon how the psychotherapist is located in the internal models of the patients.

The psychotherapist's ability to manage the transference and countertransference starts with the recognition that this is what is happening. All schools of psychotherapy recognize that the psychotherapist inevitably becomes part of the patient's system of relationships and therefore of the patient's emotional world. Important divisions arise, first over the significance of this, second over how far to allow this to develop (in so far as it is within the ability of the psychotherapist to control it), and third over whether to explain, or interpret, it to the patient. The process of containing the transference and the countertransference is a combination of abstention (the maintenance of boundaries), empathic response, and interpretation. The empathic response should not be confused with a mirroring response. The most effective empathic response may well be complementary rather than coincidental.

Bowlby justly called his trilogy *Attachment and Loss* not just *Attachment*. Attention, empathy, and attunement are important to the development of attachment, and also to the creation of the transference. Attunement includes responsiveness to the patient's anxieties and defences. These processes are to a great extent the prelude to therapy. The major work of psychotherapy is working through losses and the impact of loss. Loss in this context is a very broad term. It includes trauma, the loss of a facilitating environment, and the loss of integrity and a sense of continuing existence.

Any extensive work of this kind takes time. There are techniques that focus on particular psychic constructs that sometimes have dramatic effects. Short-term psychotherapies often create important breakthroughs—which also raise significant issues about follow-up care and support. Short-term work also offers the opportunity to

identify survival and management strategies that may be of great
value and allow reparative processes to develop in non-clinical
settings. Physiological reparative processes often take long periods
of time, may lead to less than ideal outcomes, and may leave the
patient in a condition that requires long-term continuing support.
Broadly the same is true of psychological reparative processes.

In long-term work a much greater proportion of the reparative
working through of losses will take place within the psychotherapy
relationship. This process of working through losses will revolve
around breaks, missed sessions, misunderstandings, developmental demands, harsh responses, or conflicts that coincide more or less
with the patient's past traumatic experiences of breaks and losses.
The therapeutic experience lies not just in the establishment of an
attuned attachment but in the repeated repair of breaks in the
attachment that, given the trauma of insecure attachment, is never
good enough.

Another important aspect of this management is the level of
availability of the psychotherapist and the intensity of the work. It
is difficult to assess the relationship between the level of contact
and the intensity of the work. It is important to clarify the reason-
ing behind a high level of contact. Some patients require a high
level of support and containment. This may be created by frequent
psychotherapy sessions, by a high level of availability, or by admis-
sion to a residential institution or psychotherapeutic community.
Even for those not resident in this way, attachment to groups or
institutions is undoubtedly important. On the other hand, a major
difficulty in institutional provision of psychotherapy lies in a reluctance to recognize the over-riding importance of attachment to a
specific individual.

With the great majority of patients living in the community
there are the issues of the frequency of contact and the availability
of the psychotherapist, or the team, to respond to the patient's
needs or demands. It is here that clinical decisions based on the
need for support and containment can become confused with the
extent of psychic change that is sought. There is a link in the sense
that greater change may be facilitated by greater support but the
link is not straightforward. It does not follow automatically that
more frequent contact produces greater intensity and therefore
greater psychic change.

Issues of frequency and availability are very difficult decisions in the management of psychotherapy. As so often occurs with theoretically difficult problems, rules of thumb developed that have sometimes been turned into tablets of stone. On the face of it, it may seem likely that infrequency and inflexibility will tend to foster avoidant attachment while frequency and availability will promote enmeshed attachment. However, it is not as simple as that. The patient who sees their psychotherapist infrequently may nevertheless be, consciously or unconsciously, extremely preoccupied with, and enmeshed in, the relationship. On the other hand, the patient who sees their psychotherapist regularly and frequently may have highly developed avoidant defence mechanisms.

A clinical story

What follows is a story to illustrate the nature of clinical experience in psychotherapy. This is a fictional description of a piece of psychotherapeutic work that shows how relationships shape what can be thought about and how this can develop so that changes in what can be thought about can reshape relationships. Stories are important in psychotherapy because stories are what patients bring. The relationship between the story and the theory is a key problematic in psychotherapy. It is not just confidentiality—important as that is—that demands that we address this problem at the level of stories rather than "case studies". To think in terms of stories also offers an appropriately tentative account of the status of the psychotherapist's perceptions and (explicit and implicit) interpretations.

This story incidentally touches on the link between attachment and sexual relating, and the place of the psychotherapeutic relationship in relation to other relationships. However, its central themes are the process of loosening an established structure to permit greater free association, the development of reflective function, and the establishment of new structures that permit greater flexibility and inclusiveness.

Michael is a gay man whose early attachments were disrupted. He wears clothes of hard cloth with clear cuts and sharp, dark colours.

People can see him from a distance and are to stay there. Part of Michael's motivation for coming to psychotherapy is that he has put on a lot of weight and fears that he might have a heart attack. His father died of a stroke some years previously. Michael readily accepts that the psychotherapy can not start immediately. When it does start he tends to arrive slightly early, he speaks very clearly, and he leaves readily at the end of the session.

Michael was an only child whose father worked in India and his mother would visit his father for long periods, leaving him behind with relatives and at boarding school. His narration of these events focuses on how well he had done at school and what a strong and independent character he had been. He describes being irritated, surprised, and concerned that his parents had been distressed on leaving him. He describes himself as having been calm and collected. There is no overt suggestion from him that he might have experienced loss and distress, although his narrative suggests some awareness of what he might be expected to feel.

Where distress does emerge is in one sexual relationship that developed an intense romantic dimension and in which he then felt abandoned. He has had many other sexual relationships with men. He says he has enjoyed sex, but when discussing his experiences in more detail he pulls faces expressive of a mixture of disgust and dismissiveness. The relationships have either been casual or have failed because, in his account, he became too insecure and demanding.

Since his father's death Michael has lived not far from his mother and he describes how they live parallel lives. There are regular minor conflicts but the major unresolved, and now unspoken, conflict between them is about their feelings towards his father. Michael expressed a strong concern that the psychotherapist would "make him" move away from his mother.

After about a year there is a break in the therapy created by Michael taking a holiday in Sri Lanka. Towards the end of the session just before the break he tells of a sexual assault that he experienced when he was a young man that he says he has not thought about for years. This assault occurred at that time in his life when he was beginning to identify himself as gay. He had taken his much younger cousin to a park. In an isolated area he noticed a man coming up behind him and saw that he had only a T-shirt on. He walked faster but the man ran up and knocked him to the ground. He shouted to his cousin to run, which she did. The man was on top of him and he agreed to oral sex to avoid intercourse. This took place briefly; the man heard people approaching and ran off.

The most marked element of his narrative is its dismissive quality. The psychotherapist is left wondering what to say, given the gap between the story Michael is telling and the absence of any strong feelings about it. He does express feelings related to a sense of inadequacy over not having confronted the man more forcefully and over not having wanted a prosecution. He feels that he should have been tougher. He expresses these feelings in a very distant way, as if they concerned a generalized image of how somebody should behave rather than something that very directly concerns him.

The psychotherapist feels this dissociation too. Here is this painful story but the psychotherapist feels perplexed. It seems right to acknowledge the horror of the episode but to focus too much on that would tend to reinforce the splitting off of his feelings about it from the rest of his experience. On the other hand he is describing a sexual assault, and the links with his sexual development at the time need to be considered very carefully. There are many points of interest to the story but pursuing these raises problems of intrusion and re-enactment. In the meantime his feelings seem to have run off with the child he was caring for.

The psychotherapist says, "It occurs to me that to negotiate to the point of agreeing to have oral sex you must have had some kind of conversation with this man." He replies very thoughtfully "Yes, I suppose that's true." The word conversation is deliberately chosen because of its ordinariness, because it emphasizes the creation of a relationship, however brief and unwanted, and because it links the episode to what the patient and the psychotherapist are doing in the room now. The psychotherapist could be tempted to condemn the attacker as if there is no link between the image of the psychotherapist and that of the attacker. That would avoid Michael's fears about what the psychotherapist might make him do, and how these fears are linked to his unconscious fears in relation to the break.

He comes to the session after his holiday with a new story. He was walking along a busy street in a day-dream. An elderly man approached him selling lottery tickets. He said "No" a bit angrily. The man smiled and touched the patient on the shoulder and walked on. As he walked on Michael broke down and cried. The intensity of the emotion as he tells this story is very great.

The psychotherapist suggests that there might be a link between this story and that of the assault. The interpretation of the link is: "Here was a man who wanted something, but when the patient said 'No', the man not only accepted that but touched him in a gentle and undemanding way." The patient makes the link unconsciously much faster than he makes it consciously. As an apparent *non sequitur* he says, "Well, I don't know about that, but another thing has occurred to me while I have been away. Maybe I am wrong to think that you will make me move away from my mother; maybe there could just be some changes in the relationship."

The theme that emerges through the unconscious associations concerns the metaphor of the intervention of a man (his father, the ticket-seller, the rapist, or the therapist) for his relationship to mother. Does this intervention mean that he loses both his parents, which would be close to his early experience? Does it mean that he has to split himself between an adult part that manages things as well as he can and a child part of himself that runs off?

Far from displacing his feelings away from the psychotherapeutic rela-tionship, this development creates a space in which Michael can explore some of the feelings that have arisen within the psychotherapy. The attribution of meaning and significance is central to the establishment of psychic structures. Ferenczi spoke of a confusion of tongues between adults and children as children encounter the adult world. To allow this confusion to come into the open and to be explored and clarified requires a context in which this is possible and even then there are risks.

To bring out the transference with Michael requires such a risk, but this is now building on an encounter with his internal experience that has taken place within a setting in which his sense of vulnerability and dependency in relation to the psychotherapist did not have to be faced immediately and directly. Arriving at a session shortly after the break Michael is very upset that the psychotherapist does not say his name over the entry-phone. This seems reasonable to the psychotherapist because other people use the building and not everybody wants their name announced to whoever is by the door. There is a difference in the attribution of meaning and significance. The psychotherapist is manag-ing a practical problem; the patient is bringing a state of emotional vulnerability and need. The psychotherapist asks: "Is it that it would be a sign of love if I said your name?"

Michael recognizes the truth of this immediately and then is angry with the psychotherapist both for saying this and for misleading him in the first place. Every kind word the psychotherapist has said has been taken as evidence that the psychotherapist feels towards the patient as the patient feels towards the psychotherapist and has contributed to a fantasy that the psychotherapist might love him in the same way. He feels very powerless and humiliated. Caught between a sense of rejection and foolishness, working through feelings of humiliation, is one of the most difficult tasks for patients in psychotherapy.

The idea that the child's loving feelings derived from attachment can be translated into a life-long bond by imagining the relationship as a romantic, and ultimately sexual, relationship provides a central drama of psychotherapy. There are serious dangers of taking the patient's feelings as straightforward expressions of love. An alternative danger lies in a taboo on tenderness. The psychotherapist also needs to beware of making a demand that the patient experience what the patient does not, at least consciously, feel. As Michael comes to understand that these are passionate feelings that he has avoided for a long time he feels much stronger.

Soon after this experience, Michael announces that he has rearranged his house so there is room to take in a lodger. He is open enough by now to consider seriously the possibility that this is a symbolic rearrangement signifying the fact that he is now ready to have an adult partner of his own and that his mother will not be destroyed by this. One of the most important things he can take from psychotherapy is the possibility of a new relationship. The other is what makes it possible, which is a new-found flexibility in his response to other people and to experience.

The attachment figure

The concept of a secure base raises the question of the characteristics of the attachment figure. Bowlby described attachment behaviour as seeking "proximity to some other differentiated and preferred individual, who is usually conceived as stronger and/or wiser" (Bowlby, 1977). There is a danger of idealizing the therapy relationship and obscuring the uncomfortable reality that, in Balint's terms, regression can take malignant as well as benign forms. The risks associated with regression are well known to clinicians and individual patients. They are associated with the fears of the general public and account for an element of the scepticism about psychotherapy.

There is also a risk that psychotherapists will develop an exaggerated belief in their status as the stronger and/or wiser figures that they are conceived as being. When this is coupled with a strongly held position on social, political, or religious questions there is a powerful danger of the therapist using his or her unquestioned image as a stronger and wiser figure to give authority to a supposedly definitive account of the patient's narrative, both in relation to its history and the future. However, it is clearly not possible to exclude values or to dismiss the idea that the psychotherapist is in some way offering to serve as a stronger and wiser figure—if only in a limited context.

In considering parenting, extensive research has shown correlations between attachment insecurities in parents and attachment insecurities in children. Research by Dozier and others has found that insecure psychotherapists (that is psychotherapists classified as insecure through the Adult Attachment Interview) tended to reinforce their patients' insecure attachment styles, whereas clinicians rated as secure were likely to redress these difficulties (Dozier, Cue, & Barnett (1994). In the story of Michael it required a sense of security in the psychotherapist to recognize Michael's appeal for love but contain the psychotherapist's own emotional response to this appeal (which could either be rejection and withdrawal or a reciprocal falling in love). This sense of security was also required to risk talking about it with Michael and facing his disappointment and anger.

In describing psychotherapists as secure or insecure it is important to recall the nature of these attachment styles (about which more will be said below). Sroufe and Waters offered a useful comment on their status: "Attachment is not viewed as a static trait; rather it has the status of an intervening variable or an organizational construct . . . In this view, behaviour is predictably influenced by context rather than constant across situations" (Sroufe & Waters, 1977a). Attachment figures—whether psychotherapists, parents, or any others—do not have to be paragons. They do have to be able to function securely in the particular contexts in which others are dependent upon them.

An important function of psychotherapy is to create a positive process in which the development of greater felt security supports the development of reflective function that supports a stronger sense of felt security. This does not proceed smoothly. Felt security is experienced in relation to exploration and possible threat. A feeling of safety that is based upon a tacit agreement between the patient and the psychotherapist to indefinitely exclude what is difficult is a form of insecurity. As the process develops it will be possible to encounter and reflect upon experiences, or aspects of experiences, that were previously excluded. These may be remembered or imagined in the future, but they will have some kind of representative in the present encounter in the consulting room. These encounters may, at least temporarily, throw the process into reverse as there is a feeling of threat and insecurity. The psychotherapist has to have a strong enough sense of felt security of his or her own to work through this negative reaction and sustain the exploration of the difficult experience and the patient's internal world.

The hierarchy of attachment

Attachment research supports the view that different attachment relationships are formed with different figures and that these are hierarchically organized. The present state of research points to a range of attachment internal working models that, in so far as they are not integrated, are also in some way hierarchically organized. These models will incorporate basic choices in attachment relationships and will interact with each other. This is less immediately evident in Michael's story, as a dominant avoidant attachment style reflects an avoidant relationship with both central attachment figures. There is evidence of an underlying enmeshed relationship with his mother, but also with his dead father.

One of the tasks of the psychotherapist is to recognize the kind of attachment figure that they are being invited to be. A strong theme early on in the story of Michael is the strange figure that makes him do something that he does not want to do. The psychotherapist as this figure is associated with his father and with his parent's removal to India. This figure reappears in the sexual assault, and then in the form of the lottery ticket-seller. A partial resolution of his fear and hatred of this figure allows another figure to appear. This is a figure who does not love him enough and treats him as just part of the day's work. In the story this appears not so much as a maternal figure but as an integrated image of both parents—who were away for long periods in India together.

The hierarchy of attachment may shape the figures identified in later life as capable of reshaping the internal working models of attachment formed in early life. This may have an impact on both an individual's choice of therapist and on which attachment experiences are reworked primarily within the therapy setting and which are primarily reworked outside it. In an anxiety to demonstrate the psychotherapeutic process at work, the importance of the patient's experiences and relationships outside the psychotherapeutic relationship is often overlooked. There is a school of thought that only values what is worked through within the therapy. In this view the psychotherapist must be at the top of the attachment hierarchy so that the conflicts are worked through in the clinical setting.

It is hard to see why this is necessarily so or indeed that it can ever be absolutely so. It may be that the idea of the centrality of the analyst is in part the result of confusion over the significance of the much stronger idea that any conflict is somehow represented in the consulting room. Working through the conflicts outside the clinical setting may have attendant risks but there are people other than the therapist capable of sustaining negative transferences and working through experiences of separation, whether as partners or colleagues or teachers. The lottery ticket-seller represents all of these figures.

This is not to deny that the psychotherapist always needs to be open to the patient's conflicts being worked through in the psychotherapy relationship. This means, in particular, looking at what the therapist is doing to avoid them; that is to say, what the therapist is doing to avoid intimacy or to avoid conflict. The response to Michael as he tells the story of the assault is an example of this. A formulaic response to the horror of the assault would have avoided a possible conflict associated with not taking it seriously enough, and the latent conflict over the role of the psychotherapist. However, it would also have avoided the intimacy of the felt experience. The response to Michael over the entry-phone is another example. The creation of a context in which risks can be taken is not necessarily achieved by increasing the number of sessions. It is not necessarily best promoted by an insistence that the significant transferences must appear within the psychotherapeutic relationship. This approach will frequently be experienced as oppressive and foster a strong negative reaction. There is likely to be a further struggle if this negative reaction is then interpreted as a manifestation of the transference.

Attachment styles and the development of felt security

Much of the research effort based on attachment theory has focused on the delineation of attachment styles—secure, insecure avoidant (also referred to as dismissive), insecure enmeshed (also referred to as preoccupied or resistant), and insecure disorganized (also referred to as chaotic or fearful—the latter term referring to fear of the attachment figure himself or herself). Researchers have explored the question of the stability over time of these attachment styles and their intergenerational transmission.

Attachment styles are not indispensable to attachment theory but they have become a key element of its development. The questions of their validity, status, and clinical implications have to be addressed if the theory is to develop in a way that is adequate to the phenomena that it seeks to explain. For many research purposes these styles are treated as classifications, and it is important to understand the relationship between this use of the concept and the perception of attachment security and insecurity as psychological positions that we may all occupy at different times. The value of the concept of attachment styles in the experience of clinicians is an issue that ought to concern researchers as well as clinicians themselves.

The avoidant style is more controlled, distanced, and verbally coherent but possibly emotionally inauthentic. It is traditionally associated with father. The clinical picture of avoidant attachment includes resistance to entering the psychotherapy relationship, denial of the need for help, distraction from emotional issues, a focus on practical issues, turning away from difficult emotions if they do start to appear, and missing sessions. The enmeshed style is emotionally present but verbally incoherent and pre-occupied and is traditionally associated with mother. In psychotherapy these individuals often appear as very needy, dependant, uncontained, and demanding a lot of the psychotherapist. These characteristics will sometimes appear briefly and intensely in the person with an avoidant style but be quickly suppressed. Linking the Adult Attachment Interview (the standard method of assessing attachment styles) with home studies and monitoring of cardiac arousal also suggest that enmeshed attachment characteristically underlies avoidant attachment (Ainsworth, Blehar, Waters, & Wall, 1978; Sroufe & Waters, 1977b).

The story of Michael presents an avoidant man—out of touch with his feelings about the departure of his parents, and distant from sexual partners and others who might be intimates. He lives close to his mother but maintains an emotional distance from her. He is physically carefully presented in a way that discourages a warm or intimate connection. This avoidant position is not sustained through the psychotherapy.

The construction of classifications into which people can be allocated has always created difficulties for psychotherapists. Classification may be found to be useful for purposes of assessment and diagnosis but the experience of clinicians is that in the clinical setting the limits of any such system are exposed. This is the case with attachment styles considered as classifications. Attachment styles manifest at the original interview are not maintained consistently over the course of the therapy. In many cases different defensive formations appear as the therapy unfolds and the defensive formations themselves become more fluid. Indeed, part of the aim of psychotherapy is that they should become more fluid, and therefore more responsive, without collapsing into disorganization. That the therapist should offer a secure base is a commentary on what is required of the therapist, not on the attitude to the therapist of the patient.

Attachment styles—including secure attachment—are developed structures through which the experience of the world is made manageable. It is important not to consider attachment styles as necessarily rigid classifications but to see them as psychological positions that are available and are more or less habitually taken up, fallen into, or refused. Their appearance of rigidity derives from the power of developed structures discussed earlier. An individual has a number of internal working models for attachment, one of which is usually dominant. Thus, there are alternative attachment styles available. This is quite compatible with a high level of consistency in the attachment styles observed by researchers.

The significance of Michael's avoidant attachment style is that there is an internal conflict that is not openly expressed. His ready acceptance that he could not start in psychotherapy straight away pointed to his reluctance to engage in this conflict. He would have been in some ways relieved if he had not been able to do so at all. Consistent with the avoidant style, he is clear in his statements and commitments and in his determination to do things properly. He does not show reluctance to leave but there is a hint of an unresolved need in that he arrives slightly early. This does not leave his need exposed as much as resistance to leaving would have done.

However, this avoidant attachment pattern has to be understood in the context of a hierarchy of attachments and Michael's reluctance to explore new relationships. Alongside the avoidant presentation Michael's location might suggest a significant current of enmeshed attachment to his mother. As the psychotherapy develops it also becomes clear that there is a strong,unconscious, enmeshed attachment to his father. Michael says that he and his mother get on very well. They have conflicts but they don't discuss his father. They are both locked into a conscious avoidance and unconscious enmeshment with his dead father: an unresolved mourning. Michael knows that his mother will die, sooner or later. Until that time she is a bulwark against any other close relationships that will disturb his established attachment system.

The repeatedly expressed concern that the psychotherapist will make him move away from his mother can reasonably be interpreted as an indirect expression of a wish. He says that he is not prepared to move for his mother's sake. He accepts that this thought may be a reflection of his own fears but he excludes this thought by treating it as an academic observation. It makes no immediate difference to his mental picture of his relationship with his mother or his image of what he has to fear from the psychotherapy. However, the idea gradually becomes more manageable. It is in this context that the encounter with the seller of lottery tickets could be understood as representing a belated blessing from his father and the beginnings of an acceptance of the separation.

Anxious attachment, rigidity, and exploration

Individuals build up more than one internal working model. What happens to old internal working models as new ones develop is an important theoretical question. Older and more fundamental internal working models are retained—often unconsciously—even though later, more sophisticated, internal working models are also adopted. The reversion to earlier internal working models can be triggered by experiences.

The pattern of an avoidant style giving way to an emerging enmeshed style is representative of a great many clinical reports. It is important to recognize that this process works in the other direction also. The apparently needy and dependent patient may have a highly distanced and functioning aspect to them that appears in other areas of their life. From time to time an event may occur that appears to require a practical response. This may have the effect of making this functional aspect visible to the psychotherapist where it is normally hidden. The recognition of the enmeshed patient's capacity to manage and to sustain themselves in the face of the other (often experienced as hostile) is as important as the provision of a space in which the avoidant patient's dependency can emerge.

The common theme is that through these movements between different positions and the development of reflective function there is an overall move towards greater security. Alongside alternative internal working models coming forward there is also a process of the grip of internal working models weakening. The weakening of the grip of established internal working models has important clinical implications. It is important to consider risks. The giving up of habitual patterns of organization is likely to be painful and associated with efforts to achieve a radical and urgent response to the experience of disorganization and pain. The story of Michael is a story of the containment of these emotions and the risks that they bring. The story could have been one of a more disintegrative crisis.

Mary Ainsworth spoke of the "continuity linking the organisation of attachment to the mother with the organisation of social–emotional behaviour" (Ainsworth, 1982). The kernel of the development of all three insecure attachment styles is the separation response observable in infants and young children. The sequence identified by John Bowlby and Mary Ainsworth is protest–despair–detachment. This sequence corresponds to enmeshed attachment–disorganized attachment–avoidant attachment. This sequence is retraced and worked over in psychotherapy. The transition through a painful state of dependence is a powerful motive for resistance in psychotherapy. Moreover, the state of disintegration and despair is intensely threatening and is the ground for self-destructive and suicidal acts. The sequence of separation responses both illuminates how it is that attachment styles become unclear in the therapeutic process and goes deeper than the cognitive issues in accounting for the strong resistance to change.

The distinguishing features of secure and insecure attachment are the level of anxiety and rigidity present. Secure attachment in adults means the acceptance of separation and the establishment of internal working models of available attachment figures in both the internal and the external world. Secure attachment offers flexibility and openness to exploration. Insecure attachment, in whatever form, constitutes the continuing active presence of outmoded working models. These are the models that shape the pressures that form the transference. Whether conceptualized as ego strength, a reduction in transferential pressures, the establishment of the depressive position, empowerment, autonomy, or an ability to learn new models of behaviour—a relative freedom from outmoded and restrictive internal working models—has long been recognized as a key goal of psychotherapy. However, the progress to this desired end is far from direct.

Whether the focus is on the gains in freedom and flexibility or on the risks the difficulty is that in any long term extensive work there is no counter-factual. The work is so individual that stories play a key role in transmitting understanding of the psychotherapeutic process. Patients (and those who care about them) are left with questions: would I have felt better anyway?; would I have had a period of disintegration anyway?; were the emotionally difficult disintegrative experiences worth the gain?

At the start of this paper there was reference to the need to establish what we meant by psychotherapy working. The objectives of psychotherapy within the framework of attachment theory could be described as a greater sense of secure attachment. This means that there is an internal model of attachment figures available when sought, and a corresponding greater ability to identify attachment figures in the external world and to turn to them when they are needed. The counterpart to this is a diminution of the anxieties and rigidities of insecure attachment patterns. The consequence of this greater sense of security will be a greater willingness to explore.

The Adult Attachment Interview is a well-tested methodology linked to this clear—and necessarily incomplete—conceptualization of the aims of psychotherapy. The problem of the evidential base for psychotherapy, including the debate about what constitutes evidence, and the limitations of particular forms of evidence, will remain with us for a long time. The Adult Attachment Interview offers one means of carrying out broader studies on the effectiveness of psychotherapy—and of particular psychotherapeutic approaches.

Conclusion

This paper started with the claim that it is essential to carry forward our thinking about how and why psychotherapy works. It went on to consider the contribution that attachment theory can make to this endeavour. Just as attachment theory does not claim to be a complete theory of the personality so it enables the setting of more limited and specific objectives for psychotherapy—and therefore of criteria against which to assess whether psychotherapy is working.

The attachment bond is fundamental to early life and to the practice of psychotherapy. Attachment theory offers an elegant account of the fundamental link between relationships, feelings, and cognitive processes. This account is constructed in such a way that it makes it possible to take the research effort beyond the individual clinical account drawn from the consulting room without breaking faith with a clinical sensibility.

References

Ainsworth, M. (1982). Attachment: retrospect and prospect. In: *The Place of Attachment in Human Behaviour* (p. 9). London: Tavistock.
Ainsworth M., Blehar, M., Waters, E., & Wall, S. (1978). *Patterns of Attachment: A Psychological Study of the Strange Situation*. Hillsdale, NJ: Erlbaum.

Balint, M. (1964). *The Doctor, the Patient and the Illness*. London: Tavistock.

Bion, W. (1977). *Seven Servants: Four Works*. New York: Aranson.

Bowlby, J. (1969). *Attachment (Attachment and Loss*, vol. 1). London: Hogarth Press and the Institute of Psychoanalysis.

Bowlby, J. (1977). The making and breaking of affectional bonds. *British Journal of Psychiatry, 130*: 203.

Bowlby, J. (1979). *The Making and Breaking of Affectional Bonds*. London: Tavistock.

Dozier, M., Cue, K., & Barnett, L. (1994). Clinicians as caregivers: role of attachment organisation in treatment. *Journal of Consulting and Clinical Psychology, 62*: 793–800.

Matte Blanco, I. (1971). Review of *Attachment. International Journal of Psychoanalysis, 52*: 199.

Sroufe, L. A., & Waters, E. (1977a). Attachment as an organisational construct. *Child Development, 48*: 1184–1199.

Sroufe, L. A., & Waters, E. (1977b). Heart rate as a convergent measure in clinical and developmental research. *Merill-Palmer Quarterly, 23*: 3–27.

CHAPTER TEN

The big picture

Carol Holmes

The fact that the discipline of psychotherapy is recognizable by over four hundred competing models attests to its lack of a unified theory and it is this feature more than anything else that underlines the fact that we don't know how psychotherapy works. What we do know is that these factions in psychotherapy are implicitly or explicitly committed to a particular philosophy of human nature that informs their conception of health and their method for achieving this satisfactory state. Existential psychotherapy, for example, is grounded in existential philosophy, and the phenomenological method and its practitioners view the recognition of anxiety as an indication and positive sign of the person's understanding of their uncertain and mortal position in the world. Psychoanalysis, on the other hand, considers the prevalence of anxiety as an indication of unconscious conflict and psychopathology that requires psychoanalytic intervention. Each school within the profession is therefore underpinned by a philosophy that determines its conceptualizations of both mental health and pathology. Furthermore, unlike the scientific tradition, the schisms that characterize the field of psychotherapy are further compounded and estranged by a general lack of dialogue and cooperation between therapists and researchers from these competing hypothetical approaches. As Feltham points out "It is arguable that the field of twentieth-century psychotherapy has been fundamentally characterised by serious disagreement on views of human nature, aetiology of psychological dysfunction, treatment rationales and goals" (1997, p. 1). Feltham further claims that these divisions interfere with the likelihood of systematically examining these significant inconsistencies and suggests that we have difficulty in questioning our assertions of truth and reality: "It seems to me that we are as least as resistant to examining our therapeutic truth claims as our clients often are to examining their longstanding and unproductive scripts and narratives" (ibid., p. 2). I believe that it is not the lack of certainty that inhibits our ability to better understand how psychotherapy works, but the certainty with which psychotherapists from these clannish schools cling tenaciously to their denominational positions. From my own experience there also seems to be a general lack of courtesy, regard, and modesty on the part of psychotherapists for any position other than their own.

There have been numerous systematic investigations (both quantitative and qualitative) to show the benefits of psychotherapy from different therapeutic perspectives. Yet many researchers who have studied the methodological soundness of these enquiries assert that there are far too may uncontrolled research variables to be able to adequately appraise their effectiveness (Kline, 1984, 1992). In a similar vein Howard argues that "The counselling industry has reached (much) too far beyond its current ability to define, develop and assess its theories, practices and purposes" (1999, p. 270). Holmes and Lindley (1989), examining the value of psychotherapy, found that no one form of psychotherapy could be considered to be more effective than any other. Even though there is some agreement across the schools that a positive therapeutic outcome is related to the quality of the therapeutic relationship, each tradition is prone to define and describe therapeutic efficacy from their inimitable perspectives.

The notion of bias implies a preference, and although we would prefer to believe that our choice of therapeutic approach and the theories of human nature that inform them are based on objective criteria, it would not be unreasonable to conjecture that our choice of model—either for our own treatment or training—is likely to be based on personal beliefs and philosophies.

There is also an ongoing dispute between the schools about whether psychotherapy should be aligned to the arts and considered a creative pursuit, or whether it should conform to the more exacting principles that govern the physical sciences. However, as evidence from studies carried out in the field of quantum physics has revealed, the physical world and its contents is in itself produced and sustained by a process of essential interconnectedness, entanglement, paradox, and uncertainty, which scientists themselves admit that they do not understand (Bohm, 1980; Bohr, 1958; Heisenberg, 1958). The scientific community is, therefore, not only prepared to acknowledge the absence of a unified theory of science, they also endorse the significant subjective influence that the observer has on the subject under observation in terms of outcomes. It would seem, therefore, that science has more in common with the creative process than is suggested by the empirical method. Furthermore, scientific knowledge, unlike psychotherapy has progressed by a succession of world-views.

I believe that it is important to acknowledge that this paper is therefore a summation of my own considered, albeit idiosyncratic, beliefs and ideas about what kind of interpersonal issues may help to tentatively explain how I view the function of psychotherapy. Given my own interest in the interface between science, psychotherapy, and the creative process, I have chosen to use the metaphor of the hologram as a symbolic means of illustrating my own interpersonal perspective, which originates in the communicative approach to psychotherapy developed by Langs. The case study presentation will also be explored from this same holistic, relational position. First, however, I will summarize some related theories of psychotherapeutic cure that, in my opinion, form part of the surrounding philosophical field in which this approach is located.

Psychoanalysis is a one-person approach in so far as one individual, the analyst, is expected to be able to analyse the unconscious, aggressive, sexual impulses and disappointments (related to the past) that are interfering with another person's (the patient's) capacity to relinquish their familial ties and to develop and maintain satisfying mature personal relationships. The concept of transference is the principal meta-psychological tool that powers the psychoanalytic process. It refers to the patient's tendency to transfer and distort unconscious beliefs and wishes related to early significant figures on to the analyst. The concept of countertransference, introduced by Freud in 1910 (1910d) and described by him as the analyst's "blind spots", implies a degree of symmetry between patient and analyst. However, Freud believed that with regular periods of self-analysis these countertransference reactions could and should be overcome. Paula Heimann (1950), a Kleinian analyst, pioneered the new trend that focused on the efficacious and perceptive nature of the analyst's countertransference reactions. The innovative concept of projective identification, developed by Klein in 1946, and Bion's (1959) subsequent scholarly contributions, helped to clarify the interpersonal elements of the analytic process, the mother–infant interaction, and some of the complexities of countertransference. However, it would appear that although the analyst may on occasions be subject to their own transferential experiences, they are, in the main and in contrast to the patient, considered to be able to differentiate them from the incisive facet of countertransference due to their lengthy training analysis. Within this theoretical framework, the psychoanalytic process is therefore based on the difference between patient and analyst, as the patient's relationship to the analyst is based primarily on a misconception that is rooted in the past. Through a process of exploration and interpretation the analyst is expected to enable the patient to become more aware of the source of their idiosyncratic interpersonal distortions, how they are impinging on the here-and-now encounter and their current relationships outside of therapy.

Robert Langs (1973) is known primarily as the founder of the controversial and radically contrasting approach to psychoanalysis referred to as the communicative psychotherapy. Langs' model is informed by ideas from systems theory and evolutionary psychology. Communicative psychotherapy is diametrically opposed to psychoanalysis, in so far as the notion of transference is replaced by unconscious perception, which is the patient's innate ability to comprehend interpersonal reality. Therapist madness, on the other hand, unlike its countertransference counterpart, clearly acknowledges the practitioner's inevitable resistance to consistently manage the boundaries of the therapeutic relationship. Therapist madness is explained by Langs as follows: "The psychotherapist is involved in a situation where his or her greatest vulnerabilities and psychotic anxieties are certain to be evoked from time to time.

Because of this, a measure of error—an expression of madness—is inevitable" (1988, p. 192). The communicative paradigm also diverges with classical psychoanalysis in its assertion that it is the patient's, rather than the analyst's, curative capacity that guides the treatment process. According to the communicative model, the unconscious mind is programmed to make rapid and perceptive judgements about other people. The significance of unconscious communication is endorsed by research carried out in the field of cognitive psychology (Haskell, 1999), and studies from experimental psychology (Dixon, 1971). Unconscious perception is expressed primarily through the mechanisms of displacement and disguise, and can be recognized as stories or narratives that refer to the behaviour of people and situations that are overtly unrelated to the clinical situation but that are considered to be accurate depictions of the patient's unconscious interpersonal concerns about the immediate encounter. In essence, communicative technique is organized around the therapist's recognition and confirmation of the patient's unconscious perceptions of the therapist's management of the relationship. The technique of communicative psychotherapy is characterized by its systemic and interpersonal focus in which both parties are viewed as giving and receiving interpersonal insights, although the individual roles that typically distinguish the therapeutic relationship are seen as less clearly defined, often interchangeable, and more complementary. The approach therefore endorses the dynamic, fluid, and paradoxical qualities of both members' roles within the interaction.

In his attempt to address some of the criticisms levelled against psychoanalysis Langs has seen fit to almost totally reverse the aptitudes that have been applied to the patient and analyst. Unconscious perception, which is a capacity applied to the patient in communicative psychotherapy, corresponds to the definition of countertransference as a form of resonance and affective insight that is applicable to the analyst in psychoanalytic psychotherapy. Therapist madness differs from transference and the original meaning of countertransference in so far as it is not based on distortions linked to the past. Instead, it is viewed as inherently connected to ontic and ontological issues, such as death-anxiety and concerns about separateness and intimacy that define the human condition. These factors have led me to reconsider the interface between the apparently disparate schools of existential philosophy and communicative psychotherapy (Holmes, 1998, 2001).

Although the communicative paradigm is at odds with the major tenets of psychoanalysis, Langs' convictions have led to similar criticisms as those levelled against Freud. Both Freud and Langs are joined by their allegiance to science and in their need to establish the truth of their distinctive theories of human nature. Freud employed the hydraulic method of late nineteenth-century physics as a symbolic means of demonstrating the credibility of his metapsychological theory of the mind. Langs has attempted to establish his model by applying knowledge drawn from twentieth-century physics. However, although he has insisted that his principles are universally applicable and readily testable, he has neglected to provide the necessary data to support this assertion. In my opinion Langs' prescriptive, technical, and clinical procedures have undermined the more important dynamic, relational, creative, and interconnected scientific components of his work, which are intimately linked to the ongoing vicissitudes of human relating that have also been highlighted by philosophers of the existential tradition.

In the main, people seek therapeutic help with problems that tend to interfere with their day-to-day existence, which inevitably include relationship difficulties.

Existential psychotherapy is concerned with helping the client to differentiate between their assumptions, which are often values unknowingly borrowed from significant others, and their own personal values. Existential psychotherapy is grounded in the European tradition of existential philosophy, dedicated to the examination of the dilemmas and paradoxes of the human condition. The approach gives credence to both the limits and opportunities of existence and the link between the two. As existential psychotherapy is concerned with the ontological, rather than psychological, realm of being, it is pledged to the phenomenological method, which allows the client to cognitively reflect upon and explore with the therapist how they experience themselves in the physical world and with others. The aim of existential psychotherapy is described by Emmy van Deurzen-Smith: "The objective is not to make all the suffering go away, but rather to welcome it as evidence of one's particular position in the world, which can reveal our possibilities and limitations to us" (1997, p. 188).

Being-in-the-world by necessity entails being with others, as without other people there would be no existence. Being-with-others is therefore a primary constituent of human existence and as such is fraught with difficulties (Buber, 1958; Sartre, 1943; Tillich, 1952). The notion of "bad faith", developed by Sartre, has become a common term to represent the human tendency towards deception. Bad faith from a Sartrean perspective is the automatic defence mechanism that human beings employ in order to remain detached from themselves and others. Sartre pessimistically represents other people as a major threat to our freedom, which is why we are compelled to objectify them before they do the same to us. He further claims that this tension and struggle for power is a fundamental constituent that fuels our interactions with other people. The challenge of this aggressive and futile state of human affairs first and foremost requires the individual to humbly confront their own fears and self-deceptive ploys, which is hoped to stimulate their ability to experience others in a more benign and less biased way, with less fear of domination or the need to dominate.

In the main, existential psychotherapy is focused on the client's world-view and concentrates on relationships that are external to the therapeutic arena, with little consideration given to the therapeutic interaction itself. This tendency is supported in the writings and case study material presented by existential practitioners such as Spinelli (1989) and Cohn (1997). However, it is suggested by this author that this unilateral application is rather surprising, given that the approach is founded on a philosophy of human existence that gives precedence to being-with-others in the here-and-now. From this author's perspective the interpersonal axioms that govern communicative principles are supported by the relational propositions of the human condition that are fundamental to the European tradition of existential philosophy.

The following section is a summary of the mechanisms that are responsible for generating a holographic image. The analogy of the hologram is utilized as a means of illustrating the unified and interdependent qualities of the therapeutic relationship.

In 1947 Dennis Gabor established the ideas that led to the invention of the hologram. A hologram is produced by a process that is referred to as interference, i.e., the tangled pattern that emerges when at least two wave-like events in the medium of water, light, or radio, spread through and disturb each other. A hologram is created when a single laser beam—found to be an ideal medium for producing interference—is split into two separate beams. The initial beam is then reflected on to an object, and an interference pattern is created when the subsequent beam interacts with the reflected light of the first. This interaction is recorded on a portion of photographic film. At this stage the object is invisible, but as soon as another beam is flashed on to the film an image of the original object appears in a three-dimensional form. Those of you who have encountered this phenomenon, or who have seen a three-dimensional film, will know how uncannily tangible and realistic these images appear to be, even though there is really nothing there but a disembodied, non-existent representation, which immediately dematerializes when you try to touch it. But the most breathtaking and amazing characteristic of the hologram is the fact that if you cut a piece of the film containing the holographic image and then pass a laser beam through it, each piece of film still contains the whole image. No matter how much one continues to fragment the picture the image still retains its integrity and can still be seen in its entirety on each scrap of the film, although the picture will become progressively less clear.

The eminent neuropsychologist Karl Pribram is noted for his extensive work into the hologram-like nature of memory. Pribram (1966) hypothesized that the myriad of neurons in the brain, which are electrically charged and entangled with each other, might be acting to produce an incessant interference pattern like an internal hologram (remains open to question). Experiments carried out by Pribram (1991) have attempted to demonstrate that both memory and vision are stored holistically throughout the brain.

Although his work has been endorsed by a series of ingenious experiments carried out by Pietsch (1981), Pribram's holographic hypothesis remains open to question by those involved in the relatively new field of brain research. The hologram has also been used as an explanatory metaphor to understand both forgetting and remembering.

The ability to swiftly discern familiar faces and situations has been subject to scrutiny by van Heerden, a researcher at the Polaroid Research Laboratories in Massachusetts, who developed a holographic theory of memory known as *recognition holography* (1970). As Talbot explains

In recognition holography a holographic image of an object is recorded in the usual manner, save that the laser beam is bounced off a special kind of mirror known as a focusing mirror before it is allowed to strike the unexposed film. If a second object, similar but not identical to the first, is bathed in laser light and the light is bounced onto the film after it has been developed, a bright point of light will appear on the film. The brighter and sharper the point of light, the greater the degree of similarity between the first and second objects. If the two objects are completely dissimilar, no point of light will appear. [Talbot, 1996, pp. 22–23]

There have been a variety of other holographic procedures and research studies carried out by psychologists and neuroscientists, such as interference holography, which have examined how we are able to identify and detect any slight changes in known people and places from our distant past. The interference method reveals that any changes that have occurred after the original figure has been preserved will mirror the light in a different way.

The quantum physicist David Bohm is noted for his hypothesis that the entire universe functions as a hologram. The discovery that the electron, which is the most basic element of matter, can behave as either a particle or a wave and then reverse again, and the astounding realization that an electron only manifests as a particle when it was observed, led to Bohm's theory of the essential inter-connectedness of all matter (1980), which he refers to as *quantum wholeness*. Further investigations and experiments persuaded Bohm that the entire universe itself could be understood to conform to holographic principles. Bohm asserts that an electron is distributed throughout space in a similar way to the holographic image, which remains intact even when it is fragmented. He further avers that this metaphor helps to explain the fluidity and interchangeableness that exists between the observer and the observed. Nevertheless, Bohm acknowledges the problematical nature of holism and the difficulty of viewing the world in this undivided way, which contrasts with the irresistible human urge to fragment our experiences.

The metaphor of the hologram has also had an influence in the field of psychology and has been cited to help explain Jung's theory of the collective unconscious. The American psychiatrist Montague Ullman (1987) is known for his experiments into dreams; he believes that, in contrast to our waking life, dreams are character-ized by care and represent the individual's connection to the wider world in a holographic way. Levenson (1975) believes that dreams, in contrast to traditional psychoanalytic principles, are perceptive and sophisticated, rather than primitive experiences. He also suggests that the interpersonal experience of resonance that can occur between patient and therapist can help to explain the changes that occur in psychotherapy, and that it is resonance that enables unconscious holographic experiences to surface in a similar way to the emergence of the hologram, which is created from laser wave interference.

A vortex is a physical phenomenon, which can be exceedingly rigid while spiralling chaotically in a turbulently flowing river, and has been used as a metaphorical vehicle to explain the intractable thought processes that patients often struggle with. (Shainberg,, 1987). In David Shainberg's opinion, the rigid aspect of the vortex can be likened to sedimented thoughts and belief patterns that are frequently presented in psychotherapy. These structures interfere with the free-flowing movement of creative thought that is vital to mental and emotional well-being. This inflexible pattern not only creates divisions within the self, but also prevents the person from being in the world and with others in an open and unified way.

The following case study presentation will consider the way in which holographic principles can help to elucidate the intercon-nections between patient and therapist. The clinical example was kindly donated by a supervisee, and in order to maintain the patient's anonymity we shall call her Lorna.

Case study

Lorna is a female artist in her thirties, who has presented for ther-apy at the suggestion of her company, where she is employed to offer art classes to underprivileged children. She is also in the process of compiling an art exhibition of her own paintings. Lorna had been given the therapist's name and phone number by her boss, who was also paying for the sessions, and was to be seen in the therapist's private consulting rooms. The therapist said that she could offer her a twelve-week time-limited contract. The client replied that she didn't know exactly what to expect, as she had never been in therapy before. The therapist suggested an initial meeting.

First session

The client opened the session by saying "My boss said that coming to see you for a few sessions would be very useful." She went on to say, in a very charming way, that she didn't think that she was a particularly good candidate for therapy as she wasn't messed up enough, although she did have a high regard for therapists. She said she thought she would go along with her boss as there were a few things in her life that were troublesome. She talked about being an artist and the difficulty of making a living from it and that although her family was supportive, they didn't really approve as they felt she should have entered a proper profession such as law. She went on to talk about working with children and how rewarding she found this.

The therapist reiterated the basic ground rules of time, place, day, and number of sessions. A discussion about payment then ensued. Lorna said that the company would pay the therapist; however, she agreed when it was suggested that she should make the payments herself. She then went on to say that she didn't think that she would need twelve sessions. The therapist replied that this was the contract, but "Let's see how we go." Lorna laughed and seemed to indicate again that twelve sessions wouldn't be necessary, but agreed to go ahead starting from next week. Just before the time was up she mentioned that her brother had been killed six months ago and that she and her family were coping with it quite well. She seemed startled when the therapist said "It's time to finish."

Second session

Lorna said on her arrival that she nearly didn't come for the session as the weather was so awful and it was a long journey but she felt that she owed it to the therapist to turn up.

Brief silence.

Lorna: "What happens next? Are you going to ask me questions?" She got up from her chair and went to the window. "You notice that I have to bend my head to come in here." [Lorna is about six feet tall.] "Of course this is something I am used to." She also mentioned the slippery stairs.

Therapist: "Although you said you came for me you also mentioned other difficulties about the distance, the weather, and the stairs, and seem to be telling me what an effort it has been for you to attend this session."

Lorna sat down and said, :Yes. Yes, I wondered what I was going to say and whether I really wanted to say it." She then began to talk about her brother but said she didn't really want to talk about him, but she knew that this was probably why she was coming here. She went on to say she had lots of good friends with whom she had talked about her brother but it still hadn't made any difference.

Pause.

She then related how her brother, aged twenty-eight, had been killed in a car crash by a drunken driver and continued to talk on this subject until the end of the session. She said that her brother was perfect: very good-looking and very talented. She was the middle child and her older brother was not coping well as he was rather introverted. She mentioned that he had a girlfriend who was unhelpful and whom she disliked intensely. She said that her younger brother was the parents' favourite and that they were driving her crazy, as they were very demanding. She continued by saying that there was a court case pending and that her parents wanted her to set up a trust fund for him, then mentioned that her older brother had opted out of all this so the responsibility for the parents' demands fell on her shoulders.

Therapist: "It's time to finish."

Lorna: "I can't believe I talked so much."

The client stayed for the entire contract and always arrived on time.

Sixth session

Lorna said that she was finding the sessions very helpful but didn't understand why and that when she talked to friends they always had similar stories to tell of their own lives. Her friends said that she needed to go through all the stages of grieving but Lorna didn't believe them and thought it was a corny thing to say.

Sessions seven to ten

Lorna talked mostly about her art, which she connected to her brother's death.

The therapist connected her brother's death to the impending end (death) of their relationship. The client said she had begun to realize from her art that the theme of death was very prominent in her work, not only in relation to her brother. She said that as an artist she knew this intellectually but now she had a "raw awareness" of it.

Eleventh session

Lorna talked about preparing for her exhibition and about the preview, which her parents had attended. The client continued by saying that her mother was very angry and upset with her because she had spoken about the links between her art and her brother in relation to death, which her mother felt was unnecessary. The therapist then connected the client's associations to death to next week's final session and to the client's narrative of feeling unsupported. Lorna cried for the rest of the session.

Twelfth session

On her arrival Lorna said she wasn't going to talk about her brother as it was the last session. She then said that she had found the therapy very helpful, which had surprised her. She went on to say that she had decided to let her parents make the memorial for her brother on their own and she would do what she felt was right for her, even though she knew they would be angry and disappointed with her. She also said that she had not told her boss anything about her sessions, although her boss seemed very curious to know and had asked her on a few occasions how the therapy was going. At the end of the session Lorna shook hands with the therapist and thanked her.

During the early part of the therapy the therapist was only dimly aware of the impact that Lorna's material was having in relation to her own recent loss of her mother. Not only had the therapist at one time owned an art gallery, but the therapist's mother had also been an artist. As the therapy progressed the therapist realized that she had a strong desire to want to discuss art in general; she was also very curious to know more about the client's art and artistic ability.

Due to her own grief the therapist was aware of the.solipsistic nature of mourning. She also recognized that she felt a strong impetus to comfort and sympathize with the client, but felt she was more able to contain this affect when she could connect it to her own recent bereavement.

In the sessions Lorna had talked at some length about issues connected to ambivalence, of the difficulty of needing to be independent but also of the need for an intimate relationship. At various points in the therapy she had talked about being an artist, which required her to be isolated, and she wondered if this meant she wouldn't be able to have a close personal relationship. The client also felt ambivalent about being with her friends and the need to be alone.

The therapist also felt ambivalent about the inclusion of a third party, the client's boss, who was paying for the therapy, and concerned about the lack of privacy, as the boss had contacted the therapist for information about the client. She was also unsure whether it was appropriate to see the client as the therapy was instigated by her boss rather than herself.

Themes of the fear of exploitation and lack of support were also woven into the client's material in relation to her parents, boss, and the therapist. The therapist was also concerned about her own lack of support in terms of supervision, as she was at that time in the process of changing supervisors.

Unconscious communication, which is concealed in the client's narrative associations, can be likened to the enfolded holographic image, which is at first invisible to the naked eye and can be illuminated by the therapist if she is able and prepared to consider the holistic implications of the client's material. That is, to focus on the essential interpersonal elements of the therapeutic process, which will inevitably entail a consideration of the wider existential implications that are fueling the dynamics of the encounter. The therapist's task is to illuminate and connect the client's unconscious relational concerns to the therapeutic interaction. This free-flowing communicative attitude may then enable the client to spontaneously link the here-and-now issues between herself and the therapist to current interpersonal concerns outside of the therapy as well as to relational issues rooted in the past. It is proposed that the therapist's interventions symbolically impact on the client in a similar way to the interference of an external source of energy, or light wave, as it can help to link the client's here-and-now communications in a three-dimensional, holographic way.

The themes that are hidden in narrative communication reveal the connections that exist within the therapeutic encounter, which are also intimately linked to the client's other relational concerns and to ontic and ontological issues. These aspects of the human condition are also highlighted in existential philosophy, such as separation and death and the tension between freedom and its limitations, although the connections to universal themes may be experienced more obliquely by the client (as well as the therapist), like the fragmented holographic image, which becomes less clear but nevertheless retains its durability in a holistic way. Furthermore, if the therapist is able to accept the fluid nature of her role and acknowledge the client's curative capacity to guide the treatment process, both client and therapist can benefit from the encounter. In this respect, the therapist's interventions should be focused on the client's associations regarding her concerns of not being able to maintain an intimate relationship, her ambivalence about the need to be close to others contrasted with the need to be alone, as well as the theme of exploitation and lack of support. These reflections are considered to be authentic comments, which signify the client's current concerns in relation to the therapist. For example, the patient's concerns about not being supported may appear also to allude to the therapist's reluctance to provide an ongoing and intimate relationship and the client's dismay at being left high and dry, given that the contract was time-limited.

The therapist's confirmation of the client's perceptive interpersonal communications may enable the client to loosen the vortices that are blocking her emotional progress. It is postulated that this kind of relational experience can allow the client to encounter herself in a more flexible and creative way, that is, not merely as a client but also as a person who can enable the therapist to understand her (the therapist's) interpersonal contributions.

According to Langs, encoded communication is both insightful and interpersonal, and its expression should alert the therapist to his or her own areas of interpersonal psychopathology and

vulnerability ("therapist madness"). However, unlike countertransference, the communicative therapist is consistently expected to
withstand and accept their shortcomings, as these flaws will then
form the basis of the therapist's ensuing intervention. Therefore, an
intervention that acknowledges the brevity of the relationship (as
mentioned above) may also prompt the therapist to consider why
she has opted to work on only a short-term basis with this patient.

Conclusion

It is hoped that this paper, however challenging, has made some
small contribution to the ongoing contentious debate on the question of how psychotherapy may work. By conjoining ideas taken
from competing paradigms, such as communicative tenets, existential philosophy, and holography, I believe that I have demonstrated
my allegiance to the principles of holism. The rudimentary ideas
tendered in this paper also endorse a belief in the need for the
conflicting schools of psychotherapy to consider how all of our own
stubborn vortices may be contributing to the incessant focus on
differences rather than similarities and interconnections. In conclusion, it is my cautious hope that this work in progress will encourage, rather than deter, this timely open dialogue.

References

Bion, W. R. (1959). Attacks on linking. *International Journal of Psycho-
Analysis*, 40: 308–315.
Bohm, D. (1980). *Wholeness and the Implicate Order*. London: Routlrdge.
Bohr, N. (1958). *Atomic Theory*. New York: John Wiley.
Buber, M. (1958). *I and Thou* (2nd edn), R. G. Smith, Trans.). Edinburgh:
T. T. Clark.
Cohn, H. (1997). *Existential Thought and Therapeutic Practice*. London:
Sage.
Deurzen-Smith, E. van (1997). *Everyday Mysteries*. London: Routledge.
Dixon, N. (1971). *Subliminal Perception: The Nature of a Controversy*.
London: McGraw-Hill.
Feltham, C. (Ed.) (1997). *Which Psychotherapy?* London: Sage.

Feltham, C. (Ed.) (1999). *Controversies in Psychotherapy and Counselling*. London: Sage.

Freud, S. (1910d). The future prospects of psycho-analytic therapy. *S.E.*, *11*: 141–151. London: Hogarth.

Haskell, R. (1999). Unconscious communication: communicative psychoanalysis and subliteral cognition. *Journal of the American Academy of Psychoanalysis*, *27*: 471–502.

Heisenberg, W. (1958). *Physics and Philosophy*. Suffolk: Penguin.

Heimann, P. (1950). On countertransference. *International Journal of Psycho-Analysis*, *31*: 81–84.

Holmes, C. (1998). Bad faith in psychotherapy. *Journal of the Society for Existential Analysis*, *9*(2): 24–34.

Holmes, C. (2001). *Relational Patterns of Being in Communicative Psychotherapy* (PhD Thesis). Middlesex University: Published Works.

Holmes, J., & Lindley, R. (1989). *The Values of Psychotherapy*. Oxford: Oxford University Press.

Howard, A. (1999). Psychotherapy and counselling as unproven, overblown and unconvincing. In: C. Feltham (Ed.), *Controversies in Psychotherapy and Counselling* (pp. 269–277). London: Sage.

Klein, M. (1946). Notes on some schizoid mechanisms. In: *Envy and Gratitude. The Writings of Melanie Klein*, Vol. 3 (pp. 1–24). London: Hogarth Press, 1975 [reprinted London: Karnac, 1992].

Kline, P. (1984). *Psychology and Freudian Theory: An Introduction*. London: Methuen.

Kline, P. (1992). Problems of methodology in studies in psychotherapy. In: W. Dryden & C. Feltham (Eds.), *Psychotherapy and Its Discontents* (pp. 64–86). Philadelphia: Open University Press.

Langs, R. (1973). The patient's view of the therapist: reality or fantasy? *International Journal of Psychoanalytic Psychotherapy*, *2*: 411–431.

Langs, R. (1988). *A Primer of Psychotherapy*. New York: Gardner Press Inc.

Levenson, E. A. (1975). A holographic model of psychoanalytic change. *Contemporary Psychoanalysis*, *12*(1): 1–20.

Pietsch, P. (1981). *Shufflebrain: The Quest for the Holographic Mind*. Boston: Houghton Mifflin.

Pribram, K. (1966). Some dimensions of remembering: steps toward a new neuropsychological model of memory. In: J. Gato (Ed.), *Macromolecules and Behaviour* (pp. 165–187). New York: Academic Press.

Pribram, K. (1991). *Brain and Perception*. Hillsdale, NJ: Academic Press.

Sartre, J.-P. (1943). *Being and Nothingness* (H. Barnes, Trans.). New York: Philosophical Library, 1956.

Shainberg, D. (1987). Vortices of thought in the implicate order. In: Basil J. Hiley & F. David Peat (Eds.), *Quantum Implications* (pp. 396–413). New York: Routledge & Kegan Paul.

Spinelli, E. (1989). *The Interpreted World. An Introduction to Phenomenological Psychology*. London: Sage.

Talbot, M. (1996). *The Holographic Universe*. London: HarperCollins.

Tillich, P. (1952). *The Courage to Be*. London: Fountain.

Ullman, M. (1987). Wholeness and dreaming. In: Basil, J. Hiley, & F. David Peat (Eds.), *Quantum Implications* (pp. 386–395). New York: Routledge & Kegan Paul.

Van Heerden, P. (1970). Models for the brain. *Nature*, 227, 25 July.

CHAPTER ELEVEN

Is the psychotherapist's authenticity a crucial key to therapeutic change?*

Dianne Campbell LeFevre

> "Bion was very aware in his later years that psychoanalysis
> was not effecting change in patients. He was very aware of
> patients who looked as though they had changed; those who
> had put on the clothing of an analysed person, but remained
> unchanged within. In particular, he was conscious of those
> patients who subtly copied the analyst, took on his words,
> outlook and attitude, but in whom there was no change
> within. In other words there was an absence of alpha func-
> tion and the articulations of the patient were an evacuation
> of beta elements. He tried to probe into this problem and his
> investigations into foetal life were one of his attempts to do
> so. The problem, however, remains unsolved"
>
> (Symington & Symington, 1996, p. 173)

The subject being considered in this chapter is whether authenticity
might be a key to therapeutic change, whether it contributes to
what works, whether it helps—to use Wittgenstein's metaphor—

---

*Lecture transcript

the fly to escape from the fly-bottle. Such a proposal carries the dangers of the author being seen to be encoding the message: "Am I not the most authentic, the most virtuous of you all?" and, like the ugly sister, getting the deserved reply. Similarly, presenting case material always carries the danger of exhibitionistically flouting one's strengths or masochistically advertising weaknesses.

Nevertheless, the risk may be justified if consideration of this quality of authenticity, which is difficult to define, leads to thought. The current political climate of fear seems to engender the urge to settle back into the cosy club mentality that disallows members of institutions to think beyond the boundaries of the institution (political, psychoanalytical, medical, and so on). And the interpretations of evidence-based medicine have been distorted by politicians (both medical and political), insurance companies and the like to a point that considerably reduces the usefulness of research overviews.

So what is authenticity? Is it simply the genuine article, the real thing? Something that is not an imitation or counterfeit? I have a professional background as a physician, have worked as a psychiatrist and psychotherapist, and I run a unit specializing in treatment of severe and enduring mental illness, including chronic psychoses. This unit attempts to combine medical–nutritional, psychotherapeutic, and psycho-educational treatment for illnesses that involve multiple systems—physical, psychological, and social.

Nina Coltart (1992) discusses the nature of authenticity in *Slouching Towards Bethlehem* in *Manners Makyth Man*. She says

> the basis of it, deep in ourselves, must, I think be founded on a personal philosophical study of what we consider to be the good and the true for ourselves, and how these are incorporated and can best be practised in our chosen vocation. Then perhaps, as we try to summarise how manners and personal style operate at their level of maximum skill and authenticity in our lives and work, we cannot improve upon Polonius' advice to Laertes.
>
> > "This above all: To thine own self be true,
> > And it must follow , as the night the day,
> > Thou canst not then be false to any man."
> > Hamlet, 1. iii. 78

[Coltart, 1992, p. 142]

The practitioner of psychoanalytical psychotherapy would be wise to take this recommendation.

In this presentation I want to examine a number of ways to unravel the question of authenticity as a therapeutic tool and to ask what one is intending to bring about in the patient? And how might the concept be useful in identifying the psychotic process, or the cohabiting other, that is present in all people?

Neville Symington (Symington & Symington, 1996) refers to his endeavour to put a *real* understanding of the mind and the patient before the model of the mind. He reflects that "a personal act of understanding is, in its very nature, subversive or potentially subversive of received teaching" and quotes Koestler, who, in his *Act of Creation* (1975), explores how new revolutions turn into new orthodoxies:

> The new territory opened up by the impetuous advances of a few geniuses, acting as a spearhead, is subsequently occupied by the solid phalanxes of mediocrity; and soon the revolution turns into a new orthodoxy, with its unavoidable symptoms of one-sidedness, over-specialisation, loss of contact with other provinces of knowledge, and ultimately, estrangement from reality. We see this happening—unavoidably it seems—at various times in the history of various sciences. The emergent orthodoxy hardens into a "closed system" of thought, unwilling or unable to assimilate new empirical data or to adjust itself to significant changes in other fields of knowledge. [Symington & Symington, 1996, pp. 10–11]

Let us now consider what the work of Wilfred Bion brings to this discussion. Bion himself, talking of the expectations that he would become Melanie Klein's successor and aware of the charges laid at his door, said:

> I am always hearing—as I have always done—that I am a Kleinian, that I am crazy. Is it possible to be interested in that sort of dispute? I find it very difficult to see how this could possibly be relevant against the background of a struggle of the human-being to emerge from barbarism and a purely animal existence, to something one could call a civilised society. [Bion, 1992, p. 337]

In order to get to the barbarism within each one of us, to experience it, I would like to propose that is necessary to go beyond the subject–object divide. Bion clearly felt that the desire for cure was an obstacle to the analysis, just as cure or healing is a by-product of analysis. "The tendency to equate psycho-analysis with 'treatment' and 'cure' with improvement is a warning that the psycho-analysis is becoming restricted", he claimed (Bion, 1967, p. 157). He believed that all such desires restrict the possibility of intuitive understanding, by which he means analytically and philosophically informed intuition rather than wild speculation. Coltart says in her paper on assessments that the individual who wants freedom from pain without gaining understanding will probably not benefit from psychotherapy (Coltart, 1987).

In an optimum state, when the non-psychotic psyche is functioning, the psyche is in a fluid, dynamic state, moving up and down the paranoid–schizoid/depressive axis, and adjusting itself to the requirements of outside reality (Ogden, 1994, Chapters One and Three). Grotstein (1994) talks of a normal particulate state, where parts of the self are arranged to function in relation to what is presented to it. So we are in one mode at work, in another mode with someone close, and so on. He calls it the particulate self. In the healthy state this process is flexible and adjustable (LeFevre, 2002).

On occasions when wholeness is a possibility there is a sense of being at-one when it is possible to move on to experience what Bion called O. O is the moment of *being* in the practice of psychotherapy. It is a transcendent moment of being at-one-in-time and at-one-qualitatively with the being-patient; it is the point of intuiting. That point can be transforming and Bion argued that reaching this experience of O could only be achieved within the relationship with another. He was very keen to stress the importance of having the experience itself, as opposed to relating or thinking about the experience.

He said it is necessary for the therapist to make that leap for his patient. The therapist needs to be ready to be changed by his patient and has to be able to derive genuine satisfaction from being with that person. The patient, in turn, chooses to be in the therapy with a particular therapist and must be capable of deriving satisfaction from his work with that therapist. This truthfulness is essential for the process of making sense—that is, not sense as meaning in the sense of inference, but a process of making sense with the opening of possibilities and the propensity for further growth. It is necessary for the therapist to be a real person with real feelings. He has to be able to *be*.

> It is impossible to know reality, for the same reason that makes it impossible to sing potatoes: they may be grown, or pulled, or eaten, but not sung. Reality has to "be been": there should be a transitive verb "to be" expressly for use with the term "reality". [Bion, 1965, p. 148]

Bion has proved to be right, considering the growing body of information from the neurosciences, to place thinking (Lansky, 1993) at the centre of the pathological mechanisms found in mental problems, and particularly in psychosis, which can be seen as arising as a very early defence against the pain of contact with the other (originally primary carer, later therapist). I use the terms "psychotic process" and "other mind" to mean the same phenomenon as that described as "internal cohabitation" by Michael Sinason (2001), who first outlined this model and who has influenced my thinking on the subject. The reason why I have used the word "process" is that it indicates the dynamic nature of all mental processes, their perpetual motion and therefore the possibility of change. And it is in tune with current neurophysiological findings.

Let us now consider what one is looking to bring about in the patient. Since the concept of cure is inadequate to describe the outcome of psychotherapeutic experience, how can one think of what psychotherapy might be expected to provide for a patient?

First, let's consider this as far as the whole individual is concerned: in order to arrive at a place where the individual can function reasonably well in areas of relationships, work and social life, and experience, at least sometimes, a subjective experience of belonging in the world, a realistic sense of being creative and a sense of being at peace must be in place. In Klein's terms, we might be thinking of the reinstatement of lost inner objects; in Fairbairn's framework, the provision of a matrix of good experience through the therapeutic relationship. Bollas and Winnicott might say we aim to bring the "unthought known" to the area of narrative play and Bowlby might talk of achieving an experience of attunement (Holmes, 1999).

Let's now consider the therapeutic aim when a psychotic process is involved. The essential task is to tackle the point of anxiety at which the "other mind" takes over, usually the point at which a contact is made, perhaps with an internal or external other, or any contact which indicates need or longing. We need to recognize this point with the patient and then to deal with the shame of the discovery. We then need to work with the patient to understand the purpose and reason for the existence of the other mind, which in very general terms, is to avoid the pain of relating in any way with a significant other. We then proceed to detail every characteristic of the other mind and to differentiate it as clearly and precisely as possible from the healthy self. We work towards the gradual erosion of the substance and the power of the "other mind", and to strengthen the healthy self.

If we assume that there is a psychotic and a non-psychotic process or "other mind" in every one of us, then it is relevant to those interested in being authentic to know how to recognize this lest it diminishes the ability to apprehend truth about oneself and about the other. To be authentic, one has to know oneself, one's own barbarism and the hatred, fear, dread, futility, hopelessness, shame out of which it has arisen. Fortunately, these affects are not always in the forefront of consciousness, but they should be accessible if the therapist is to be of use to the patient who suffers them. In a healthy and flexible psyche, it is possible to access such painful affects when required, and to bring them into the arena of thought.

There are times when the individual gets into a position where current mental activities are no longer in the realm of fruitful thought; for example, in the states of sleep and dreaming. However, this is also possible in wakeful states. Imagine that you are tired and with someone you like and respect. You make a gaff and say some-thing really clumsy and hurtful and there is no opportunity to put it right. You go home and curse yourself for being so idiotic. You curse the person for being there just at the time when you were not thinking straight. Anxieties about the thoughtless statement go round one's head like an obsessional rumination. You go to bed and wake up and the thought jumps out at you. You can't pull the ideas into a cognitive structure where you might realize that you were tired at the time, and that a bit of explanation to the person concerned might put it right. In fact fear and shame prevent you entertaining that possibility. There is, in effect, a switching off of the light of the reflective capacity, and so self-consciousness, meta-cognition, the observing self acting with the dynamic, flexible healthy self (the non-psychotic personality), is replaced by the darkness of an internal closed circuit, which is rigid and inflexible caged within the closed circuit. This inflexibility distinguishes the "other mind" from the healthy self or non-psychotic process. This "other mind" is forced to regard a mental apparatus which utilizes self-reflection, and consciousness of internal and external reality, as an anathema.

At this point, most of us—because we do not have a psychotic illness—would confide in a friend, who would probably say, "So, you were tired! You haven't killed anybody. Go and apologize and explain." With that help and containment, you would then be able to think about the matter and discuss it, make the apology and the whole thing would be rapidly forgotten. However, if the potentially healthy self were very vulnerable and depleted, and there were organic factors that might predispose you to psychosis, and stressors and glucocorticoids had increased, then this could theoretically develop into a recognizable psychotic illness. It would do this by hypercathecting, hypertrophying, and fuelling up the "other mind". Then the effect of stress is to stimulate already present but dormant cerebral anomalies into action, to produce, for example, hallucinations, which would be given meaning "borrowed" from life experience (LeFevre, 2002)

The quality of the experience is worth some reflection. The addictiveness of the rumination process, its dream-like quality, the rigidity, the inevitable attack on the self and the third party, and the difficulty in moving the attention to something new and fresh— these qualities are all noted by people experiencing an active " other mind" in a psychotic illness. In this state, persecutory anxiety dominates, guilt is not accessible, and primitive defence mechanisms predominate.

The experience described is not a psychotic illness. It merely serves to illustrate a very mild occurrence of the other mind, and the difference between flexible thinking and possible movement. It illustrates the rigidity of the state of being in the other mind, which exclusively uses what I will later describe as calculative thinking.

It is likely that the other mind becomes established in very early infancy as a result of trauma. A state not dissimilar to post-traumatic stress disorder gives rise to the cohabiting other mind, which can remain under wraps until the covers are swept aside at the point when the individual is faced with leaving the protective home environment by which the trauma is concealed.

At this point it would be useful to describe the history of a patient with very early trauma who was seen in twice-weekly psychoanalytical psychotherapy. She had had a chronic psychotic illness for many years. The identity of the patient is concealed and the patient has given permission for me to produce this material. Her story illustrates how her traumatic early history led to a fully functioning other mind.

> The patient, Margot, has been seen for several years twice a week. Her biological mother, who was a sixteen-year-old alcoholic who suffered from a nervous disorder, tried to abort her using a knitting needle, and then starved herself. Margot was born prematurely and suffered low birth weight, and alcohol withdrawal. After being born she was immediately put into an incubator, where she lived for some weeks. She was fed first by nasogastric tubes and later by spoon, and was never suckled.
>
> After about four or six months, Margot was adopted by a couple who physically and emotionally abused her and failed to notice that she was being sexually abused by a seventeen-year-old from the age of four until eight. She was troublesome throughout her childhood, crying a great deal, with temper tantrums, difficulties at school, and so on. She was seen by a psychiatrist in her early teens for behavioural problems. She killed a small animal by biting its head off and kicked a few more to death. She experimented with drugs, ran away from home at the age of thirteen, and worked as a prostitute. She self-harmed and regularly shop-lifted. She learned to drive and loved it. For a short time she did a job that allowed her access to the morgue and she would spend her lunch hour watching post-mortems. She loved watching the organs, especially the heart, being removed and put into bags. She loved the fact that the body could not get away. It had to just lie there and be cut all the way down the middle.
>
> The first of her many hospital admissions, some under a section of the Mental Health Act, was after the birth of a baby for whom she had no loving feelings. She had a plethora of psychotic symptoms, including hallucinatory voices and occasional visions, hearing her own thoughts out aloud, delusions, third-person hallucinations with voices talking about her, thought broadcasting, passivity where she would be impelled to do something against her will, thought reading that

prevented her from looking at others, and so on, all part of a chronic psychotic illness (a term I prefer to schizophrenic illness).

It is difficult to imagine that any form of psychotherapy would work where there are such traumatic early circumstances, unless mental processes are dynamic. But neuroplascticity is a fact. There is a growing body of research to indicate that indeed the brain can change as a result of relational experience—such as therapy. For example, it is reported that some Buddhist monks really are happier (*The Times*, 22 May, 2003) due to increased electrical activity in a region of the left prefrontal cortex of the brain. Meditation and practice of compassion requires being in the moment. Increased activity in this part of the brain, especially the orbito-frontal area, has been shown to be associated with positive affects (Davidson, 1994, 2000; Davidson & Irwin, 1999), less liability to mental illness and more NK (natural killer p-1203) activity, which increases immunity (Davidson, 2000). This seems to demonstrate a very clear interaction between the body, in particular the brain, and the environment.

This would give weight to Fonagy's (1999, 2003) view that therapeutic gains are made by interpreting the here-and-now situation of the immediate transference and not by elaborating the past. He seems to me to be advocating being in the present with the patient, and it is not possible to "be" inauthentically! This certainly provides food for thought.

I would like to talk now about thinking. First, I will tell you a story in which two types of thinking are demonstrated by the tale of the man who discovered the benzene ring (Herbert, 2001). Kekulé had been working on the structure of benzene in his laboratory. He returned home and sat exhausted in front of a fire. He let himself "be" in a state akin to reverie. As he looked at the fire in a sleepy state, he saw smoke curling into a ring, like a snake eating its tail. He had a sudden awareness that this was the structure of the benzene ring with its alternate double bonds, and the six carbon atoms with hydrogen attached. The basis of organic chemistry was born out of meditative thinking. When, later, Kekulé had to grapple with the task of proving the point at which he had arrived by meditative thinking, he needed then to use calculative thinking. We could say he moved from "being without memory or desire"—to use Bion's construct—to the metapsychological state of calculative thinking in which we communicate in words. He transformed beta elements into alpha elements (Symington & Symington, 1996, p. 140).

Understanding thinking helps us to understand what might determine our ability to live life creatively. It also provides an understanding of psychoses, perversions, obsessive compulsive disorder, borderline personality disorders, and so on. Kant's third proposition (Joad, 1957, pp. 359–401) suggsts that concepts without intuitions are empty, and intuitions without concepts are blind. Thinking that leads to truth is meditative thinking and it involves combining concepts with intuitions. It involves an openness, and receptiveness. It does not have an objective. It is not aimed at demonstrating an end point. It is different from meditation. It requires right-brain to left-brain communication. It indicates the importance of understanding brain lateralization, the consequences of its malfunction and the role of the integrity of cell membranes in this process (Crow, 1995; Horrobin, 2001; Peet, Glen, & Horrobin, 2003).

Meditative thinking requires the ability to tolerate the state of not-knowing, of ever changing, and of ambiguity. It has to be learned over time. Calculative thinking (Heidegger, 1966, 1968) is necessary both for the development of meditative thinking and for scientific rigour. But in contrast to meditative thinking, it has an objective. At one end of the spectrum it is essential for scientific rigour. At the other, it is the exclusive mode of thinking in psychosis and perversions; in the middle it is common in spin-doctoring, institutional discourses, political correctness, statistics, and so on. It adumbrates the thinking of symbolic equation, of which it can make full use, as well as symbolic representation. It is possible to prove that the moon is made of green cheese with calculative thinking. The "other mind" uses calculative thinking exclusively, mainly to make the point that relating with a needed other, that recognizing need or longing, is not allowed.

Although Heidegger called metaphysics the "death of thought" we need metaphysics, or the metapsychological model (in this case the psychoanalytical model), around which to drape our communications and as a starting point for understanding. However, we have to put theory to one side in order to "be" with the patient in the treatment setting.

Siegel's (1999) work and, in particular, his paper (1996) on how cognitive neuroscience informs psychotherapy may be helpful in emphasizing the importance and the difficulty in therapy of "being" in the present, since the present may be, for the patient, a re-experiencing of being in an incubator. At birth, prior to the development of the hippocampus, memories are pre-symbolic, and pre-linguistic, laid down as notions or sensations, as non-declarative implicit memory with a direct encoding of experience, later expressed as feelings or behaviours, which are not sensed as being remembered. It is possible that these notions and sensations contribute a great deal of content to the "other mind". After the age of two the memories become symbolic, experienced as images, ideas, and categories. When language has properly developed memory becomes symbolic and experienced in words and as remembered content. In these two later developmental phases explicit–declarative (semantic and episodic) memories are available. These will all be enacted within the transference and need to be experienced by the container/therapist and held until they can be understood and safely returned. The earliest experiences of dread with futility, hopelessness, despair, annihilation, rage, hatred, terror, confusion, emptiness, thought disturbance, and so on, are forcibly projected into the therapist, who must not distort the countertransference experience or run away unless there is a real and unmodifiable threat to life.

The experience of living in a box, the incubator, feeling terrorized by every sound as a potential indicator of more pain (another intravenous drip or nasogastric tube and so on), occasionally the comfort of hearing the quiet burble of my voice—all in pre-symbolic, pre-linguistic memory—was experienced by both therapist and patient in this case study.

To convey the essence of working with Margot I have extracted some material from three sessions, each of which is necessarily abbreviated and disguised. The sessions for the first few years were often largely silent. She named her "other mind" Bod (for the purposes of this chapter).

> I saw her on a Friday, having missed a Monday bank holiday. She came in very angrily saying that she hated me and didn't want to be there and wanted to kill me. (Issues of wanting to cut my heart out emerged on and off.) She initially denied that Bod was around but later admitted that Bod was there and was telling her that she hated me. Bod told

her that I had abandoned her and didn't care about her. For this reason she deliberately didn't answer when I phoned to remind her that I was alive, as we'd agreed I would. This was to punish me. I remembered, however, that when I phoned and left a message on the answering machine asking Margot to phone back, she did so almost immediately.

Later in the session she angrily said, "Bod has taken over my life, she is ruining my life." Being careful never to criticize the other mind, and to help with the development of self-observation, of which there was very, very little, I spoke with her about the idea that Bod thought she was protecting the patient from what Bod thought were the hazards of relating to me. I said that the break had been very difficult for her, Margot, and that Bod came on board because the patient was so afraid of her need for me and because of her fear that she would lose me.

At the next session she came in looking apprehensive. She glanced at me briefly. The session took place with long silences between the verbal interchanges. There was fear in the room as she sat in silence.

M. I'm afraid/

DL: I can see. [Silence.] What is that about?

M: I don't know.

DL: You're afraid of me?

M: Nodded.

DL: What are you afraid that I will do?

M: Shrugged her shoulders.

DL: I think you're afraid that I will hurt you and abandon you and leave you on your own.

M: Nodded

[Silence]

DL: I think this is related to the fact that there was a break. I think that you were afraid that I would never come back and I would leave you for ever.

M: (Nodded.) I want to kill you.

DL: Is it you who wants to kill me or is it Bod who is telling you that you should kill me?

M I think it's me.

DL: Fair enough. And how would you kill me?

M: Stab you

DL: Where would you stab me?

M: In the chest.

DL: Do you know why you want to stab me in the chest?

M: Shook her head

DL: I think you feel that I'm a heartless bitch. That I go away and leave you when you need me.

M: Nodded.

DL: I think that is when you make yourself heartless, so that you don't have to feel anything and you don't have to be aware of needing me. That's when you become aware that you can't love anything, you can't love anybody, you can't allow yourself to need anybody—in fact you have no feelings except hatred for anybody.

M: Nodded

DL: You feel as if I have cut your heart out with a knife by deserting you.

M: It is when you won't hear. When you don't want to look after me and you don't want to be my mum.

DL: You feel that I don't want to look after you or be your mum and you feel that your heart's been ripped out of your chest. You are left without any good feelings. So you believe that I'm a heartless bitch and you're going to take a knife and rip my heart out and cause me the same pain as you have endured.

M: Yes, you don't want to be my mum and you don't want to look after me.

DL: Who says I don't want to?

M: Bod does.

DL: Yes—I wondered if it was Bod rather than you who stripped you of all your feelings of needing me and of fear that I would not come back. I think you know that I do want to look after you, otherwise I wouldn't be here. And in the context of being here in the therapy, it is as if I'm your mum. I wouldn't continue seeing you if I didn't want to look after you. However, seeing you like this doesn't feel like enough.

The therapy is only fifty minutes twice a week and you go home and have to put up with life all on your own and that's just too painful.

I went on to say that we were working together so that she could take home a Me in her head, and the memory of being with me and feeling cared for by me. She could think about it when she's at home.

She said almost blissfully that she'd sit in the sun at home because she felt warmed by the sun. I said she felt held by the sun just as she felt warmed and held by me in the session.

Her whole body language changed in the middle of the session and she looked more relaxed. What came to mind was seeing a baby in an incubator relaxing after the heat is turned up. Margot confirmed that she was feeling less fearful. At the end of the session she said she didn't want to go and that she felt good being with me in the session.

I knew there would be trouble ahead as this had been a good exchange and the "other mind" would object. In Rosenfeld's terms there would be a negative therapeutic reaction.

Session held three days after the last. Margot had phoned before the session saying she didn't want to come, that she wanted to stab me. She came in and looked violent. She wore an anorak and was almost rumbling with an ominous energy. She made occasional flashes of eye contact. She was virtually silent throughout the whole session. I was aware that she was in a different world—stuck in the "other mind". I knew immediately that we were on the edge of something dangerous. I felt afraid, imprisoned and unable to get up, rather as she must have felt in her incubator. The fear was accompanied by a feeling as if my skin was being pierced by sharp objects and a pain in the chest.

I said very gently that I was glad she was able to come so that she could talk about her feelings about me rather than acting on them. I wondered aloud if she was afraid. The silence went on and on. I became increasingly uncomfortable and felt I had to exercise great self-control and hang on to my ability to think. At the same time I wondered if we were going to weather this—whatever it was.

Then, after a good while, her muscles relaxed a bit. I felt a loosening up and she said she felt bad. I felt relief and very sad. Immediately I felt that the grip of the "other mind" had loosened. After I had made several attempts to find out why she felt bad, she revealed that she had a knife hidden in her sleeve. [Whenever I write this I feel a need to cry—it must have been a relief to her to be able to cry with grief rather than rage and she has said many time how she wishes she could cry.]

I continued to speak quietly with her about how courageous she was to actually get to the session despite her feelings. After a bit more time, there was a marked change in the air in the session. She relaxed a bit. Her eye flickering stopped. She looked at me briefly and said she wanted to take the knife out and give it to me. I agreed because I felt the danger had passed. She pulled out a knife that was at least a foot long with a long, thin, eight-inch blade and handed it to me. I put it in the filing cabinet next to me and pushed my chair against the drawer.

I spoke about her feeling that my not seeing her between sessions and not phoning her was cruel and it made her heart-broken. I said that Bod had taken over, rendered her heartless as she felt I had been, and persuaded her that the way to solve the problem of missing me between sessions would be to get rid of me and actually kill me. So she was persuaded to bring the knife as she had done to get rid of all the aggravation she had had to endure by being connected with me.

I said I thought that she, her healthy self, wanted me to feel how unloved and heartless she felt. Because of the work she had done with me, her healthy self was able to gain strength and was able to communicate with me. I said it was understandable that she would feel that missing sessions was terrifying and heart-breaking. It was an achievement that she had been strong enough to return to those feelings in this session with me.

Conclusion

To be authentic is to be able to *be*, and to be in tune in time and space with the patient's experience. To be first requires that the observing self of the therapist has an unobstructed view of both the non-psychotic process and the "other mind". This requires the mirror of another, a therapist for the therapist, who has similar aims and a good training and independent mind. From this, the capacity for meditative thinking and self-reflection that leads to a sense of what is true within oneself may develop. I believe this is necessary in the practice of psychotherapy with patients with severe illnesses, in whom there is a great deal of uncontrolled pre-symbolic content.

Authenticity fosters a humility that allows the psychotherapy to be an integral part of a number of simultaneous treatment strategies, necessary in a multi-system illness, as is the case with chronic psychoses (Horrobin, 2001). Opening one's mind to all the possibilities that are appearing on the horizon in a truthful and open way is stimulating, enlivening and, as one stands back to observe the whole, meditative thought is startled into action by wonder and awe.

I stated earlier that concepts without intuition are empty, and intuition without concepts are blind. Wittgenstein said that it is possible to be imprisoned by concepts. Learning comes to an end where one cannot see a situation differently. Nowhere is that more true than in our professions as psychotherapists. A man can be imprisoned in a room where the door opens inwards as long as he keeps trying to push it outwards. The therapist can be imprisoned by omnipotence and omniscience and remain imprisoned by rigid defence mechanisms with the patient although the exit is visible. To avoid this, meditative thinking, with all its pain and uncertainty, must be worked towards. Knotty problems arise, of course, but in Bion's words, "Thought needs friction over a rough ground". And, as Nietszche said, "Have you suffered for your knowledge?"

The living whole constantly changes and evolves in a ceaseless evolving process. This is so for the individual, for the therapeutic dyad, for the society, and the universe. All are interrelated. Authenticity is a wholeness that one constantly strives for, to enhance one's life and the lives of others. As to whether authenticity—in the sense of having a sense of the whole and a longing for truth—is important in the discussion about what works, the answer is, of course, yes, if one values truth and the practice of compassion, as love that does not seek to change or own its object. To ask whether authenticity alone works has its answer embedded in this talk. It is a contradiction in terms, as authenticity adumbrates wholeness and relatedness within oneself and without.

To end with another Bion quote:

Nobody can tell you how to live your life, or what you are to think, or what language you are to speak. Therefore it is absolutely essential that the individual analyst/psychotherapist should forge for himself the language which he knows, which he knows how to use, and the value of which he knows. [Bion, 1987]

References

Bion, W. R. (1965). *Transformations*. London: Maresfield Reprints.

Bion, W. R. (1967). *Second Thoughts. Selected Papers on Psychoanalysis*. London: Maresfield Reprints.

Bion W. R. (1987). Evidence. In: *Clinical Seminars and Four Papers* (pp. 239–246). Abingdon: Fleetwood Press.

Bion, W. R. (1992). *Cogitations*. London: Karnac.

Coltart, N. (1987) Diagnosis and assessment of suitability for psycho-analytical psychotherapy. *British Journal of Psychotherapy*, 4(2): 127–134.

Coltart, N. (1992). *Slouching Towards Bethlehem*. London: Free Association Books.

Crow, T. J. (1995). A Darwinian approach to the origins of psychosis. Review article. *British Journal of Psychiatry*, 167: 12–25.

Davidson, R. J. (1994). Asymmetric brain function, affective style, and psychopathology: The role of early experience and plasticity. *Developmental Psychopathology*, 741–758.

Davidson, R. J. (2000). Affective style, psychopathology, and resilience: brain mechanisms and plasticity. *American Psychologist*, 1196–1214.

Davidson, R. J., & Irwin, W. (1999). The functional neuroanatomy of emotion and affective style. *Trends in Cognitive Science*, 3(1): 11–21.

Fonagy, P. (1999). Memory and therapeutic action. *International Journal of Psychoanalysis*, 80(2): 215–223.

Fonagy, P. (2003). Rejoinder to Harold Blum. *International Journal of Psychoanalysis*, 84(3): 503–509.

Grotstein J. S. (1994). Endopsychic structures and the cartography of the internal world: six endopsychic characters in search of an author. In: J. S. Grotstein & D. B. Rinsley (Eds.), *Fairbairn and the Origins of Object Relations* (pp. 174–194). New York: Guilford Press.

Heidegger, M. (1966). *Discourse on Thinking*. New York: Harper and Row.

Heidegger, M. (1968). *What is Called Thinking?* New York: Harper and Row.

Herbert, J. (2001). *The German Tradition. Uniting the Opposites: Goethe, Jung and Rilke*. London: The Temenos Academy.

Holmes, J. (1999). *John Bowlby and Attachment Theory*. London: Routledge.

Horrobin, D. F. (2001). *The Madness of Adam and Eve*. London: Bantam Press.

Joad, C. E. M. (1957). *Guide to Philosophy*. New York: Dover Publications.

Lansky, M. R. (1993). Philosophical issues in Bion's thought. In: J. Grotstein (Ed.), *Do I Dare Disturb the Universe? A Memorial to W. R. Bion* (pp. 427–440). London: Maresfield Library.

LeFevre, D. C. (2002). Psychosis as jack-in-the-box. In: H. Affillé & J. Cooper (Eds.), *Dilemmas in the Consulting Room* (pp. 117–136). London: Karnac.

Ogden, T. H. (1994). *Subjects of Analysis*. London: Karnac.

Peet, M., Glen, I., & Horrobin, D. F. (2003). *Phospholipid Spectrum Disorder in Psychiatry and Neurology*. Marius Press.

Siegel, D. J. (1996). Cognitive neuroscience encounters psychotherapy. Lessons from research on attachment and the development of emotion, memory and narrative. www.kerygma101.com/text/neuroscience.html

Siegel, D. J. (1999). *The Developing Mind. How Relationships and the Brain Interact to Shape Who We Are*. New York: Guilford Press.

Sinason, M. (2001). *Icon Critical Dictionary of Psychoanalytic Thinking*.

Symington J., & Symington, N. (1996). *The Clinical Thinking of Wilfred Bion*. London: Routledge.

INDEX

relational, xvii–xviii, xx, 15,
    25–26, 32–33, 35, 43–45, 113
psychoanalytic/al, 4, 6, 15–21,
    25–27, 30–31, 43–44, 51–52, 60,
    63–64, 87, 116, 142, 167, 172,
    180, 188–189, 194, 213, 215–216,
    217, 222, 232, 233, 238, 240
psychopathology, 30–31, 227
psychosis, xxii, 232, 235, 237, 240,
    246
psychosomatic, 8, 55, 113, 119
psychotic, xxii, 2, 57, 169, 216, 233,
    235–236, 238
  illness, 237–239

Racker, H., 59, 67, 179, 182
Rank, O., 22–23, 50
real relationship, 26
reality, 25, 29, 33, 138, 143, 153, 155,
    157, 166–167, 190, 193, 214, 216,
    233–235, 237
reflection, 27, 69, 90, 116, 131, 178,
    189, 207, 227, 237, 245
regression, 103, 107, 142, 148, 151,
    153, 155, 157, 194, 201
Reich, W., 142–143
relatedness, 3, 11–12, 63, 121–122,
    246
relationship(s), 4, 10, 24, 31, 34–35,
    37–38, 44, 54, 57, 60–62, 65,
    72–73, 76–77, 81, 86, 89–91,
    93–94, 96–100, 113, 118, 120–122,
    125, 128–129, 131, 133, 139–140,
    147, 150, 152, 160, 165, 167, 179,
    188–189, 192–193, 197–201,
    203–204, 207, 210, 215–216,
    218–219, 226–227, 234–235
  with therapist, xv–xvi, xxi, xxiii,
    18–19, 26–27, 42, 45–46, 61–63,
    65, 69–82, 86, 88–89, 92, 97, 100,
    102–103, 105–106, 113–114, 118,
    121, 123, 127–128, 133, 142, 147,
    149, 151–153, 157, 167–169,
    173–174, 179, 194–197, 200–201,
    204–205, 214, 216–217, 219, 225,
    228, 235

reliability, xvii, 5–7, 12
remembering detail, xvii, 8–9
reorganization (of self), 85–86, 88,
    90–92, 94–95, 97, 103–104,
    106–108, 114, 121, 130
repeat, 18, 30, 72, 74, 78, 101,
    121–122, 129, 173, 175, 196, 207
repetition/repitition compulsion,
    72, 74–75, 103–104, 121, 141,
    145, 175
represent/representation, 70, 103,
    118, 124–125, 130, 174, 190–191,
    204, 207, 240
repression, 138, 142–143, 174
resistance, 2, 15, 21–25, 32, 58, 95,
    192–193, 205, 209, 214
rhythm/rhythmic, 85–109, 117
risk-taking, 79
Rose, S., 143–144, 162
Rosenfeld, H., 180, 182, 244
Rothschild, B., 153, 162
Russell, J., 173, 182
Rustin, J., 152, 161
Rutter, P., 173, 182

safety, 95, 103, 167, 203
Samuels, A., 25–26, 46, 50
Samuels, S., 87, 111
Sander, L., 116, 134
Sandler, J., 77, 83
Sardar, S., 85, 87–88, 101, 109, 111
Sartre, J.-P., 219, 230
Schacter, D., 144, 162
Schafer, R., 23, 50
Scharff, D. E., 109, 111
Scharff, J. S., 109, 111
Schore, A. N., 60, 67, 87, 94, 107,
    109, 111, 117, 134, 148–149, 162
Schwartz, J., xviii,51, 56–57, 67, 70,
    83
Schwartz-Salant, N., 92–94,
    101–102, 111
science/scientific, xxii, 33, 45, 52,
    60, 87, 88, 109, 148, 179, 188,
    190–191, 193, 213, 215, 218, 233,
    240